PRAISE FOR
IMPOSSIBLE TO IGNORE

"This is the book marketers have been waiting for—and it couldn't come at a better time. With the massive focus on technology's role in marketing, we can't forget what drives people to make decisions. Dr. Simon's insights remind us that choice is a reaction to stimuli. As marketers, we need to think about what's most important to us, what we want consumers to do, and to really be intentional about the stimuli we're showing them!"

> **—KEVIN LINDSAY**, Director of Product
> Marketing at Adobe

"It does not matter how much our audiences forget; what matters is that we impact the little they remember. Ensuring we do not leave our audience's memories to chance is a skill of the future and an important premise of this book."

> **—RONA STARR**, Director of Supplier
> Workplace Accountability
> at McDonald's Corporation

"This book will help you leverage Dr. Simon's brain science techniques to make your content and training not only more memorable but also more actionable."

> **—JEFF CRISTEE**, VP of Global Sales
> Training at Cisco

"Today, 53 percent of clients base their decisions on the sales experience. Carmen provides memorable insights on how you can differentiate yourself from your competition and make you stand out. This is a must-read in today's highly competitive market!"

—**ELI BOUSHY**, Director of Sales
Operations-Central at Xerox Canada, Ltd.

"Rewire how your audience thinks and behaves. Carmen shows us how to make your content count—by deliberately leading your audience to remember, and then to act."

—**JEREMIAH OWYANG**,
CEO of Crowd Companies

"With more and more presentations delivered remotely or online, it is increasingly critical to 'get it right.' *Impossible to Ignore* provides proven techniques to ensure your presentations, whether in person or online, are impossible to forget."

—**MALCOLM LOTZOF**, CEO of Inxpo

"Anyone in marketing should understand the brain science of attention, memory, and decision-making. *Impossible to Ignore* describes complex concepts in a very engaging manner and offers practical examples to help translate psychological principles into application."

—**LEAH VAN ZELM**, Vice President of
Audience Strategy at Merkle

"Selling is about getting people to buy. The more we stay in their memory, the easier it is for them to decide. Carmen Simon explains how we can make our content quickly memorable—and that sells!"

—**JACK DALY**, author of *Hyper Sales Growth*

"True leadership is impossible without influencing other people's memory."

—**CHARLENE LI**, Founder and Principal
Analyst, Altimeter, and *New York Times*
bestselling author of *Open Leadership*

"Our agency spends every day building and delivering experiences that are impactful and memorable. Dr. Simon reveals a breakthrough approach to influencing other people's memories of the future as a way to shape their behavior. *Impossible to Ignore* will become an essential part of our strategic planning process."

—**CHRIS MEYER**, CEO, George P. Johnson
Experience Marketing

"It is important to dream big about resolving important issues: climate change, alternative energy, boosting the economy. And in that process, others must remember your dreams. Big dreams are never accomplished solo. Dr. Simon's book points to the benefits of social memory: it is only when others remember us that we impact important issues and become impossible to ignore."

—**REX R. PARRIS**, Mayor, Lancaster, California

IMPOSSIBLE TO IGNORE

Creating Memorable Content to Influence Decisions

Carmen Simon, PhD

NEW YORK   CHICAGO   SAN FRANCISCO   ATHENS
LONDON   MADRID   MEXICO CITY   MILAN
NEW DELHI   SINGAPORE   SYDNEY   TORONTO

2 3 4 5 6 7 8 9 0   QFR   21 20 19 18 17 16

ISBN: 978-1-259-58413-8
MHID: 1-259-58413-5

e-ISBN: 978-1-259-58414-5
e-MHID: 1-259-58414-3

Library of Congress Cataloging-in-Publication Data

Names: Simon, Carmen, 1973– author.
Title: Impossible to ignore : creating memorable content to influence
    decisions / Carmen Simon.
Description: 1 Edition. | New York : McGraw-Hill Education, 2016.
Identifiers: LCCN 2016011861| ISBN 9781259584138 (hardback : alk. paper) |
    ISBN 1259584135 (alk. paper)
Subjects: LCSH: Business presentations. | Cognitive psychology. | BISAC:
    BUSINESS & ECONOMICS / Business Communication / Meetings &
Presentations.
Classification: LCC HF5718.22 .S556 2016 | DDC 658.4/52—dc23 LC record
available at http://lccn.loc.gov/2016011861.

McGraw-Hill Education books are available at special quantity discounts to use as premiums and sales promotions or for use in corporate training programs. To contact a representative, please e-mail us at bulksales@mheducation.com.

To your memory

CONTENTS

CONTENTS

ACKNOWLEDGMENTS

I am grateful to the following people who did not forget to help me when I needed it most: Caesar Simon, James Luyrika Sewagudde Jr., David Hill, Evelyn Lee, Mike Lee, Tom Hogan, David Nason, Hartly Nason, Colleen Donovan, Jim Morris, Elana Morris, Paula Pedrosa, Jennifer Parkinson, Mike Parkinson, Rick Altman, Paul Clothier, Amy Nason, Iris Varga, Ron Berndt, Danielle Daly, Dwight Larue, Livia Teixeira, Bruce Kasanoff, Scott Adams, Leah van Zelm, Joni Galvão, Marioara Taran, Holly Gilthorpe, Constantin Taran, Kevin Lindsay, Casey Ebro, Jann Basso, Erich Gerber, David Evans, Cindy Turner, Chelsie Park, David DeVisser, Chad Sweazey, Shri Nandan, Mary Ann Sabo, Iriny Amerssonis, Danielle Araujo, Elaine Parrish, Bill Besselman, Nicolas Rivollet, Diana Andone, Thomas Been, Josipa Caran Safradin, Bob van Duuren, Mitchell Levy, Steve Gleave, Ernie Simon, Jack Daly, Mark McDaniel, Chris Taylor, Jeff Cristee, David Purdie, Hugo A. St. John III, James Lani, Mark McDaniel, Pablo Teixeira, Tom Lewis, Lucian Bure, Marina Demant, Rob Nachum, Ashok Kanjamala, Gabriella Giamundo, Patricia Simon, Mark Damiano, Hoang Luxius, Adele Revella, Rogerio Chequer, Kasey Morris, and Patricia Wallenburg.

AUTHOR'S NOTE

There are 15 variables you can use to influence other people's memory: context, cues, distinctiveness, emotion, facts, familiarity, motivation, novelty, quantity of information, relevance, repetition, self-generated content, sensory intensity, social aspects, and surprise. All are discussed in this book, but some variables dominate in particular chapters. Specifically:

Chapter 1: distinctiveness

Chapter 2: cues, emotion, motivation, social aspects

Chapter 3: facts, familiarity

Chapter 4: cues, distinctiveness, familiarity, relevance, sensory intensity, social aspects

Chapter 5: context, distinctiveness, familiarity, novelty, surprise

Chapter 6: cues, emotion, familiarity, motivation, novelty, relevance, social aspects, surprise

Chapter 7: familiarity, motivation, novelty, relevance, repetition, social aspects, surprise

Chapter 8: distinctiveness, relevance, self-generated content, sensory intensity

Chapter 9: context, emotion, facts, familiarity, relevance, sensory intensity

Chapter 10: facts, familiarity, relevance, quantity of information

Chapter 11: familiarity, relevance, social aspects

You don't have to use all 15 variables in a message. The combination is up to you. The following chapters will enable you to explore and experiment. Soon you'll be impossible to ignore.

Shall we get started?

CHAPTER 1

MEMORY IS A MEANS TO AN END

Why Memory Matters in Decision-Making

Would you tour a museum naked? You may consider it if you visit the Museum of Old and New Art (MONA) in Tasmania, Australia. MONA is an extremely innovative museum, increasing its financial viability each year and disturbing many conventions in the art world. While typical museums are aboveground, this one is underground. While typical museums are easy to access, this one is on an isolated island, in a working-class district. You don't access MONA by ascending massive staircases or passing between marble columns. You enter it via a tennis court.

Art exhibits conventionally have labels. MONA has none. There are no signs or directions, no logical route that visitors must take, and nothing is displayed across a timeline. The museum is a theater of curiosities, from a sculpture of a grossly fattened red Porsche, to rotting cow carcasses, to a library with blank books. Dark walls dominate with the intent to undermine the standard white gallery. An Australian magazine described MONA as "a mash up between the lost city of Petra and a late night out in Berlin." The museum's daring themes of sex and death are in blunt contrast to the people of Hobart, Tasmania's capital, who are modest and courteous. For an extra thrill, you can join the "naturist" tour in the buff after 9 p.m. The guards and guides will also be naked.

This unconventional approach to art belongs to David Walsh, a mysterious multimillionaire and mathematical savant, who came out of obscurity in 2007. Walsh made his money gambling, not in a James Bond, sexy kind of way, but rather in an applied mathematics kind of way. While pursuing a degree in math, he figured out that you could make money at casinos if you knew how to play within reasonable limits. The odds are always in favor of the house, but *some* money can still be made with low-yield, low-risk betting, backed up by a large amount of cash. Walsh found a partner to provide the financial backing, and wrote an algorithm that proved profitable in computerized gambling, with a focus on horse racing. As he made a fortune, he overcame a lingering social awkwardness from a sickly childhood and decided to "go public," opening his quirky hobbies to the world and hoping for an audience.

While Walsh is atypical in many ways, he is quite normal in one way that marks all mentally healthy individuals. At some point, we all create something and hope that other people will act on it: read it, listen to it, like it, buy it, or recommend it to others. We want to influence people's choices. But how do we get others to act in our favor in an age of increasing competition, complexity, and noise? This book reveals how to spark action by using an overlooked variable: memory.

People act on what they remember, not on what they forget.

The concept of memory is refueling the efforts of scholars and neuroscientists who are deepening the understanding of human behavior. The latest scientific findings place *memory* at the heart of adaptive behavior and *decision-making*. Scientists are also increasingly worried that our society is being stripped of the responsibility to remember much. We have increasingly more devices and programs that remember for us. Our phones store people's numbers, social apps remind us of birthdays, slides prompt us on what to say in presentations, and more recently, plants can use Twitter to remind us to water them. At this rate, we are grooming generations of amnesiacs.

It is useful to have machines that remember things for us, but—at least for now—humans are responsible for evolving our society, and organic memory is at the core of what happens next. Particularly in business, if we don't have a systematic way of getting *others* to remember what is important, we have to rediscover the formula for success every day.

Forgetting hurts business. Before MONA, Walsh had bought a two-acre property with two houses on it and converted one of them into a small museum. He remembers creating a venue that was "elegant, white, understated, and, basically, generic." In other words, forgettable. Does this resemble business content you see?

Initially, Walsh considered the idea of a small museum out of necessity, and then out of guilt. He and his partner had won $18,000 at a casino in South Africa and discovered that legally they could not take that much money across the border. So he spent the money on an antique door instead, and that kindled his appetite for art collecting. One piece led to another, and before long, his house was filled to overflowing. When one of his cats broke an expensive piece, he knew he had to do something with his art collection.

He liberated the original bland museum by turning it into a venue that people could rent for work events or social functions. He enjoyed watching people experience parties within the context of a museum, and that combination stayed on his mind when imagining MONA. He kept asking obsessively, "What will happen if I alter the purpose of visiting a museum?" "What would get people through the doors?" "What will be memorable?" He even asked, "What if no one comes?"

These questions are natural because when we aspire to be a part of people's future decisions, we implicitly ask what the future will bring. The attempt to anticipate the future is mandatory in understanding how to influence others' memory. This is because all neurologically intact people are relentlessly on fast-forward. The brain has evolved to be a prediction engine because natural selection favors those who can accurately predict the future. At some point this morning, did you predict how your day would unfold, when your body might need food, and what you might do in the evening? And did you select specific actions based on these predictions in such a way as to maximize rewards?

What matters most is what happens next.

If the brain is a prediction engine, memory is its fuel. We can argue that the only reason we need memory of the past is so we can inform the future. In our everyday life, we make behavioral choices that maximize our biological fitness, which is why our brains have evolved to pick up key features in the environment, predict the rewards of these features based on past memories, and use this information to compute the most favorable decision.

In the past decade, with improved brain imaging technologies, we have reached a deeper understanding of how memory works. We're at a point where we can see thoughts moving and images being formed and even spot the birth of a memory. There are limitations to these technologies. Some are better able to capture neuronal activity very quickly, but they do not reach far or deeply into the brain. We are still decades away from being able to fully decode the brain or download our memories and post them on social media. There may come a time when we can fit an MRI machine into a smartphone. But for now, there are many exciting insights into how the brain processes information, remembers, and decides what to do next. The purpose of this book is to translate current memory research into practical techniques you can apply today to help others remember and act on what you consider important.

Let's start with what people remember naturally. Studies show that when we choose an action, we rely on memory to predict rewards and to guide our behavior in three ways:

1. A *reflexive* way, through which we subconsciously alter behavior to ensure biological fitness. It takes only one experience with a hot surface (stimulus) to remember what to do next time to prolong survival (reward).

2. A *habitual* way, through which we repeat actions that proved rewarding in the past. Unlike the reflexive route, where rewards have innate, biological value, habitual decisions involve learning and remembering arbitrary associations. In scientific experiments, after trial and error, animals learn to turn left or right to receive food and go on autopilot afterward; we do the same after we initially exert cognitive effort to find the best way to get to work and follow it without thinking once it's proved suitable.

3. A *goal-oriented* way, through which we anticipate outcomes based on the past but are willing to change our minds in light of new information. For example, we may take a *new* road to work because the habitual one is under construction, or we may apply for a new job because the old one does not pay as much.

All three routes to our next move have strengths and weaknesses. Sometimes they work cooperatively; other times they compete against each other. However, all of them are adaptive and predictive and are fueled by memory.

To be on people's minds, you must become part of their reflexes, habits, and/or goals they consider valuable.

Scientists have compiled a list of stimuli that are *biologically* rewarding (whether seeking something pleasant or avoiding something unpleasant) and that elicit reflexive responses. Think of the automatic responses you have to sweet taste, putrefying odor, proper body temperature, pain, physical touch, snakes, flowers, an aggressive tone, play, courtship, sex, crying infants, sleep, novelty, altruism, or control over your own actions. These stimuli are considered primary reinforcers, meaning that they are prewired, not learned, and generate an automatic response. Contrast them with secondary reinforcers, such as money or promotions, which are learned and which require, at least initially, cognitive effort to generate action.

MONA is memorable because the subject matter is associated easily with what's naturally on people's minds and causes automatic actions. At MONA, there is plenty of novelty, stimulation, and playfulness that *reflexively* invite a response. The "no-label" policy for the exhibits is meant to allow visitors to be in full control over their actions and free them from what the curators call "the tyranny of instructions." Walsh believes that the more words near a work of art, the worse the art. He also believes that forcing information on people makes them want to reject it, whereas inviting them to search for information makes them interact and remember.

To search for information at MONA, visitors have the option to use an iPod Touch, nicknamed the "O," which displays context-aware content. As people walk through different exhibits, the information on the O adjusts to show more details about each piece. Walsh anticipated that at some point people would *habitually* look for some information about the art. Creating the O was a multimillion-dollar investment. Its context-aware content required a GPS system, but the museum is underground. The curators adapted technology used in the mining industry that enables miners to keep track of each other's locations without GPS. The effort paid off. If you're part of people's habits, you've become part of their memories.

We also act based on *goals*, which, unlike reflexes or habits, allow us to change our minds in light of new information. Studies show that when rats learn the routes on a maze that lead to food, some are able to change their route when the food is placed elsewhere. The adaptive rats form a cognitive map of the maze and realize that different actions lead to different outcomes. Goal-oriented behavior produces

adaptation based on a remembered mental representation (the cognitive map). MONA takes people off autopilot by removing any logical order in the exhibits or indications of what direction to take. At
some point, visitors have to pay attention to where they've been and
where to go next. The building does give you cues about your location
within it, so you build a mental map of its scale, but for the most part,
its design is intended to get you lost, so you think your way out and pay
attention. If you do take the naked tour, as *Smithsonian* writer Tony
Perrottet confesses, once you figure out what to do with your hands
and eyes, "You've never been more alert to the art itself."

The mistake some people make when trying to influence others'
memory is that they overestimate the importance of goals and under-
estimate the impact of existing reflexes and habits. Imagine this: Chris
is an executive who believes that everyone in his organization must
complete a new sales training program. He frames it as a program that
will help each individual make more money, assuming that surely all
share that goal. It may not be the most exciting training ever, but the
novelty of the program has people jazzed. After a week, however, they
revert to their old routines. It's almost as if the training hadn't happened. Did they forget that much? Yes. When there is too much novelty but no integration with existing reflexes and habits, as well as no
reinforcement and no immediate rewards, forgetting is inevitable. To
avoid this, either Chris must integrate a few of the novel techniques
with some older ones that are still effective, or he must eliminate the
kinds of cues that are likely to trigger old habits (e.g., old PowerPoint
files that will prompt the old way of selling).

All the efforts to consider people's reflexes, habits, and goals are
paying off at MONA. Here's how MONA stacks up against the competition: At the Metropolitan Museum of Art in New York, visitors spend
an average of 32.5 seconds gazing at a work of art. The *Mona Lisa* at the
Louvre captures a visitor's attention for approximately 15 seconds. In a
study of 100 museum exhibitions across America, results showed that
visitors stayed an average of 20 minutes. In contrast, at MONA, people
stay over six times longer than the average. Many spend as long as five
hours, and 30% of visitors return the next day. Despite its controversial

collection and its label of a "subversive Disneyland," the museum constantly receives awards for architecture, tourism, design, and technical innovation.

Tony Perrottet observes that while the most striking impact of the museum is financial—it has pumped more than $200 million into the fragile Tasmanian economy since MONA's inception—the more potent effect is psychological. While Tasmanians once believed that the most important events always happened elsewhere in the world, they now have a clearer sense of their image and know they can be widely recognized as significant. As Adrian Franklin, author of *The Making of MONA*, puts it, the museum has helped Tasmania graduate from wilderness to sophistication. *Lonely Planet* agreed that it is making Tasmania "rise from its slumber." We can make any business content rise from its slumber, too. And we don't need millions of dollars. We just have to understand how memories are formed and how different variables contribute to influencing memory and compelling people to act.

Is it even possible to influence *other* people's memory when we can barely take care of our own? It is possible because we now have more brain science research we can apply, and we naturally put more effort into leaving an impression. For example, business people don't go to work and think, "Today I will spend 30 minutes to improve my memory." But they do think, "Today I am going to spend 30 minutes to figure out how to win Customer X." This thought is implicitly about how to influence someone else's memory because people make choices based on what they remember. So we can count on the fact that we are more likely to put effort into influencing other people's memory than working on our own.

In addition, it is impractical to study individual memory in isolation; enhancing our own memory is nice but not sufficient to guarantee a significant improvement in our lives. People function and evolve in complex systems. Even when we use autobiographical memory and reflect on individual experiences, many of those are a result of interacting with others. Behavior and success are shaped by social memory. It is not only possible to influence *other* people's memory; it is crucial to human progress. When we share great ideas, and others remember and act on them, we progress. When we have great ideas and others forget them, we stagnate.

———

What are the variables that influence other people's memories, and how should they be used? Let's put them in perspective by learning from a classical parody and the discipline of math.

Charles Dodgson, a conservative mathematician at Oxford University, did not like the direction that math was taking in the nineteenth century. There was a new and abstract approach to algebra, in which you could use letters to denote numbers. There were procedures that made it possible to extract the square root of a negative number. And there was the new concept of projective geometry that made it possible to bend a shape into another shape if it retained the same properties (for example, a circle could be turned into an ellipse or a parabola).

This was too much for Dodgson to take. He believed in traditional algebra and Euclidian geometry and had a hard time reconciling with the new proposition that $A \times B$ was not equal to $B \times A$. He found the perfect venue to vent his frustration. He adopted a pseudonym, Lewis Carroll, and wrote *Alice in Wonderland* (more formally, *Alice's Adventures in Wonderland*). One of the most popular books of all time (by some counts, surpassed only by the Bible and Shakespeare), *Alice in Wonderland* has been evaluated as a satire on language, political allegory, a parody on children's literature, or a Freudian descent into the world of the subconscious. However, new scholarly research points out the hidden math in the book, revealing Dodgson's yearning for Euclidian geometry that had served the world well for 2,000 years. *One of these findings is particularly relevant to how we can influence others' memory.*

Melanie Bayley, an Oxford scholar who has dedicated her doctoral thesis to the hidden math in Dodgson's fiction, points out how the book rebels against the new math logic. For example, Dodgson makes the Cheshire Cat disappear, leaving behind only its grin, with the intent to show the increasing tendency toward the abstract in the field. He parodies the fact that cause and effect are no longer linked, by posing unanswerable questions such as "Why is a raven like a writing desk?" He mocks projective geometry by turning a baby into a pig.

In a way, Dodgson's reaction to his new reality is not that different from the reactions we sometimes have to our current reality. We live in an age marked by complexity and change, some of which we don't understand or are not ready to accept. Despite his bitterness, Dodgson offered a wise coping technique for times of complexity and change: focus on proportions rather than precision.

Throughout the book, Alice moves from the logic of traditional arithmetic to a world where her size varies from nine feet to three inches. In one chapter, the Caterpillar is sitting on a mushroom, smoking a hookah, and Alice tries to restore herself to her original size but ends up shrinking so quickly that her chin hits her foot. The Caterpillar shows Alice how eating the mushroom can make her smaller or larger, depending on which side of the mushroom she eats. Alice nibbles from different sides, and parts of her become smaller and others larger. "Keep your temper," the Caterpillar advises Alice. Scholar Melanie Bayley points out this was not intended as an invitation for Alice to stay calm. At the time, the phrase "keep your temper" had a different meaning. Intellectuals considered it as "proportions in which qualities are mixed." The advice was to keep proportions, regardless of the size.

Consider influencing others' memory through the lens of proportion rather than precision.

The concept of proportion binds all the practical techniques in this book because there is no single factor that makes something memorable. It is a *combination* of elements, used in the proper *ratio*. If you put one spoon of sugar in your coffee, it will taste better. Three spoons of sugar will make it taste awful. It is the same with memory. *Surprise,* for example, is memorable, but too much of it can be disconcerting. An audience may still remember a surprising segment but not for the proper reasons or with the intended emotion.

What are some elements that we can combine to influence memory? To make recommendations on the proper ratio of variables, we must first agree on what memory is, as it means many things to many people.

Memory is the picture that comes to mind when you think of your last vacation; it is the ability to swim in a pool even though you haven't done it in a while; it is being nauseated thinking of food you hate; it is taking the same route to the grocery store without thinking; and it is the knowledge that the *Mona Lisa* has no eyebrows. We have multiple memory systems to account for this array of memory types, and one of the formal ways to study memory is to look at it as the process we use to encode, store, and retrieve information. We can also study memory by its duration (short term versus long term) or by whether it is declarative (you can put it into words) or procedural (such as habits or skills).

Regardless of type, all memories consist of an association between neurons, so that when one fires, others fire, creating a pattern. Memory research shows multiple variables impacting memory. Some are under our control when we want to impact what people remember, and others are not. Overall, I have identified 15 variables we can use to influence others' memory: *context, cues, distinctiveness, emotion, facts, familiarity* (tied to integration with reflexes and habits), *motivation, novelty, quantity of information, relevance, repetition, self-generated content, sensory intensity, social aspects,* and *surprise.* It is impossible to control how much sleep your audiences are getting before they listen to you, how much other content they just consumed or will view later, how similar this content is to yours, how long after content exposure specific memories must become active, how stressed they are, the mood they are in, or the drugs they are taking— all of which influence memory, too. However, we can focus on using the variables we *can* control in proper proportions.

We don't have to remember all 15 variables by heart; various chapters of this book will address them in smaller combinations. A small dose of these variables makes a difference in memory. Consider popular decks available on slideshare.net. We can tell which ones influence others' memory because people act on what they remember. Good decks stay on people's minds long enough for them to "act" by sharing, liking, downloading, commenting, or embedding them in other sites. I analyzed a sample of the most popular SlideShares of 2015. The top 50 SlideShares contained, on average, 9 of the 15 memory variables, and 39.7% of the slides were categorized as "intense," i.e., containing at least 7 of the 15 memory metrics that we can control. The SlideShares that utilized intense slides 40 to 60% of the time had roughly the same outcomes (i.e., shares, likes, downloads, comments, and embeds) as SlideShares that utilized intense slides 80 to 100% of the time. This means that we don't have to work so hard on making every single component in communication materials intense. A small dose of these variables can still lead to action.

Memory needs sidekicks.

David Walsh could have built MONA anywhere in the world. He could have chosen New York, for instance. But he contends, "If this was New York we'd probably get a lot more visitors but have a lot less impact. So it would be drowned out by what I once described as the scream of cultural bland. There is so much going on [in New York] that no one would notice that this was interesting. It's like eating chocolate after you eat a jelly bean."

We often start creating content from a place of abundance. To avoid the temptation of including too many stimuli, set a *framework* and then decide the degrees of distinction within that framework (more about this in later chapters). When there is a framework, let's say a set of slides in a PowerPoint presentation, some items can become distinct relative to their "neighbors." Scientists call this *salience*. Items with less salient neighbors will be more distinct than items with more salient neighbors. This view challenges the belief that the beginning and ending of a sequence are always more memorable than what happens in the middle. It is possible that the beginning and ending of a sequence are salient because of their privileged position: no neighbors on one of the sides. However, you can rescue any middle in your communications (presentation, blog, e-mail, marketing campaign, training program) if you establish a framework first and then determine neighboring items around the ones you want to make memorable.

To be memorable, you must accept memory trade-offs.

Hugh Hefner took advantage of the concept of salience. Some issues of *Playboy* included pieces by John Updike, Arthur Miller, John Irving, Ian Fleming, and Ray Bradbury. In the 1960s and 1970s, *Playboy* was appealing to a literate, daring reader, appreciative of in-depth articles. It wasn't unusual to read an essay about Hemingway by his son Patrick, and even the first English translation of a poem by Goethe. In recent years, the magazine has showcased investigative journalism and quality fiction. At some point, Hugh Hefner is known to have told the Playmates that "Without you, I'd be the publisher of a literary magazine." The articles served as quality sidekicks to the pictures intended to be salient points, offering some justification for the famous claim "I read it for the articles." In 2015 *Playboy* announced a new policy of no full nudity, so it will have to find new ways to distinguish what is important and what should serve as sidekicks.

David Walsh and Hugh Hefner could afford to include sex in their frameworks as salient points. When creating corporate or academic content, it's not so easy. However, it's not the *type* of stimulus that counts but how a stimulus relates to others within that framework. It's

{ DECIDE THE SALIENT POINT
AND REPEAT IT }

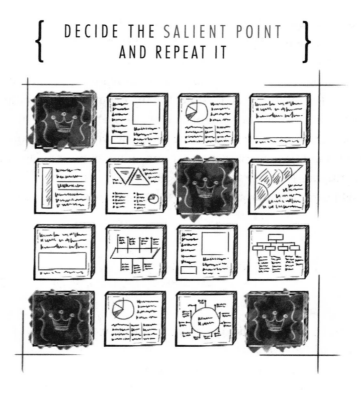

about nibbling from the mushroom in the proper ratio. As you investigate the content you share with others, look at the ratio between different stimuli you're including (text, pictures, videos, etc.). Ultimately, every component in your communication has the potential to be remembered. Even a complex chart can be memorable if it appears after a string of simple text-based elements because it is seen as a surprise that breaks a pattern.

How do you establish proportions when the variables that impact memory are imprecise? After all, few things are "fully" surprising or "fully" new. And something that is surprising may also be perceived as new. A modern approach in analyzing what influences memory comes from *fuzzy logic*, which embraces imprecise variables. Fuzzy logic is an area of math that focuses on reasoning that is approximate rather than precise. Contrasted with crisp logic where variables are true or false, 0 or 1, in fuzzy logic, variables may have a truth value that ranges from 0 to 1. This provides a way to arrive at a conclusion based upon vague, imprecise, noisy, or missing input information.

As you use the guidelines in this book, consider that depending on the context, a stimulus (text, graphic, video) may have a surprise rating of .8 or an emotion rating of .6. These ratings can be higher in one context and lower in another. We don't have to assign specific numbers to our content, and there isn't one stimulus that influences memory more than any other. When we are open to this type of approach, we will find it easier to embed the recommended variables in our communications because the fuzzy approach mirrors reality more closely. Few things in life are fully surprising, relevant, or novel and deserve a score of 1. It is not their individual precision that matters; it is their combination in the proper proportions that matters. It is about "keeping our temper," using the variables that work for us, and distributing them across a communication sequence in such a way that salient items have less salient neighbors.

Learn how to vary the proportions of imprecise and unconventional stimuli, and you will enjoy the rewards of staying on people's minds and compelling them to act. That's what this book will show you how to do. Essentially, you will find out how to metaphorically balance Euclidian logic and the Cheshire Cat to get others to remember you and act in your favor.

Clothing optional.

KEEP IN MIND

- People act on what they remember, not on what they forget.

- What matters most is what happens next. People need memory to predict their next move.

- Memory guides action toward maximum rewards.

- To be on people's minds, plug into their:
  - Reflexes
  - Habits
  - Goals

- Establish a framework, and then decide which items must stand out. Weaken their neighbors.

- Consider memory from the standpoint of proportions, not precision.

CHAPTER 2

A BUSINESS APPROACH TO MEMORY

Three Steps to Influence Memory and Decisions

n June 2014, ultra-runner Kilian Jornet Burgada raced up and down 20,320-foot Mt. McKinley in 11 hours and 48 minutes. It takes the average mountaineer two weeks to ascend and descend the same mountain. When interviewed by *Outside* magazine about his remarkable record, Kilian talked about his trip in a reserved, humble tone. On the way up, he says, he skinned the steep slopes on skis and then put on crampons for the more technical parts. He spent 10 minutes at the summit before he put his skis back on and raced down. Although Kilian makes it sound easy, he does talk about extreme weather and snow conditions and how at times he had to ski more by feel than by sight.

In the same reserved tone, Kilian confesses he completed his almost 12-hour trip on only one liter of water and one energy gel. He'd packed one other energy bar that he did not eat. Back at base camp, he remembers sleeping for the day, eating some dried food and chocolate bars, and then going back up to 14,000 feet to celebrate his record with his team: three friends, experienced mountaineers, who had been waiting to applaud him. He is energized as he talks about being at the forefront of the latest trend in ultra-endurance athleticism: FKTs (fastest known times), which have no rules and no schedules—you just pick your window and go. He is proud to have established some FKTs by moving fast and light, believing this new trend is not about winning but about improving. Kilian gets emotional as he mentions the peak of his team's adventure before leaving the mountain: skiing the Orient Express (a near 45-degree slope) under the midnight sun. When asked about his future mountaineering plans, Kilian estimates that he will conquer Everest, bottom-top-bottom, in about 55 hours. Most people take five weeks just to acclimate. He wants to get the whole thing done in one weekend.

If we could put Kilian in an MRI machine as he is relating this story, we would be surprised by what we see: most of the brain areas involved in reminiscing about the past are the same brain areas involved in planning for the future. Understanding this overlap will impact the way you communicate to be remembered.

When Kilian is thinking about his past mountaineering adventure and imagining a future one, he is drawing from similar types of information. For instance, when he constructs a scene from the past such as the trip to Mt. McKinley, he combines these components into a coherent narrative: vivid visual imagery (skis, snow, midnight sun, skinning the slope, putting on crampons), contextual information (the mountain, Orient Express), facts (details about his three friends, his location), conceptual information ("It's all about improving, not winning"), personal meaning (he is at the forefront of a growing trend), and emotions (elation when meeting with friends and skiing in a surreal place together). An MRI machine would show us that these processes activate modality-specific cortical areas (e.g., visual, motor, sensory, planning) and that these are the same neural networks that contribute significantly to his description of a *future* trip to Everest.

We know that thinking about the past and thinking about the future are linked not only because of MRI studies but also because of studies on patients who have damage in the areas responsible for relating past experiences. Many amnesic patients who have trouble with the past are also likely to have difficulty picturing the future.

Of course, there are some neural differences between remembering the past (*retrospective* memory) and "remembering" the future (*prospective* memory). The obvious difference is that the two systems have a different temporal orientation. Past memories are also more vivid and more detailed. And when engaging in prospective thinking, we may combine older pieces of information in new ways. But for the most part, past and future memory draw from the same neural resources.

This is important because it makes us rethink the way we consider memory, especially when we want to influence it in other people and become impossible to ignore. What if memory has evolved to keep track of the future, not the past? After all, there is little evolutionary advantage for humans simply to recall the past. It would do Kilian no good merely to reminisce about his previous mountaineering adventures. The advantage of remembering the past comes from using it to preexperience his future, to predict and prepare for what happens next.

Remembering the past becomes useful if it gives us insights into future outcomes.

A MODERN APPROACH TO MEMORY: THE PROSPECTIVE MODEL

What are the three most important memory problems you experienced last week? This is a question scientists often ask people when they investigate memory issues more deeply. A series of research studies have found that 60 to 80% of our memory problems are related to forgetting to execute on a future intention. Yesterday you may have intended to give someone a call, send a specific e-mail, or stop by the store to buy milk, and only remembered these today. Some unfulfilled intentions linger for a longer time. How many books have you promised yourself you will read on your next vacation . . . for the past five years? We have good intentions but forget to execute on them, or if we remember them, the reward is not compelling enough to get us to act. Our audiences are no different. They listen to us, and they may agree that what we say is helpful. When they leave, they might still remember something from what we had said but don't do anything about it. We can address that by changing our approach to how we view memory.

Instead of viewing memory as merely recollecting things from the past, let's look at memory from the lens of the future. This shift is useful for three reasons. First, our audiences' brains are on fast-forward anyway; as they listen to us now, they are by default anticipating the future. The brain has evolved to be a predictive engine because survival is more likely when one can accurately predict what happens next. We can see evidence of our inclination to anticipate the future in many activities: completing other people's sentences, salivating before taking the first bite, or laughing just *before* someone is about to tickle us.

Second, we constantly look to the future to *extract value* for our present actions. Yale psychologists George Newman and T. Andrew Poehlman have studied the human brain's tendency to look to the future and identify value for the present. They sampled 240 YouTube videos showing a child prodigy and an adult performing the same song. In a side-by-side comparison, the child performances garnered 10 times as many views. Some explain the larger viewership as a result of novelty or awe or the skills being incongruent with the kids' age. Some ascribe the youths' talent to a divine source. Consistent with findings on the topic of "conceptual consumption," psychologists estimate that we consume not only the product or the experience in front of us, but also an idea of its future. For child prodigies, we may wonder, "If they are so good right now, imagine where they will be in the future." These projected images about future achievement generate positive emotions, which translate to the feeling of value in the present.

The third reason it is useful to approach memory with the future in mind comes from communicators sharing content with audiences now, hoping they remember and *act on it* later. Imagine that we share content at Point A, and we hope people remember and act on it sometime in the future, at Point B. This "future" can be as close as two minutes from now, two days, two weeks, or longer. So it is pragmatic to ask, what is happening in people's lives, and what do they intend to do at Point B? If we know this already at Point A, we can prepare for Point B so we can become part of people's memories and intentions.

WE SHARE CONTENT HERE Ⓐ　　　　Ⓑ THEY REMEMBER AND ACT HERE

Getting people to act on what they remember always starts with an intention—an intention they already have or one you wish to place in their minds. Everyone intends to do something next. Our intentions range from trivial to serious and from automatic to goal oriented. We intend to eat, send e-mails, check Facebook, create documents, revamp a software platform, attend meetings. Dr. Mark McDaniel, one of the most influential researchers in the area of memory and an academic authority on the subject of intentions, says, "I am out of orange juice and I can't expect that it will magically appear in the fridge. I have to set an intention and go get it." Even if the fridge were to order it for him, McDaniel would still have to remember to set the command.

Everyone intends to do something. Kilian intends to do Everest in 55 hours and is already starting to plan for his Point B. The sooner we identify people's existing intentions or clarify a new intention they would benefit from having, the better we can plan on how to be part of their memories.

Prospective memory, which means "remembering a future intention," has remarkable advantages for any business because it keeps us viable: we stay in business when we become impossible to ignore—when people remember what we say and act on it in the future.

You are a choreographer
of delayed intentions.

Sometimes when we tell other people what to do, they forget, but the consequences are benign: "Call me at 4:30"; "Send me that file"; "Pay me back later"; "Take the meat out to defrost." Failed prospective memory hurts when others forget to call us indefinitely, ignore all our e-mails, don't set up another meeting, and later we find out that they picked another consultant/vendor/lover. Ouch.

The last few decades have given us more rigorous research findings on prospective memory, revealing specific techniques that increase the likelihood of people acting on what they remember. Most research on prospective memory is carried out by scientists who work with subjects either in laboratory experiments ("Remember to press this button on a keyboard when you see a certain color or a word") or in real-life situations related to simple goals ("Remember to write down in a journal when this specific event is happening"). The more serious prospective memory research has been done in clinical studies, where it is important for patients to act on future intentions, such as taking medication or showing up for doctors' appointments.

In advertising, brands are also researching prospective memory because it hurts business when companies spend a large marketing budget and customers remember the ads at the point of purchase, but they either don't buy that brand or, worse, choose a competitor's product. From a wider business perspective, whether we work in sales, training, marketing, finance, or IT, we can use findings from research on prospective memory and extract practical insights to help others act on future intentions.

Research reveals that when people act on future intentions successfully, they complete these three steps, sometimes within fractions of seconds:

1. *Notice cues* that are linked to their intentions

2. *Search their memory* for something related to those cues and intentions

3. And if something is rewarding enough . . . *execute*

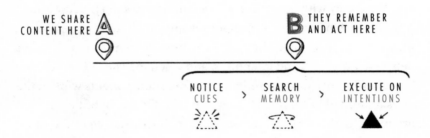

Let's say you have a dinner party and want to buy some wine on your way home from work. You tell yourself in the morning, "When I drive by the store tonight, I must stop and buy the wine." The intention is to buy the wine, and the reward is your guests will think of you as a wonderful host. On your way back, you see the store (*notice cue*); you think, "What was I supposed to do? Oh, yes, buy wine" (*search memory*); and you pull into the store (*execute on intention*).

Now consider your own content and imagine you must help your audiences go through the process described. With this prospective memory model in mind at Point A, you can prime your audiences with the proper cues, help them to keep in long-term memory what is important, and make it easier for them to execute on intentions at Point B. Currently, in the business world, the process of prospective memory is left to chance, and as a result, our audiences forget a lot, and the little they may remember does not always lead to action. We can fix this.

The three steps of prospective memory—*noticing cues, searching memory*, and *executing on intentions*—have a few things in common. They are all tied to the brain's tendency to seek rewards and avoid punishments. When we speak about future intentions, what we picture is a reward we will get from either moving toward something positive or away from something negative. From an evolutionary perspective, we become more adaptive every time we learn and remember what's rewarding and what's not. Any time you ask people at Point A to act on a future intention, they strike a tacit deal with you. They implicitly say, "I will stay with you to Point B as long as you keep me rewarded." And they will be on the lookout for rewards at all three stages: when they notice cues, when they do a memory search for connections between those cues and intentions, and when they decide to execute. No rewards, no action. In addition, all three components work in the ways identified in Chapter 1: they can be reflexive, habitual, or goal oriented. In other words, they are *automatic* or *strategic*. The more automatic they are, the faster they happen. The less cognitive effort is involved, the greater the likelihood of action.

How do these concepts apply in business practice?

I remember working with an executive to create a sales presentation. The goal was to sell his company's platform, which made a website more efficient by enabling the user to create content anywhere (using a tablet, smartphone, or computer), distribute it everywhere (various media, including TV), engage viewers (e.g., chat capability), and monetize content (e.g., add a shopping cart for products). The title of the presentation was "Can Your Website Do This?" and it listed these four capabilities. But then we asked, "What will prospects see or hear on their jobs, days *after* the presentation, when they will be more likely to make a decision whether to buy a new platform? What cues will they notice, what memories should come to mind, and what would prompt them to call him back?"

The audience for this presentation was composed of chief marketing officers (CMOs). We asked, "What do CMOs care about?" After a survey, we discovered CMOs considered three things to be important for corporate websites: content, community, and commerce. So we reorganized the structure of the presentation to reflect these three items instead of the original four. These three words were already on listeners' minds and later could act as cues to trigger memories of this presentation. To make the purchasing decision easier, the presentation heavily emphasized a concern that CMOs have each time a new system must be implemented: Does it fit with what exists? CMOs consider smooth integration rewarding. The presentation provided ample evidence of how this platform was distribution-, tool-, and system-agnostic, as well as its ease of use and customization at an enterprise level. Most of this evidence was based on case studies and third-party testimonials.

The biggest lesson for the presenter in this case was that to craft memorable content, the techniques go beyond beautiful graphics and well-organized information. To become impossible to ignore, we must learn how to create cues, bring important memories to an audience's mind, and help listeners execute on intentions at a future point. Here is a general description of each of the three steps. The descriptions will prompt you to shift your thinking about what memorable content really is and how to create it so that it influences decision-making.

1. How Cues Help Memory

Cues serve as signals that something must be done at a specific time or during a specific event. For example, the boss sends a reminder to an employee to "call at 1 p.m." (*time-based cue*) or "call when you get to the office" (*event-based cue*). The effectiveness of cues depends on how strongly they are related to a desired intention and how salient they are to draw attention at the time of remembering.

For example, in the spirit of sustainability, we are being asked on TV, radio, or social media to bring our own shopping bags to the store. This is "Point A" messaging because we're sitting on the couch or in front of the computer when we see the public service announcement, and yet the sponsoring organizations want us to act on a future intention, at Point B, which materializes at a different time and in an entirely different context. Many of us have made it as far as having extra bags in the car. But how often do you find yourself already in the store, thinking, "Darn it. I left the bags in the car." Some stores have recently started to display giant signs *in the parking lot*, which read, "Bring your shopping bag." That's a great cue to remind us what to do *at a time when it counts*. That's Point

B messaging. It is *these signs* that we should see on TV or social media, at Point A, associated with the action of bringing the bag into the store. This early priming would make it a lot easier for us to notice the cues at the point of remembering. After all, even with those signs in the parking lot, there is still the possibility that they may compete with other signs in the same parking lot or with the fact that people may be looking at their phones or talking to their companions when they get out of their cars and therefore behave in a state of partial attention.

For cues to work, they must be distinctive enough and tied to an intention people care about. In business contexts, where content creation and delivery are concerned, either one of these two conditions is missing. Sometimes our audiences notice cues at Point B but don't care enough to act. Or they care enough to act, but the cues are not strong enough to be noted and they forget. For example, after attending a training program, people return to work and fail to apply the new information they've learned because cues back on the job are not distinctive enough to remind them of the new skills or cues are not strongly tied to a reward. We must ask constantly at Point A, what will they likely see at Point B that is distinct enough and relevant enough to trigger memories and action?

You may be only as memorable as your cues.

People always intend to do something next. It is more likely they will pay attention to cues linked to *their* intentions versus *your* intentions. Connecting the proper cues to the proper intentions is the first entry point toward influencing others' memory and actions. Chapter 4 presents additional guidelines on how to build proper cues.

2. Memory Search: Bridging Cues and Action

If the cue and intention are sufficiently associated when we first present people with information, and if the cue is sufficiently noted when it counts, then the prospective memory process is effortless. People can act on what you consider important even when they are busy doing something else. In the parking lot, when we see the sign "Bring your bag," the cue may be linked to the stored memory of "bag = sustainability" or "bag = savings." If we consider this memory relevant and rewarding, even if we've walked away from the car, we're more likely to turn around and grab the bag.

Proper cues moderate access to existing memories.

The question is, how are memories formed, stored, and retrieved at the right time? This is important to answer because even in the prospective memory process, at Point B, *retrospective* memory counts. We still need the past to execute on the future.

Our brains experience stimuli through our senses. The hippocampus, along with parts of the frontal cortex, determines whether the stimulus is worth *encoding*. If it is, the memory trace is *stored* and *consolidated* through a process called long-term potentiation, which can take days, weeks, or even years.

We *retrieve* our memories when we are prompted to recall something via an external cue, such as the "Bring your bag" sign in the parking lot, or we retrieve memories on our own accord, through free recall. Cued recall is easier than free recall. A cue asks us to recognize a stimulus we've seen in the past; this narrows the search in our memory inventory. In free recall, the search is wider and requires more effort. This is why we prefer multiple-choice tests to essays. And, of course, the greater the association between the cue and the memory, the greater the chance for retrieval.

I recently helped a startup executive create a one-day workshop on best practices for hiring great talent. Initially he wanted to divide the workshop into sections that tackled attracting candidates, drafting job descriptions, interviewing, screening, and making acquisitions. We used the prospective memory method and asked, "After the training is over, at Point B, what will participants see and use when they are expected to apply what they learned in the workshop?" He mentioned an online tool that would walk recruiters step-by-step through the hiring process. So we created the presentation to mimic the structure of *that* tool. Since the executive had control of the tool itself, we designed the training so it would contain no more than four main components and was easy to navigate. We changed the flow and the labels of each section in the training to match the new tool. The tool would provide strong cues at Point B, and we encoded them at Point A to increase the likelihood that people would retrieve the proper memories and act on them.

When analyzing your own content, ask this: When you are no longer in the room with your listeners, what type of cues will be available in their lives to trigger the appropriate memory and entice them to act? Prime their brains with those cues at Point A, so they are recognizable and will prompt the right memories at Point B.

Also ask: Will they have sufficient cues to remind them of what you consider important, or will they have to recall something *on their own*, without any external help? There is no right or wrong answer, but clarifying this at Point A increases the likelihood that you'll be satisfied with what happens at Point B.

Sometimes people like to choose what they remember, and sometimes they prefer to be reminded what to do (in other words, to be given cues). At work, for example, we expect managers or executives to tell us what to do, so we often externalize our memories to them. When we want to influence other people's memories, we must consider whether they take control over their own remembering process or expect other people to remind them of action items. For instance, in prospective memory studies, older people perform *better* in natural settings compared with younger adults because they naturally take control of a task. However, in laboratory settings, older people expect an experimenter to tell them what to do, and their prospective memory is worse.

When we take control of a task, and if the task is relevant, we encode more stimuli and therefore form more memory traces, which we are more likely to remember in the future. When Kilian reflects on his experiences on Mt. McKinley months later, it is easy for him to retrieve past memories without any cues because he was there. He encoded vivid images (skiing under the midnight sun), specific actions (skinning a 45-degree slope), and meaning ("It's not about winning; it's about improving"). These techniques help with our own memory, but how about influencing *other* people's long-term memory?

If we can't rely on external cues to reactivate specific memories in people's minds, then we have to use additional techniques to make sure they store information long term and retrieve it on their own at Point B. These additional techniques include the variables mentioned in Chapter 1: *context, cues, distinctiveness, emotion, facts, familiarity, motivation, novelty, quantity of information, relevance, repetition, self-generated content, sensory intensity, social aspects,* and *surprise.* Details about each are included in later chapters. We don't need to use all of them at once when we communicate, but a combination of several (nine, according to my research) is sufficient to influence others' long-term memory. Why is it important to go through the extra effort? Because memories fuel execution, and this is the third step in the process of prospective memory.

Memory matters because it influences action.

3. Executing on Intentions

It is possible for people to remember what we tell them but still forget to act. Lots of businesses capitalize on this human tendency. I am sure you know people who:

- Bought products for the rebates but never claimed them

- Have automatic renewal payments for services they no longer need

- Are going to switch to a cheaper health insurance plan or rebalance an investment portfolio that currently has high service fees "some day"

Most of us are humble about our memory for the past, but just as many of us overestimate our ability to remember to do things in the future. Harvard University professor Keith Ericson recently completed a series of studies on our *overconfidence* in remembering future effort. In one experiment, he asked participants to make a choice between receiving larger payments that depended on remembering to claim them six months later or smaller payments that would be sent to them automatically after the same time delay. Participants were allowed to use memory aids and were clearly shown whom to contact in order to claim their payment. Out of the group who selected the larger payments, 76% of participants estimated they would remember to claim the payment, but only 53% did. Even though we assume memory aids can be used, people tend to underutilize them.

Forgetting the future is visible in many fields. Here is a review of a hotel in New York, posted on TripAdvisor: "Stayed 6 nights . . . Had to ask for towels for 4 days. Had to ask for soap for 3 days. Sushi bar in downstairs restaurant was excellent. Restaurant food was excellent. Buffet breakfast included with room was good, but hard to find napkins, silverware on many mornings. Great views of NYC. Good shuttle service to NYC, neighborhood industrial but safe. Housekeeping needs a list for each room to make sure towels, glasses and soap, shampoo, etc. are restocked daily. We had 3 rooms on different floors and we all had to ask for these things VERY often. Bring sticky notes to leave for housekeeping to remind them." You can sense the reviewer's honesty and frustration as the description keeps coming back to failed prospective memory. I am sure the hotel's housekeeping meant well. The future of staying in business will be to bridge the gap between meaning well and doing well.

The ideal way to study what influences action is to understand it in relation both to memory and to its two close cousins: emotion and motivation. Together, the three processes compute the rewarding or punishing features of a stimulus. Some scientists believe that this combination—memory, emotion, and motivation—is at the basis of the brain's design. We process stimuli around us with our senses, and in the process, we identify the value of those objects that we can use for a specific outcome. We evaluate which stimulus is associated with which reward, or we form a new association, and then we select an appropriate behavior. *Stimuli do not lead to action. Stimuli contain value codes, which activate emotional states, and these states may lead to actions.*

Let's consider the following definitions, which are gathering consensus from scientists:

- *Emotions* are states elicited by rewards and punishments.

- *Motivation* is the state we are in when we are willing to work to receive a reward or avoid a punishment.

- *Memory* is the process that leads to the selection of appropriate action to obtain a reward or avoid a punishment.

Remembering rewards and punishments is how we are able to cope efficiently in a complex and changing environment. As scientist Edmund Rolls states, "We guide our behavior toward stimuli that are useful and away from those that are not." For example, we are motivated to work to obtain rewards such as affection, praise, physical touch, or money. The emotion we feel when we obtain these rewards is happiness. We are also willing to work to avoid negative emotion, such as a boss being disappointed by subpar performance. We feel emotions when we expect a reward and don't get it, such as frustration when someone else gets the credit for our work. Or we feel relief when a punishing stimulus stops, such as someone quickly answering a cell phone that interrupts an important conversation.

Memory, emotions, and motivation are impacted by the presence, absence, or termination of rewarding or punishing stimuli.

Ponder your own communication efforts right now: Are you making it clear how your content enables others to move toward something rewarding, such as accomplishments, affiliation, efficiency, excitement of discovery, prominence, or freedom from worry? Alluding to any of these motivational drivers in your content increases the likelihood for action. Here are some examples of message changes that participants have made during my brain science workshops. Notice the difference when they switched from a question of topic to a question of reward:

- "Processing Nonretirement Distributions" versus "How to Process Distributions Quickly and Avoid Errors." The new message works because it alludes to the rewards of efficiency and freedom from worry.

- "4-Step Goal-Setting Process" versus "Earn More Money with Goal Setting." The new message invokes the reward of accomplishments.

- "Delivering a First-Class Care Webinar" versus "Improving Patient Outcomes Through Increased Patient Education." The new message works because it intensifies a reward: it is more satisfying to improve patient outcomes than to deliver a great webinar.

- "Challenger Selling Overview" versus "Selling: Are You Doing It Wrong?" The new message alludes to the rewards of discovery and the avoidance of something negative, such as using the wrong process.

Influencing behavior becomes more complex when people can choose among several alternatives, each associated with different rewards. For example, imagine you are one of four vendors proposing a new marketing platform to a potential client. How do you steer the decision makers in your direction, especially when you may not know specifics about their reflexes, habits, or goals? Despite complex situations and moving variables, there is something that stays the same: the brain's quest for seeking rewards or avoiding punishments. People execute on intentions, taking into consideration the following variables:

- *Effort.* "How much work am I willing to do to obtain rewards?"

- *Time delay.* "For how long am I willing to wait before I receive rewards?"

- *Risk.* "How much uncertainty am I willing to accept?"

- *Social aspects.* "What are the outcomes of *other* people's actions in relation to my actions?"

The four variables—effort, time delay, risk, and social aspects—are well balanced in Kilian's case. On the one hand, he is willing to put in a lot of effort to reach his goal of conquering Everest in 55 hours. However, based on his memories of past excursions, he realizes that while there is some risk involved, his past successes predict a high ratio for the likelihood of his success in the future. In addition, he does not have to wait too long to see the rewards of his work, and he knows there will be a lot of social advantages once he accomplishes his extremely ambitious goal. The *Outside* magazine article in which he is featured, starting tongue in cheek with the words "FKT up," already treats him with reverence for planning to run up and down Everest, with no oxygen, in one weekend.

Simply put, when it comes to executing on intentions, our brains are after maximizing rewards while minimizing effort and risk in a socially desirable way. In later chapters, we will learn more about these aspects and what pushes people into action in complex situations, when alternative choices are available.

KEEP IN MIND

- Prospective memory, which means *remembering a future intention*, has remarkable advantages for any business because it keeps us viable: we stay in business when people remember what we say and act on it in the future.

- When people act on future intentions successfully, they complete these three steps, sometimes within fractions of seconds: they *notice cues* that are linked to their intentions; *search their memory* for something related to those cues and intentions; and if it is rewarding enough, they *execute*.

- The effectiveness of cues depends on how strongly they are related to a desired intention and how salient they are to draw attention at the time of remembering.

- Memory, emotions, and motivation are influenced by the presence, absence, or termination of rewarding or punishing stimuli.

- People execute on intentions according to the following variables tied to rewards: effort, time delay, risk, and social aspects.

CHAPTER 3

CONTROL WHAT YOUR AUDIENCE REMEMBERS

Practical Ways to Avoid the Hazards of Random Memory

S o far, we have noted that it is practical to approach memory from a future perspective for three reasons: (1) the brain is constantly on fast-forward to stay adaptive, (2) we look to the future to extract value for our present actions, and (3) when we communicate at Point A, we aspire for others to remember and act in the future at Point B. Prospective memory, which means remembering to act on an intention in the future, includes noticing cues, searching memories, and executing on intentions. If we have prepared an audience for these three steps at Point A, we increase the likelihood of action at Point B.

When we want to influence others' memory, we must start with this question: What is it exactly that we want them to remember and act on? In asking this question, we implicitly ask another: *How much* would we like others to remember? We realize it is not ideal for our audiences to remember *everything* we do or say. There are situations when we would prefer that people forget something we did or shared.

Budweiser may want people to forget a controversial Bud Light bottle that read "The perfect beer for removing 'no' from your vocabulary for the night." Urban Outfitters wants us to forget its women's T-shirt that read, "Eat less." Amazon and Sears want us to forget that at some point they carried swastika rings on their sites. JCPenney pulled out of its shops a girls' T-shirt that read, "I'm too pretty to do homework so my brother has to do it for me," apologizing to consumers and admitting that the T-shirt "does not deliver an appropriate message."

There are times when we make blunders or cross the line, and the human tendency to forget helps us stay in business and retain customer loyalty. There are also times when forgetting is intentional because we want to move away from the old and toward the new. Imagine you just created a new training program on communication techniques for a global company. The techniques work in one country but don't in another. When we don't forget an impractical past, we form bad habits. Luckily, people are good at forgetting what does not serve them well.

Discarding an impractical past serves us in the future.

Intentional forgetting is helpful. Accidental forgetting is what we must avoid. To stay viable in business, it is critical for us to help audiences keep in mind valuable information—and just as critical for us to stay humble about the quantity of information we aspire for others to remember.

HOW MUCH DO BUSINESS AUDIENCES REALLY REMEMBER?

For over a century, scientists have been investigating how much people remember after being exposed to new information and, equally important, how much they forget. A concept called the "forgetting curve" hypothesizes that we lose information over time *when we make no effort to retain it.* The forgetting curve is exponential after the first session, meaning that in the first few days after exposure to content, we forget most of it, up to 90% by some accounts. Even memories that are strong at first are fated to be forgotten.

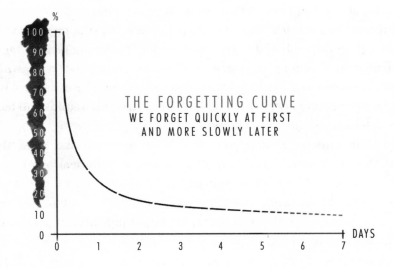

The little that we do keep in our minds stabilizes over time. Let's call this the *metaphorical* 10%, since it is difficult to measure definitively how much business content people really remember, because they don't typically consume it with the intent to memorize. Sometimes, they may retain 1% from a stimulus, sometimes 20%, and when the stakes are high, they may retain a lot more.

What erodes existing knowledge? Forgetting typically happens for three reasons: People don't pay attention to what we tell them in the first place (failure to encode). Even if memories do become encoded, people may still forget because their memories are not consolidated. Consolidation of a memory trace takes a few days or weeks—sometimes even longer—and is influenced by sleep, stress, anxiety, or exposure to more information after we speak to that specific audience (this causes interference and failure to store). Even when memories are encoded and stored, people may be missing the proper cues to bring those memories to mind (failure to retrieve).

The forgetting curve should not be confused with the myth that people remember 10% of what they read, 20% of what they hear, 30% of what they see, 50% of what they see and hear, 70% of what they see and write, and 90% of what they do. No study has found such conveniently progressive statistics. This memory pyramid is not supported by science (how is "reading" different from "seeing"?). Donald Taylor, chairman of the Learning Technologies conference, notes that "those who prefer copy-and-paste to reflect-and-consider" have been perpetuating this memory myth with a series of Technicolor pyramids and bar graphics, which have no validity.

The forgetting curve, which is backed by science, reminds us that retention decreases quickly at first and more slowly later. Psychologists and mathematicians have joined forces to create a mathematical formula that expresses the nature of the forgetting curve. What we know so far is that the forgetting curve depends on the strength of the initial memory trace and the difficulty we have in retaining that memory over time. For example, if we learned an array of nonsense syllables, we may be able to recite them well immediately after learning them (the memory trace is strong), but we will have difficulty retaining those memories for a long time. However, if we had a discussion with a loved one, even weeks later, the strength of the initial memory may be weak, but we are still somewhat familiar with what took place during the conversation, even though we don't recall the details ("I vaguely remember you mentioning that interior designer and the witchcraft").

Despite a lot of forgetting, there is the opportunity for a small percentage—that "10%"—to become part of our audiences' long-term memory, and it is important not to leave it to chance. I've been asking this question of business professionals—"What is your 10%?"—to challenge them to identify the critical message they want to make memorable to their audiences. Here are 10% messages I still recall from business presentations I've attended in the past few months:

- The top four mistakes we won't make in Q4

- Generating business value from machine data

- Good data guides smart business decisions

- Big Data was so last week

The memorable communicator practices content restraint and has a strong 10% message. In his book *Essentialism*, Greg McKeown points out an intriguing fact. Each year at the Academy Awards, the most distinguished prize is the best picture award. The media build up the hype for this weeks and weeks in advance. At what point during the awards ceremony do we take a break and maybe make a sandwich? Film editing. Yet ironically, there is a correlation between best picture and film editing. Since 1981, all movies nominated for best picture were also nominated for film editing. And two-thirds of those that won the award for film editing went on to win the prestigious best picture award. This is a reminder that knowing what to cut in our content and expressing an essential 10% message can have tremendous rewards in becoming impossible to ignore and getting others to act in our favor.

Ultimately, the problem is not that people remember very little. The problem is that they remember very little *at random*. Imagine you're speaking to five people. Unless *you* take control of that 10%, they will. Each person will take away a different message. After a few days, if you ask those five individuals what they remember from your conversation, you will be surprised. I confirmed the concept of random memory in a study I conducted in 2013. I invited 1,500 people to view online a PowerPoint deck of 20 slides, with one message per slide. After 48 hours, I asked them what they remembered. On average, people remembered four slides. Participants who viewed the decks in which I had not manipulated specific slides remembered four slides at random. When I consciously asked the question, "Can I control what they remember?" and changed some slides specifically with that goal in mind, participants took away what I wanted them to take away. For example, in one manipulation, some slides had a different background color than the rest. One group saw mainly picture-based slides with a few text-based slides, while another viewed the opposite. In some decks, a few slides contained emotionally charged pictures among mainly neutral pictures. For these groups, participants remembered what deviated from the pattern. Overall, manipulating specific slides did not help people to remember *more* slides; it got them to remember *specific* slides.

What happens when we don't take control of this small percentage that audiences do remember? Content creators and the recipients of that content both report unproductive meetings, rambling e-mails that are misunderstood or ignored, uninspired and anemic presentations, communication that needs to be re-created. In short, random memory exhausts time, misuses effort, and loses business.

HOW DO WE CONTROL WHAT PEOPLE REMEMBER?

People retain very little and at random. How do we control what they take away at Point A so that at Point B we can trust that they remember and act on what *we* deem important? To answer this question, we return to a concept from Chapter 1 related to fuzzy logic, which has evolved from the need to work with items that are vaguely defined but can still be analyzed with mathematical formulas.

For example, let's say we want to determine the membership of a human to a set: alive or dead. Using binary logic, we can assign someone a value of 0 or 1. This set is a crisp set, meaning that it has clear, sharp boundaries. Someone can be either fully included or fully excluded from this set. Now let's say we want to assign a value for how rich someone is: the membership to a set is not so clear. This is because it is more difficult to determine the cutoff point at which "rich" begins; the "rich-people" set does not have sharp boundaries.

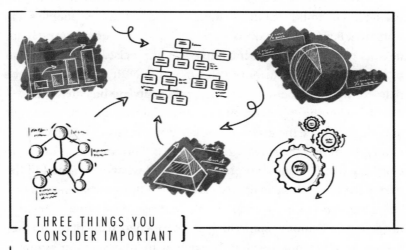

{ THREE THINGS YOU
CONSIDER IMPORTANT }

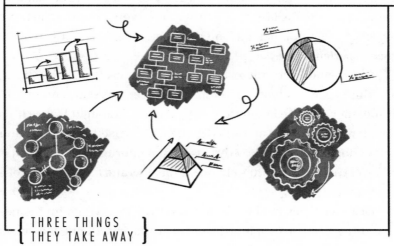

{ THREE THINGS
THEY TAKE AWAY }

CAN YOU AFFORD THE RANDOMNESS?

Using fuzzy logic instead of binary logic, a person may belong to different sets with different degrees of membership. Someone who has $1 million in the bank might have a .2 membership in the rich-people set in Luxembourg but a .9 membership in the rich-people set in Romania. Fuzzy logic makes it easier to handle uncertainty and helps us work with items that are incomplete or imprecise. Memory belongs to this category because variables that impact it cannot always be defined with the precision of a 0 or 1, especially in a business context.

The scientific approach to memory has borrowed from fuzzy logic and has produced the fuzzy-trace theory, according to which we form two types of memories: *verbatim* and *gist*. Verbatim memories are word-for-word, accurate representations of what we learned in the past. Recalling European capitals is an example of verbatim memory. These answers belong to crisp sets. By contrast, gist memories include the general meaning of something that happened in the past, and they are less accurate and specific. They belong to fuzzy sets. For example, thinking back to the last hotel you stayed in, you may not remember the exact room number, but you may remember whether you had a good experience.

Gist memories result in a sense of "familiarity" with the stimulus. This is why students sometimes fail on exams that require precision: they mistake familiarity for verbatim. "I thought I knew it" is their typical response at a failed grade. Gist is tied to meaning, and it does not always map directly to verbatim information because it is relative. We consider a 20% chance of rain low and a 20% chance of a heart attack high.

Gist memories tend to be longer lasting than verbatim memories. This is because people go in and out of paying attention to others every 12 to 18 seconds. During these segments, we engage in an internal dialogue that is more valuable and more rewarding than the details of the stimulus. Our internal dialogue has a stronger chemical signal, a natural high. During these moments, we formulate a meaning, and because of the stronger chemical signal, it is longer lasting than the precise details around us. A few early readers of this book wrote me to say that they enjoyed the section on "clues" (instead of "cues") and that they appreciated the idea behind the "exactness" of words (their way of describing the word "verbatim"). People don't remember what we say; they remember what they *think* we say, and this is the foundation of an enduring gist memory.

We may not remember what we experienced, but we remember what we understood.

The 12- to 18-second internal process of making meaning must not be confused with mind wandering, which is the experience of not remaining focused on a topic. My friend James, from Uganda, says, "I am in a business meeting and a few minutes into it, I am crossing Lake Victoria with my father." In this example, the meeting moderator did not manage to hook into a reward that is strong enough for James, so he simply exited the conversation, not even trying to make sense of it. This can be dispositional (some people are more prone to mind wander than others) or situational (the meeting participants or the materials presented are boring).

Verbatim memory is a bit harder to keep intact for a long time. How many books did you read only once in school and now vaguely remember the plot but not the characters' names? Influencing others' verbatim memory for the long term is not impossible; as we will see in later chapters, verbatim memory requires stimuli that people can process easily (e.g., simple words or actions that are reflexive or habitual) or more intensive and repeated exposure for stimuli that require cognitive effort.

It is not entirely true that "people will not remember what you said, but they will remember how you made them feel." Think of a recent argument with your spouse or close friend, and it is likely you remember a combination of what they said and how they made you feel. Some words may be running through your mind still. In the PowerPoint memory study mentioned earlier in the chapter, 86% of participants remembered *precise words* from the 20-slide deck. The rest used a combination of words from slides they had seen, along with their own words, to describe the four slides, and were accurate in their description.

Keeping verbatim and gist memories in mind, at Point A it is critical to decide what is more important to you and in what ratio. Are you after a gist or a verbatim 10% message, or a combination? The answer may depend on your industry. In the medical field, for example, a lack of verbatim memory may be life-threatening. Consider these drug names: Advair versus Advicor, Bidex versus Videx, Cidex versus Cedax, Dioval versus Diovan, Doxil versus Paxil, Kwell versus Qwell, Ranexa versus Prenexa. They are so easy to confuse. People have even confused Allegra with Viagra. About 25% of medication errors are related to pharmaceutical names that are barely distinguishable from others, and doctors, pharmacists, and patients report experiencing this confusion.

Do you want people to remember exactly what you say or . . . sort of what you say?

INFLUENCING EXPERTS' MEMORY

When deciding between gist and verbatim memory, it is practical to consider the expertise and age of those we address. When making decisions, experts are shown to need less information but process it less precisely. For example, using simple, gist-based representations, expert doctors have better discrimination regarding patient outcomes compared with novices. Experts know how to streamline judgment and decision-making and integrate them better with other knowledge. When we address an older and more experienced crowd, we can present many details, knowing these people will extract the gist that integrates well with the rest of their knowledge inventory.

Take caution, however. Relying on gist memory makes even experts prone to biases. For instance, let's consider the base rate of a disease to be 10% and imagine the diagnostic test for that disease is 80% accurate. If a patient has a positive test result, how likely is it that he has the disease: is it closer to 30% or to 70%? Researchers showed that for a sample of 82 expert physicians, only 31% selected the correct answer (30%). Despite almost daily feedback about how base rates combine with diagnostic test results, experts still chose an incorrect answer. This means even when we address experts, we must not rely entirely on generating gist-based memory. Verbatim memory can save lives.

WHAT TYPE OF MEMORY IS MORE IMPORTANT TO CONTROL?

How do you evaluate whether you are satisfied with what people report they remember from what you say? You have three choices:

1. Accept only verbatim

2. Accept a combination of verbatim and gist

3. Accept only gist

If you work in a courtroom or academia and specialize in topics based on hard facts, it is likely you will seek and accept choice 1. If you work in the corporate world, you're mostly fond of choice 2. You may become more particular about verbatim if the gist you offer is too similar to the gist your competition offers. If you work in a creative field (fashion, design), you will probably like choice 3; it is useful for people to remember the gist of what you say so when you are no longer in the same room with them, they can continue to create without being too attached to minute details from the past. Always recapitulating the past does not spark originality.

In the PowerPoint study mentioned earlier, there were three coders evaluating participants' responses on how many slides they remembered. We agreed ahead of time that we would accept choice 2: a combination of verbatim and gist, as long as the gist retained the meaning of a slide. The purpose of the deck was to inform participants of useful techniques when sharing their webcam during a virtual presentation. Some techniques included this kind of advice: "Don't wear white; it glows, and it becomes the most noticeable thing on the screen." "Don't wear bright reds; they are distracting." "Don't wear stripes because they dance around the screen." "Don't wear black; it is harsh and sucks up all the light." Participants' answers that simply reported "Don't wear white, black, red, or stripes" were considered correct because they got the gist of what not to do. However, here are examples of empty gist memory that is too fuzzy: "Wow, I just went blank. I remember what the presentation looked like and that I thought the information was useful and applicable to what I do and that I thought the slides were well done because there wasn't a lot of text on each slide, but I cannot recall any specific message."

This is not to say that a level of .9 fuzzy is worse than a .2 level of fuzzy. It is a matter of what you consider appropriate for your audience ahead of time. For example, I've worked with executives who said firmly: "I don't care what the audience extracts from my message, as long as they come back to hear me speak next time." A .9 fuzzy message may still lead to action.

Gist also leads to familiarity, which can lead to decisions. It is possible for people not to remember anything verbatim, but the exposure creates familiarity with us, the stimulus. The "exposure effect" makes it so that the more we are exposed to a stimulus, the more we prefer it, assuming it does not move us away from what we consider rewarding. Familiarity is a strong decision driver. For example, when people are asked to pick a face in the crowd that they consider most appealing, they tend to pick faces that are composed of all other faces (this is called the "beauty-in-averageness effect"). Think about the Save icon in many programs you're using. Even though it is such an antiquated visual, it's tough to move away from it because it has been familiar for so long.

I remember an executive from a telecom company who wanted to inspire his employees to "be at the heart of the revolution" (meaning the next phase of enhancements in telecom). His presentation had 14 points. We agreed it would be hard to control how much people would remember from the 14 points. So we focused on three items: (1) the verbatim phrase "be at the heart of the revolution," which was important to the executive; (2) where to find the 14 points after the presentation; and (3) a sense of familiarity (gist) that there are a lot of cool things happening in the field. When looking at it from this perspective, even the most complex content does not have to be daunting where memory is concerned.

Reflecting on your own content, ponder this: What is your 10% message for your next communication? Should your audience be able to repeat it verbatim or just get the gist? And if just the gist, what degree of fuzzy will work in your favor? Is a sense of familiarity sufficient for people to come back and interact with your content again in the future?

Verbatim memory is more easily accessible immediately after viewing a stimulus, while gist is more accessible after a longer time. It is then important to ask: When do we expect our audiences to make decisions on something important to us? Immediately after we talk to them or in a few days? The answer will determine whether we repeat specific details (and fewer of them) or share general information but stay on the surface.

ARE YOU ON PEOPLE'S MINDS WITH THE INTENSITY YOU WOULD LIKE?

In the movie *Casablanca*, Rick, the protagonist, talks to Ugarte, a member of Casablanca's criminal underworld who sells exit visas to refugees. Ugarte is desperate for Rick's attention and admiration but senses something is off. At one point, he asks Rick, "You despise me, don't you?" And Rick retorts, without even looking up from his work, "If I gave you any thought, I probably would."

This scene reminds me of a sobering reality. We are not on people's minds with the intensity or frequency we think we are. However, each time we communicate at Point A, we have the opportunity to impact what happens at Point B. Despite the fact that people forget almost everything we tell them, it is possible to influence the little they do remember and drive a desired action.

What exactly would you like to place in people's minds? Imagine someone in your audience with a bird on each shoulder. One bird is called Verbatim; the other is called Gist. Which one will survive longer? The one you feed.

KEEP IN MIND

- The forgetting curve hypothesizes that we lose information over time when we make no effort to retain it. We can lose as much as 90% after a few days.

- Unless we take control of the metaphorical 10% message, an audience will remember things at random.

- According to fuzzy-trace theory, people form two types of memories: verbatim and gist. Verbatim memories are word-for-word, accurate representations of what we've learned in the past. Gist memories include the general meaning of what has happened in the past, and they are less accurate and specific.

- Determine what type of memories (verbatim or gist) you would like to place in people's minds and in what proportions.

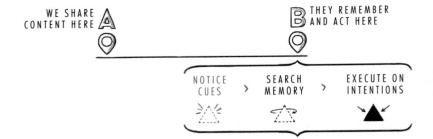

WE SHARE
CONTENT HERE A

B THEY REMEMBER
AND ACT HERE

NOTICE
CUES   >   SEARCH
MEMORY   >   EXECUTE ON
INTENTIONS

CHAPTER 4

MADE YOU LOOK
How Cues Pave the Way to Action

grew up in Communist Romania in the 1980s, a time and place of scarcity. One of the costs of communism was waiting in extremely long lines for just about anything: pencils, batteries, socks, or pork chops. My mom was firm with me: "You want chocolate? Queue up. See you in four hours." The most exasperating part of waiting in line was not knowing whether there would be enough for everyone. Sometimes store clerks would be considerate and announce early on, "We probably have enough meat for 30 people." To make the cut even more precise, they might say, "We will serve up to . . . the tall gentleman with the hat."

I remember a violently windy afternoon when a truck pulled up behind the corner grocery store, and someone screamed, "They got bananas." I love bananas; they were usually a biannual treat, so getting them deserved effort. I sprinted to our apartment, took money out of a drawer reserved precisely for these events, and put on my bright-red windbreaker, a hand-me-down from an older friend. Three sizes too large, but on those occasions, there was no time to fuss over fashion. I promptly lined up. I had been in line for about three hours, anticipating my mom's approval when I would showcase the eight bananas, a typical family ration. Four hours into the wait, I started to get antsy, picturing the bananas running out, the last ones going to someone in front of me. The line was still holding strong when the clerk came out, looked over us, and declared, "We will serve up to . . ." Usually, in those moments, I knew the battle was lost. I was just a kid, buried between large adults. No way I would get picked. And just out of nowhere, he said, ". . . up to . . . the girl with the big red jacket." I felt as if I had just been selected for the Romanian gymnastics team. My posture changed. I felt tall and important. I also felt guilty because the person right behind me was bigger, older . . . much more "banana-worthy." But most of all, I felt gratitude for my bright-red jacket that cued his attention and action at the right time.

Cues are important because they are reminders of what to do next. In an earlier chapter, we discussed how noticing cues is critical to the process of acting on intentions. The clerk had been training himself for many years to look for cues that stand out and help him make a decision easily so he could finish his work. Bright colors were likely associated in his mind with "I am going home soon."

Most people don't sit around and wait for cues. This means the cues we create at Point A and aim to be noticeable at Point B must be distinctive enough to *attract attention* and prompt a specific memory, even when people are busy doing something else. If there is one thing that neuroscientists agree on, it is that cues are signals to act, and we know that people act on three things: reflexes, habits, and/or goals. So let's learn how to build cues mapped to the same three decision factors, keeping in mind that, regardless of the cue type, the brain is in a constant search for rewards.

When the cues you use to attract attention at Point A are similar to what people encounter later at Point B, they are more likely to signal action. For example, let's say that a husband and wife must lower their cholesterol and have to take pills (a new routine). At home, they can remember to do that if they tie an old routine—drinking coffee—to the new routine of taking pills. Setting the pills by the coffeemaker helps them to act on their intention. This process is in danger when they go on vacation and the coffee drinking does not happen in the same location. Suddenly a routine that served as a cue is no longer in its place, so it's easy to forget to take the pills.

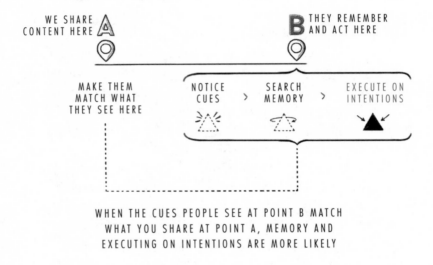

WE SHARE CONTENT HERE A

B THEY REMEMBER AND ACT HERE

MAKE THEM MATCH WHAT THEY SEE HERE

NOTICE CUES > SEARCH MEMORY > EXECUTE ON INTENTIONS

WHEN THE CUES PEOPLE SEE AT POINT B MATCH WHAT YOU SHARE AT POINT A, MEMORY AND EXECUTING ON INTENTIONS ARE MORE LIKELY

Constantly ask at Point A: Am I showing my audiences a cue that attracts attention in a similar way to what they will see on their own? It would make no sense if Colgate toothpaste used one color palette in a TV ad and a different color palette on the shelf at the decision point.

CUE PEOPLE'S SENSES IN AN AUTOMATIC WAY

The physical properties of various stimuli have the power to attract our attention to a cue, almost "despite ourselves." A bright-red jacket, a loud sound, or the unexpected touch of a lover's cold feet will get our attention in a reflexive, automatic, effortless way. This happens because humans have an outstanding vigilance system, which constantly scouts the environment through an attentional filter and zooms in on what's important for survival. This attentional filter is at work all the time, even when we sleep. Consequently, physical properties that suddenly alter our environment, such as unusual or bright colors, textures, size, motion, loud sounds, harmony, or orientation of objects, *force us* to look. This is one way we become impossible to ignore.

{ PHYSICAL PROPERTIES OF CUES, SUCH AS SIZE, COLOR, LOUDNESS, OR BRIGHTNESS, ATTRACT ATTENTION REFLEXIVELY }

In the pictures that follow, you can be certain where your viewers' eyes are going because of the use of physical properties such as color and size. Viewers can't help but look at a specific area first. And if we are certain where they are looking, we can be more certain that something may happen next, such as retrieving memories and executing on an intention.

Physical properties of stimuli are automatic attention triggers, especially when people are in a rush and attention is scarce. In 2003, in an effort to get people's attention and remind them not to smoke, advertising agency Clarity Coverdale Fury created a cigarette butt the size of Paul Bunyan. The structure measured approximately 18 feet (5.5 meters) tall and 5 feet (1.5 meters) across at the base. To make it even more attention-grabbing, a heavy billboard was placed on top of it, so it looked as if the billboard were crushing the butt into a black and equally giant ashtray. The installation was displayed in Minneapolis, and it reminded people driving back and forth to casinos to quit smok-

{ COLOR }

{ SIZE }

USE STRONG SENSORY INPUT AS CUES
TO DRAW ATTENTION TO YOUR MESSAGE

ing. Due to its giant size and strong message, the artifact was hard to miss, even at 70 mph.

Attracting attention with automatic cues works because it shifts the burden of thinking to the outside world. Attention and memory processes can easily become distracted or confounded by similar items. We can learn from what cognitive psychologists call Gibsonian affordances, after American psychologist J. J. Gibson. A Gibsonian affordance describes an object whose design features give us cues about how to use it. Affordances indicate the potential for action.

When you approach a door, do you know whether it will open in or out? When subjects in an experiment were asked, "Does your bedroom door open in to the bedroom or out into the hall?" most could not remember. That's because features of the door encode this information for us, so we don't have to think about it. When we drive a modern car, even if we're used to keys, we quickly know to push the start button. Looking at the handle on a drawer, we know how to pull it to open it. When using an oven, we immediately know how to turn a knob to increase the temperature. When we create affordances, we reduce the burden on our audience's conscious brain.

Gibsonian affordances apply to business content creation too. For example, a few years ago, I remember helping Phil Fernandez, CEO of Marketo, create a presentation about his book, *Revenue Disruption*. Out of 45 slides, 14 had key words whose size was 30% bigger than the text in the rest of the presentation. These were words related to several problems marketers were facing (e.g., "limited choices," "Mars versus Venus"—to describe the marketing versus sales dynamic, "five stages of grief"), and solutions (e.g., "create revenue," "enormous opportunity," "revenue performance management"). Marketers would encounter many of these physical stimuli later on during their daily tasks, long after the delivery of the presentation. When reinforced through subsequent e-mail reminders, a white paper, and a webinar recording, they act as cues that signal action.

Thinking of your own content, ask this: What can be externalized to the environment to cue your audiences to act? Spend time finding the answer to this question because it pays a huge reward: an increased likelihood that your audiences will act on what you believe is important.

A word of caution about stimulus-dependent attention. It may be appealing to rely on it frequently because it does not require cognitive effort on the part of the audience. However, it may be short-lived where memory is concerned. Unless we are offering our audiences a truly distinctive sensory experience, perceptual attention may not carry us far. This is because when we capture attention through the senses, the process leads to sensory memory, which only lasts a fraction of a second. If the stimulus is strongly tied to moving an audience toward a reward or away from a punishment, it may stay active for a longer time. Its length is still debatable among scientists, but short-term memory supposedly lasts from 30 seconds up to a few minutes. If we want to use cues to influence long-term memory at Point A and Point B (and in prospective memory we do), we must combine perception-based attention with attracting and sustaining attention in some other ways. Read on.

USE CUES TO PROVOKE PEOPLE'S HABITS

We often direct our attention to stimuli that serve our habits. Attention driven by habits is potent because people can sustain it on their own, and once habits are formed, they do not require much cognitive effort.

Routines such as solving a problem, finishing a project, talking to friends—we are drawn to them consciously at first, but after a while, if the process is rewarding, we are capable of focused attention for extremely long periods of time. Consider Edward Steichen, the photographer who spent a whole summer in the 1920s just photographing pears. He produced the famous *Three Pears and an Apple* shot and was credited for being the first to transform photography into an art form. That's the result of dedicated and habitual attention. Think of Steve Swingler, the graphic designer who spent a whole year photographing sinks in hotel bathrooms around the world in an effort to regain some life perspective. He returned home to create a successful philosophy project that inspired others to take time and reflect. He notes, "The constant of something as mundane as a sink intrigues, leads to questions, comparisons, and, for those who have been there, memories richer and more personal than yet another sunset or the Taj Mahal." These touching insights are the result of dedicated and habitual attention.

While awake, people are always paying attention to something. Are you where they're habitually looking?

How do we find places where our audiences are already looking? I once read about an aspiring comedian who wanted to increase his chances of finding a job as a stand-up comic or actor. He asked himself, "Where do potential employers in this field typically go?" They go to restaurants. They go to clubs. They are also in the habit of flying. So he became a flight attendant at Southwest Airlines, working mainly on routes that included Los Angeles—a hub for the entertainment industry. He could both polish his craft with an airline that endorses fun skits *and* be in a location where potential employers could be.

A startup software company with a spin on creating lightning-fast marketing campaigns does not reinvent the wheel to sell its platform. It figures out how to integrate with Salesforce.com because the startup's ideal customers are already using Salesforce. The next step is to draw their attention to a new feature within a platform they already know. With enough repetition and exposure, the new information becomes associated with old habits. This is much easier and cheaper to do than starting a task of persuasion from scratch.

I remember working with a presenter who was selling a social networking platform for corporate employees. I enjoyed his description of the application ("Facebook for the enterprise") because he was using a habitual cue (Facebook). In his pitch, the presenter mentioned that in order to accomplish anything in a work setting, business professionals circle among three items: applications, content, and people. We could have easily visualized these three things with generic icons, such as gears for applications, a folder for content, and male and female icons for people, and set all these images against a generic background. Instead, we visualized the three concepts using icons that his targets would recognize in the context of their *desktop*—a place that is *habitual* to many. Picture a computer desktop, and on it a folder called Applications, in which you see icons representing PowerPoint, Excel, SAP, and Salesforce. You also see a Content folder, with icons for Word, Adobe Reader, the intranet, SharePoint, and Jive, as well as a People folder, which contains icons for e-mail, Skype, and WebEx. We drew a circle around these three folders and introduced the name of the new application that this presenter was offering. The new application was represented by a neon-green icon, which made it hard to ignore among all the others. The approach to this introduction was to build on top of what an audience considered habitual.

Take a look at an important message you want to communicate. Can you place it in a spot where your audience is habitually hanging out? Once you know that location, you can use physical cues to direct attention to where it counts and to ensure those cues are strong enough that they will be noticed at Point B (e.g., a bright icon associated with your product, which appears in a place people cannot miss).

CUE WITH REFLECTIVE ATTENTION

In addition to cues that prompt attention to the external world, we can also provide an audience with cues directed toward their internal thoughts. Think of this question for a moment: What would you say to a former flame?

I was intrigued by this question, asked by Andy Selsberg, author of *Dear Old Love*. The book is a brief compilation of anonymous messages from people who pictured what they would say to those they once loved, dated, or divorced. The short entries in the book immediately attract attention: "I am consoled by the fact that the two of you will have very hairy children." "Please change your e-mail password. I am addicted." "How were you against holding hands? That's like hating springtime or being anti-kitten." "I liked your roommate better." Some entries are funny, some smart, and some spiteful. To create the book, the author did not have to provide visual stimulation; he simply provided a cue: a potent question that directed people's attention inward toward a specific topic.

You can do the same with your own audiences. Provide them with cues to focus on specific thoughts, and link those thoughts to your message. The advantage of this approach is that you don't always need slides or long paragraphs to draw attention.

Here are some examples of cues for reflective attention you can use in your conversations with others *to guide people toward their own thoughts.*

Reactivate old memories
"Remember what happened when . . ."

"What surprised you most?"

"What was the most fulfilling part of it?"

Note relationships between concepts
"What is the connection between your CMO and the IT department?"

Elaborate on something they learned in the past
"What did you notice after your last campaign?"

"What will you do differently as a result of this experience?"

Derive meaning
"What happened that contradicted your prior beliefs?"

"What does that suggest about your values?"

"What did the experience teach you about your strengths?"

When we engage our audiences in reflective attention, we promote long-term memory because of a process called elaborate encoding. This means our listeners are creating additional memory traces for the specific topic we are discussing. The memories become even stronger if we reactivate them on subsequent occasions over time. If there is something really important for someone to remember and we are meeting with that person in two weeks, it is useful to ask a few of the *same questions* again, along with some new questions, so the person doesn't think you are struggling with your own memory.

TIE CUES TO PEOPLE'S GOALS

Sometimes people are so focused on one point that they totally miss other things going on around them. Professor Ira Hyman from Western Washington University did a study to observe whether people looking at their phones and walking at the same time would notice a nearby clown riding a unicycle. While chatting on the phone, 25% missed the clown, who was wearing a red nose, a bright red-and-yellow costume, and giant red shoes.

These stats remind us of a humbling reality: at any given moment, people can turn away from us and choose another source of stimulation—even if we are as interesting as a clown on a unicycle.

What influences people to deliberately turn their attention to something, especially when most complain that they have such short attention spans? In addition to reflexes and habits, it is practical to link your message to people's most relevant goals. Unlike reflexes or habits, noticing cues related to goals requires cognitive effort, but it is still possible to draw attention because goals are typically fueled by needs, whose fulfillment is rewarding and which spark enough motivation for action. What are examples of these needs?

Many psychological theories on human needs have been contradicting each other for the last few decades. For each need identified by a psychologist, there has been another to claim that we need the opposite. So scientists are finally considering that we humans may have a set of *conflicting* needs:

Uncertainty ◄───► Structure

People ◄───► Privacy

Satiation/Survival ◄───► Transcendence

Think about how you may have experienced these conflicting needs in the past few months. You may have searched for a new restaurant or tried a new sport, seeking novelty and surprise. However, while in a meeting, you wanted to know the agenda ahead of time and needed structure, routine, and predictability. You may have sought time with others, perhaps over dinner, but also cherished a few moments on your own. You may have indulged in delicious food and drink but also denied yourself some desires or enlarged your sense of self by joining a social group with valuable aspirations.

The people in your audience are no different. They, too, will have conflicting needs and goals, but all are typically in the service of achieving something rewarding such as a sense of competence, attractiveness, and self-worth. So return to your message with this list of six needs in mind. Can you find ways to tie your message to any of these needs and address their opposites? For example, I once helped a client create a presentation about "making marketing more personalized." The promise in the pitch to potential buyers was that marketers would be able to create "one-to-one e-mail messages, and send catalogs only to those who wanted them." This alluded to the need for *structure*. The promise also included the ability to "start on a small budget and grow from there." This was linked to a sense of *uncertainty*, meaning that "great things may happen; you just don't know them yet." The presenter also mentioned marketers' ability to use algorithms on their own (*need for privacy*) but also join teams to learn from other experts (*need for people*).

Link your message to a human need, and you will earn attention.

Once you identify a need, consider acknowledging that the opposite may be true for the same audience.

In addition, consider tying your content to an audience's current but *unfulfilled* goal. People tend to pay greater attention to and remember more of what is not finished because the brain seeks closure—and it is seeking it now. In a recent experiment, researchers had participants search a series of pictures with a specific goal in mind (e.g., find a picture of eyeglasses followed by one of scissors). One group found the target picture sequence; a second group did not; a control group looked at the same stimuli, for the same amount of time, but was not given a goal. Later, the participants were asked how many words they could remember that were related to the target picture sequence. People from the "target-not-found" group could remember *more* words related to the target picture sequence than participants in the other groups, while people from the "target-found" group remembered very few words. Having an active goal enhances accessibility to goal-related information (in this case, words related to the pictures), but goal fulfillment reduced that accessibility. In other words, having an active goal enhances recall of relevant information only so long as that goal has not been attained. This is why soap operas and TV series are so successful; they always leave viewers hanging with one unexpected line or mysterious scene at the end that is *not* resolved.

The goal can be attainable in one shot (get a meal or a winter coat), or it can be something that is process-based and *always* lingers in the background (staying healthy or being socially desirable). Consider offering the people in your audience both something they can complete using your content and something they cannot complete during a certain amount of time, for which they will have to return to you later on. For example, "There are four steps to create an effective investment plan. Today, we have time to cover the first three."

Where goal-oriented attention is concerned, we must also consider this question: Do our listeners have enough *willpower* to either follow our guidance or direct attention on their own toward something that is important? This is a critical question, because if we are talking to people at 5 p.m. and they are already exhausted from a day of work, then it will be hard to get the type of attention that requires greater cognitive effort. They may have little willpower left. It is much more efficient to leave people a note in a large font reminding them to do something for you the next morning than to ask them to work 30 minutes overtime to finish a task, which is likely to require rework the next day.

Social desirability is one of the greatest cues of all because social motives are chronic. Impression management is constantly in the back of our minds: "Do they like me?" "Do they believe me?" "Will they hire me?" Social desirability, tied to the need for people (e.g., their acceptance or approval) is always a background motivation; it does not become satiated and does not go away. And it plays a strong role in memory because we generate cues around it internally (e.g., "When I speak eloquently, they want to spend more time with me") and we have constant external reminders (e.g., "People who speak eloquently have nice jobs").

Social desirability cues are practical to master because the mere presence of another person can help reinforce old memories and cue existing knowledge that prompts action. For example, stimuli that are related to social desirability are processed *faster* in the presence of another person, and people recall more words related to social desirability than neutral words. When we are in the presence of another person and we view ads together, we are more likely to remember those related to social desirability, such as ads for antidandruff shampoo or perfume versus those for a toaster.

Reflecting on your content, ask this: When people are likely to recall my content, will they be surrounded by others, or are they likely to recall and act on the information alone? If we expect our audiences to remember our information in groups, then it's better to present the content to a group at Point A because the presence of other people will serve as a cue for attention, memory, and action at Point B.

STRENGTHEN THE ASSOCIATION BETWEEN CUES, MEMORY, AND INTENTIONS

The purpose of our communications, particularly in business, is to have people eventually act on something we say. For example, we hope that the next time potential clients have a choice of vendors, they hire us instead of someone else. The trouble with this is that they are busy with many other things, and we may be one small speck against a crowded background.

The continuum we are after is for people to notice cues, search their memory, and act on intentions. This means we must work at creating and training the *association* between the cue, memory, and intention. At Point B, it's not just reactivating the same stimuli that counts; it is reactivating the *association* between stimuli and intention that counts. fMRI studies show that when we repeat the encoding of the same stimuli (we are shown the same things over and over), there is less activation of the hippocampus. However, when we reactivate the *associations* between the stimuli, there is greater activity in the hippocampus, and this is what leads to more accurate memory retrieval.

To encode links between cues, memory, and intentions, you can explicitly state them, or you can ask others to state their own intentions: "When I am in situation X, I will perform action Y." Both work equally well, whether stated verbally or in writing, and are superior to not having any intentions and simply expecting people to perform something from their own memory. Studies show that prospective memory is more effective when it follows the formula of written instructions + imagery. For example, "When I receive a prospect's information, I will check his or her LinkedIn profile" (and we see a picture of someone's LinkedIn profile). Any modality of instructions has the possibility to improve prospective memory when you show people "how" to do something. Research findings remind us that even asking people to imagine for 30 seconds that they will do something in the future improves the likelihood of its execution.

It is critical to encode distinctive cues that are not associated with anything else in long-term memory except you or your cause. At the point of decision, Point B, a cue must be distinctive enough so people don't confuse us with someone else, particularly the competition. We must be humble enough to realize that at Point B, people are typically preoccupied with other things: the right prospective cue is extremely important.

How do we gauge if our cues meet the mark? Consider these guidelines:

1. *The nature of the cue.* The more the cue corresponds to the memory itself, the stronger the memory. For example, if, in

your mind, Kleenex represents tissues and only tissues, then saying "tissues" may quickly bring to mind the brand Kleenex. If someone says "lightbulbs," you may not immediately think of Philips because the company stands for a lot more than lightbulbs. What we bring to mind is always cue dependent, whether we provide the cue ourselves or someone else does. Weak connections do not activate specific memories.

2. *The strength of the cue.* If someone says "beer" but you are not a beer drinker, then that cue does not bring about a particular memory. Cues become strong with enough exposure and repetition.

3. *The number of connections of that cue in our memory with other elements.* If someone says "beer," how many brands come to mind? If you address an audience and say "predictive analytics," are you the only vendor that comes to mind? Can you find a word or term that only you're associated with in your listeners' brains? People find it hard to form if-then plans if the number of cues increases.

Here is an example of how these findings are reflected in content creation.

As part of a university advertising campaign aimed at convincing students to drink less, posters around campus read, "65% of students at our university have 3 or fewer drinks when they party." It was meant to appeal to the student population using social proof: the more students were shown to follow acceptable behavior, the more students might be motivated to emulate others. Social proof may be a great decision driver, but students need to remember the message at a time and place when it matters most: at Point B, in places where they might drink, not while walking around on campus, away from the bar.

To increase the likelihood that the "drink less" message will not be ignored when it counts, imagine if university staff had placed reminder messages on coasters in bars or on entrance bracelets or hand stamps in nightclubs. In one study, bar owners were asked to place "light cubes" in alcoholic drinks. These were plastic LED lights in the shape of ice cubes that emitted flashes of red and blue light, reminiscent of the ones on police cars. Drinking diminished due to the distinct visual cues at a time and in a place where it mattered most.

With your content in mind, consider the nature of cues at both stages: encoding and retrieval. So far, we've discussed using cues for attracting attention at encoding. In the retrieval stage, cognitive scientists remind us of three criteria that cues must meet to impact memory and action when it counts:

1. People must *recognize the cues* at retrieval. In the "drink less" campaign, a more effective strategy would have been also to advertise those LED ice cubes so they don't look completely new when they are spotted in bars.

2. Once people recognize the cue, they must still *retrieve the associated action*. In the "drink less" campaign, this means that they must be reminded that the LED ice cubes are linked to "don't drink." This association is stronger at retrieval if established at encoding.

3. People must be able to *coordinate* what they are doing now and what they should be doing. In the "drink less" campaign, this means that the LED ice cubes must be placed in glasses before it's too late. For other content type, we must ask: Is the cue distinct enough for people to interrupt what they are doing now to achieve another desirable state? Is the reward obvious enough that it pushes them to switch tasks?

In attempting to influence your audience's memory and actions, using cues that will be noticed later on is one of the most important steps because that's often where memory and intentions start. Researchers are observing, "The noticing function might be more effortful than the search function. The noticing function might frequently require explicit memory or rehearsal to respond to a prospective cue, but once the cue is noticed, relatively little memory is needed for the search function to determine what to do." So once you take care of this step—helping others notice cues—your task as an effective communicator becomes easier. Just as easy as noticing a red jacket in a crowd.

KEEP IN MIND

- When the cues you use to attract attention at Point A are similar to what people encounter later at Point B, the cues are more likely to signal action.

- Physical properties of stimuli such as unusual colors, textures, size, motion, loud sounds, harmony, or orientation of objects can force people to look "despite themselves." These types of cues work because they do not require much cognitive effort.

- Create cues that are linked to existing habits (e.g., associating new information with a software application people already use). Attention driven by habits is potent because people can sustain it on their own, and once habits are formed, they do not require much cognitive effort.

- Use cues to direct attention inward and prompt audiences to focus on habitual thoughts. When you engage your audiences in reflective attention, you promote long-term memory because of a process called elaborate encoding.

- Link your message to people's most important goals. Unlike reflexes or habits, goals require cognitive effort, but attention is still possible because goals are fueled by needs. Consider acknowledging that an audience may have conflicting needs, such as uncertainty versus structure, people versus privacy, and survival versus transcendence.

- Tie your message to a current but *unfulfilled* goal. People tend to pay greater attention to and remember more of what is not finished because the brain seeks closure.

- Link cues to social desirability because impression management is a strong motivation driver. People tend to pay attention to what makes them look good in front of others.

- Ensure that people have enough willpower to pay attention to you (e.g., present important messages early in the day).

- Strengthen the association between cues, memory, and intentions.

CHAPTER 5

THE PARADOX OF SURPRISE

The Price We Pay for Extra Attention, Time, and Engagement

n 2013, Kleenex partnered with Facebook to provide care kits to users who were feeling sick. Israeli ad agency Smoyz helped with the campaign by searching Facebook for status updates in which users reported being ill. Then the agency used its online connections to find the users' mailing addresses and sent them a get-well-soon Kleenex kit to help them feel better. Surprise! People who received the kit were so touched that every single person—no exception—posted their experience and gratitude online, turning the marketing effort into a viral campaign and capturing the attention of more than 650,000 people.

Surprises are not always generous and pleasant.

In the late 1970s, Romanian ambassador Corneliu Bogdan visited Charlotte, North Carolina, to watch the Davis Cup match between the United States and Romania, and he was in for another kind of surprise. A small Army band accidentally played the old, pre-Communist royal anthem. Surprise! The Romanian ambassador was in shock. Ceausescu had been cruel to subordinates for smaller mishaps. Luckily, the music was immediately stopped, and the organizers swiftly switched to other activities and then redid the opening ceremony with the correct anthem.

Earlier in the book, I mentioned a study of the most popular SlideShares of 2015. The results showed that surprise was the single most reliable predictor of staying on people's minds long enough for them to act in our favor. When surprise was included, even a small dose (5–10% of the slides) was sufficient to compel viewers to like, share, download, comment, or embed the presentation on their own sites.

It is useful to understand the neuroscience of surprise, because when you surprise someone, whether the outcome is good or bad, you can rely on extra emotion and engagement. This chapter offers guidelines on how best to create surprises for audiences in such a way that we influence attention, memory, and action.

WHY IS SURPRISE LINKED TO ACTION?

There are two processes going on in our brains when we're surprised: a reaction and an evaluation of what just happened. The reaction is fast (150 milliseconds or less), automatic, and short-lived and is rarely a conscious process. The fast path takes the event to the amygdala, the brain region that prepares us for emergencies and assigns emotional significance to what happens. The fast track is also protective and suspicious. When faced with surprise, it is biologically adaptive to assume the worst. Evolution has taught us that it is better to exaggerate danger than it is to be realistic.

On the slower path, the surprising event takes a detour: it goes through cortex areas associated with rumination and evaluation before it reaches the amygdala. This is where the brain assesses the event, tells the amygdala to quiet the alarm, and concludes, "I won't be shot for a national anthem mishap." Since we are conscious of this slower appraisal process, we can relate to it more than to what's happening on the fast track. The two processes, fast and slow, are often in conflict because they pursue different goals: the fast one wants to enable quick reaction to potential danger, and the slow one wants to evaluate accurately to be better prepared for the next time.

Surprise is a prediction error.

Given that natural selection favors those who can accurately predict the future, our brains have evolved to be constantly on fast-forward. From this perspective, biologically speaking, surprise is always bad. This is because surprise implies a failure to predict the future. Even when an event turns out to be good, such as receiving unexpected Kleenex for a runny nose, surprise is still a prediction error.

If all surprises are biologically bad, why is it that we enjoy *some* surprises? After all, the people who received Kleenex care kits enjoyed the experience even if it was not predictable. Cognitive scientist David Huron prompted me to ask this question of clients I coach: "Suppose you could know the exact date and time when your most cherished goals would be fulfilled, would you choose to know them?" Most say no. Some of the joy in life comes from uncertainty and the surprises we face along the way. While prophecy is a source of pleasure, too much certainty can diminish it.

Since all surprises are treated initially as bad, this means they induce a state of fear or stress—even if this never reaches our conscious state of awareness. Scientists confirm that when we experience fear or stress, the body releases opiates, such as endorphins, to counteract potential pain and allow us to function and fight if necessary. Since most surprises are false alarms, the net result is that opiates are still released; we don't need them to fight, but we enjoy their effect.

So it looks like we are faced with a biological paradox: on one hand, we like to predict accurately, but on the other, we also seem to enjoy some surprises. Can we create for our listeners something that is predictable *and* surprising at the same time? To answer this, we must first understand how the human brain learns to predict and what is likely to appear surprising. For this, we turn to the psychology of expectations.

HOW DO WE FORM EXPECTATIONS?

Our brains map out everything we do. Eating, working, feeling pain, or making love—many of these activities take place in the mind first.

Neurocognitive studies have demonstrated that actions, such as a simple movement of the hand or physical exercise, take place in the brain first before they take place in reality. And we learn to predict what happens in the end by forming expectations.

The brain starts with the end in mind.

We form expectations automatically and mostly unconsciously based on what we pay attention to, memories of past experiences, and motivations and emotions we have along the way. Studies using electroencephalography and intracranial recordings suggest that the human brain has evolved to take input from our senses and run it through a hierarchy of neural networks that are constantly exchanging information and updating our past experiences and internal biases. The purpose of these complex but efficient processes is to minimize unpredictability and accurately predict what's next.

One of the ways to reduce unpredictability is to form schemas or mental representations, which are typically the result of repeated exposure to stimuli. Think of movies. We don't expect a guy named Bob to be a villain, nor do we expect a character named Beast to be selling cookies for charity. It is adaptive to form mental schemas because they allow the brain to process information quickly and respond appropriately. It would be exhausting to evaluate every single event we face, and the brain is constantly looking to save energy.

We may have schemas—and therefore expectations—for business meetings, grocery stores, airports, or our national anthem. On a home improvement show, for example, I saw a contractor showing an inexperienced homeowner how to use a glue gun. As the glue is pouring out of the gun onto the wooden panel, she observes, "It's just like frosting!" She sees something new through an existing schema.

We have expectations constantly—of how our day unfolds, how we'll react to a show, or what our partner may say after we share some news. When our expectations are met, we experience pleasure because we predicted accurately. When our expectations are not met, this prediction error is a teaching moment: we learn how to adapt. Negotiating the gap between what we expect and what happens is how the brain becomes a better prediction engine. And the value of good predictions is the most precious gift of all: living longer.

Accurate expectations = biological advantage

The terms "expectation" and "anticipation" are often used interchangeably. For this discussion, let's keep them separate; let's consider that expectations run constantly and sometimes quietly in the background, while anticipation is expectation in action. Anticipation is also linked to dopamine, which has a critical role in our ability to hold people's attention and get them to act. This is why the next chapter is dedicated specifically to anticipation. For now, let's focus on expectations, which constantly feed our future-obsessed brains, and let's see how we can use them to offer our audiences surprises they enjoy and convince them to pay attention and make decisions.

IS THERE A DIFFERENCE BETWEEN SURPRISE AND NOVELTY?

Before we look at practical ways in which to create surprise for our audiences, let's distinguish two more terms, which people tend to use interchangeably: "surprise" and "novelty." Even though the terms are related, there are some differences, and knowing these differences helps us change our approach to how we create content to attract attention. We'll define the term "novelty" as something that has not been previously experienced and "surprise" as something that occurs unexpectedly. It is easy to swap the terms because we often witness them together. For example, while working with a company on a presentation about a platform that scales marketing campaigns, we showed a first slide that displayed "The End." The intent was to tell the people in the audience this was the end of their traditional marketing story, meaning there are currently too many tasks in marketing that happen manually and would benefit from automation. Starting with "The End" was perceived as new (the presenter's audiences had not seen that before in a business presentation) and unexpected (we expect to see the phrase at the end of a sequence).

Sometimes we may experience just novelty without surprise, such as hearing various statistics related to a particular field or object. For example, according to a 2015 Bank of America report, approximately three-quarters (71%) of respondents sleep with their mobile phones. We may not have known that exact number (new information), but we're not surprised by it. Sometimes, we experience surprise without novelty, such as a presenter checking a smartphone in the middle of his own presentation: we've seen people checking their phones, but seeing someone doing so in that context is unexpected.

For the most part, however, we tend to witness novelty at the same time as surprise. And our audiences' brains are constantly looking to mitigate the tension between two states: on one hand, people want to minimize the energy necessary to process their environment and appreciate it when incoming stimuli conform to their expectations. On the other, they want to learn new things and revise their schema in order to make better predictions in the future. This is why the following guidelines are expressed from the lens of this dichotomy: offering your audiences new knowledge to stay adaptive and improving predictions to conserve energy.

OFFER FAMILIARITY BY INVOKING EXISTING MENTAL SCHEMAS

When predicting a future stimulus, our best prediction is the stimulus that has occurred most frequently in the past. I remember reading about a stylish businesswoman taking a yoga class for the first time, who admitted to hearing "Prada" (the name of the fashion designer), instead of "Prana" (the word for breath or life-giving force), because she had been exposed to the former stimulus more than the latter.

We tend to prefer frequently occurring stimuli because they improve our prediction power. Abundant literature confirms that even though they deny it, people prefer familiar faces to unfamiliar faces, familiar foods to unfamiliar foods, and familiar objects to unfamiliar objects. As much as science reflects our preference for familiarity, we are almost insulted to hear this. Surely we are more attracted to novelty! To demonstrate that people are drawn to familiarity, scientists design studies where the exposure is separated from the stimulus. The way to do that is to place participants in an MRI scanner and show them a series of stimuli (pictures, text, or food) so quickly that the conscious brain does not detect them. When people are asked afterward which stimuli they would choose between two options (one they had "seen" and a new one), they choose the more familiar option. However, if they are told ahead of time that they had seen the stimulus, they claim to prefer the novel stimulus.

Further evidence for the preference for familiarity is found in studies where there is a time delay between the moment you see something and the moment you're asked if you prefer that stimulus. After a day or days, you tend to prefer the stimulus that occurred more frequently. Familiarity wins over novelty when our conscious mental processing is disrupted or distracted. If you are tired after a day's work and you are browsing through your iTunes, with limitless choices, do you find yourself migrating toward a familiar tune? Keep this principle in mind especially when you're talking to people who are tired or overwhelmed. We constantly want to impress others with novelty, but when their conscious processing is already spent, you're feeding the fast brain, which is drawn to familiarity.

Our preference for familiarity is called the exposure effect and has several scientific explanations. When we perceive something as familiar, we can let our guard down. The lower level of arousal means that we attend to the stimulus in a relaxed state, which creates pleasure. Another theory is that we misattribute the ease of processing to the actual stimulus: "Since it was so easy to see or taste or hear, it must be good, so I will choose it." Based on these theories, we can estimate that it's not so much that familiarity gives us pleasure; it is *accurate prediction* that gives us pleasure. And we attribute that positive feeling to the stimulus itself.

I once helped a presenter deliver a pitch on the importance of predictive data at a time when the concept was just gathering momentum. He knew that the people in his audience would be skeptical of some of his revolutionary concepts, so we opted to start with what they considered familiar: bad predictions. We included prophecies from those who predicted that the car, the computer, the airplane, the telephone, or the Beatles would not become popular. The presenter observed that it's tough to be in the business of farfetched predictions. Feeding his listeners' familiarity with bad predictions opened them up to listen longer.

Ron Berndt, program manager of Worldwide Sales & Partner Training at Cisco, attended one of my workshops and used these guidelines not only at work but also in his personal life. On Veterans Day, he was invited to give a 10-minute presentation in his hometown (Lake Geneva, Wisconsin) to about 500 students, faculty, veterans, and families. To engage students, he had to use something that felt familiar to them. Too much novelty, especially from a speaker they did not know, would have been too jarring. To teach them about the importance of veterans, Berndt had a brief quiz about famous actors who served in the military. Hearing names such as Ice-T, Chuck Norris, James Earl Jones, Mel Brooks, and Clint Eastwood prepared them for some novelty later on, when Berndt presented several modern-day heroes.

Reflect on your own content and ask: What do your listeners find familiar, and what are they prone to receiving without skepticism? The link to something that confirms their mental schema and alleviates threats buys you a few more minutes of their attention.

BREAK A PATTERN PEOPLE HAVE LEARNED TO EXPECT

Although highly familiar stimulation is preferred, after some point, too much predictability leads to boredom. To mitigate the tension between the pleasure caused by predictability and the conscious preference for novelty, it means that we must break a pattern our audiences have learned to expect.

When entrepreneur Peter Thiele, cofounder of PayPal, announced that he would pay 20 kids $100,000 to pursue world-changing innovations as part of his fellowship . . . if they drop out of school . . . it created a great deal of commotion because he disrupted an existing schema we have about the importance of formal education.

Surprise is departure from an expected norm.

In order to deviate from a pattern, we must first identify a pattern that people recognize, and then we must modify it slightly. Picture the *Mona Lisa*. It is a painting you have seen multiple times in your life— whether the actual work of art or a photograph—and if you were to see it one more time, there would be no surprises. If you want to show the *Mona Lisa* to others and surprise them, you would have to break away from what they expect. If we type in any search engine "*Mona Lisa* variations," we find the classic *Mona Lisa* morphed with Miss Piggy, Lara Croft, Rowan Atkinson (Mr. Bean), Santa Claus, the Terminator, Snow White, and many others. We also see her in different outfits— Egyptian goddess, biker chick, belly dancer—and with different accessories—sunglasses, cigarettes, devil ears, gas mask, tiara, clown nose and makeup, a fat cat that she is holding, hair rollers, or no hair at all. We even see the *Mona Lisa* in a wheelchair: this image advertised an event for an organization for people with disabilities. None of these effects would surprise us if we did not have the initial schema of this classic painting. So consider giving your audience members both something they expect and something they don't expect.

When working on a presentation for Bill Ruth, vice president at General Electric Software, I was impressed by how he used the concept of the consumer Internet (existing schema) and modified it. This is what he said: "In the nineties it was the consumer industry with a billion people connected. Now think what's going to happen when 50 billion machines get connected online. There will be more machines connected than there are people connected. It's going to change the way every industry operates. It's going to change the way every industrial product or service is delivered and managed." This approach works because it builds on what people know but also takes them on a new path.

You can disrupt a variety of schemas to create surprises. Take linguistic schemas, for instance. Now check out the following line:

The old man the boats.

Known as a garden-path phenomenon, it leads you on the path of a common interpretation of each word until it disrupts a linguistic schema. You may have to reread it until you process it successfully and fit it within an existing expectation.

Think of social schemas. Give someone a hug when that person expects a handshake and watch the surprise. Creating optical illusions, such as offering multiple images within one picture, is an example of deviating from a perceptual schema. Check out Charles Allan Gilbert's *All Is Vanity*, where you first see a skull, and then within the same picture, you spot a woman sitting at her vanity table.

We can create surprises by deviating from cultural norms, too. For example, scientists in music theory wanted to see if people from different cultures have different expectations based on different musical schemas. At the University of Washington in Seattle, several researchers presented volunteers with successive tones and asked them to predict what tone would come next in a melody. When they compared results across German, Hungarian, and American listeners, they found significant differences between the three groups, suggesting that mental representations are influenced by cultural background.

Can you think of ways in which your communication materials can deviate from linguistic, perceptual, cultural, or social norms to take your listeners by surprise?

BREAK A SACRED RULE

Another way to provide surprise—and therefore attract attention by causing a prediction error—is not only to break a pattern but to break one that people consider sacred. For example, you may be familiar with a painting called *Liberty Guiding the People* by Eugene Delacroix, which he completed in 1831. The painting depicts the heroes of the French Revolution, alongside the dominant figure of Liberty. Portrayed as a goddess, Liberty is standing rebellious and confident, despite the dress that has slipped below her breasts. Her right arm is extended up, holding the French flag toward the sunlight. This is all well and good, except that her raised arm shows an extremely hairy armpit. It was this detail that caught the critics' eye at the time. A goddess was always depicted with smooth, hairless skin. Critics were appalled that an allegory should have so much realism, that a goddess should resemble a natural woman so closely. The imperfection was forgiven, though, and the painting was welcomed with enthusiasm at the Louvre in 1874. Bare-breasted Liberty became such a French icon that she appears everywhere, from posters to book jackets and postage stamps.

Bobby Fischer, American chess prodigy, is known for having broken many sacred rules. In one internationally acclaimed match, he sacrificed his queen, a bold move dubbed "Be6," that won him the match.

In any industry, there is a natural cycle: experts establish the rules, and practitioners follow them. But at some point, someone comes around and breaks a few of those rules. The unconventional approaches work until they become the new rules. In business content, bullet points used to be the rule. Now, we are shifting toward visuals. At first, vibrant visuals dominated—until someone started a trend toward black and white, with a few accent colors. Sharp images ruled, and then at some point, pixilation became an intriguing effect.

What are some of the *sacred rules* that exist in your field? Is there one you can comfortably break in order to get attention and gain an uncontested place in your audience's memory when you take people by surprise? Would you be willing to sacrifice your queen?

JUXTAPOSE SEEMINGLY UNRELATED BUT EXISTING SCHEMAS

Musical satirist Peter Schickele pairs the very familiar Symphony No. 5 by Beethoven with a sporting event atmosphere, complete with a cheering audience, a referee, and two commentators. As soon as the symphony starts—*tah nah nah nah*, the most recognizable four notes in music—one of the commentators remarks, "And they are off. The beginning of a symphony is very exciting. I don't know if they are slow or fast because they keep stopping. And it looks like . . . yes, it looks like we are coming up to a cadence here, folks . . ." The commentary resembles that for baseball games, and the two familiar but unrelated fields (classical music and baseball) reward us on two fronts: the pleasure of predictability from both fields *and* the novelty and surprise that results from their combination.

Business presenters who successfully combine unrelated but existing schemas benefit from greater attention and memory. For example, when helping a company promote its data analytics services for revenue growth, we started with a comparison between a lightbulb and a laser. In the script, we mentioned that "a bulb releases light waves at multiple frequencies, which inefficiently go in random directions. Shine a penlight at a wall during the day, and it is barely visible. In contrast, a laser releases light waves on the same frequency, going in the same direction. A laser beam illuminates across the room during the day, reads DVDs, cuts through steel walls, performs brain surgeries, and even measures the distance to the moon." We then asked the members of the audience whether their company was like a lightbulb, with brilliant people but going in different directions and operating in silos. We invited them to imagine an organization operating more like a laser: focused, synchronized, with incredible potential. And the way to make it happen was with proper data analytics. The juxtaposition between the lightbulb/laser and the concept of data analytics was perceived as new, even though each individual concept was considered familiar and easily recognized.

Look around you right now. What two familiar things can you combine that would delight listeners and take them by surprise?

Find the familiar and play off it.

FEED EXPECTATIONS BY LINKING TO BELIEFS AND TOOLS

Surprises are a function of expectations, and the expectations people form are tied to their beliefs. Expectations based on beliefs are often so strong that they turn into self-fulfilling prophecies. This has been tested and measured across a large spectrum of situations. Students who believe they will do well in school typically do. People who believe they will do well on a job typically do. People who believe they will have great relationships typically do. This means that when we link our content to an audience's existing beliefs, we increase the likelihood of action.

In addition to strong beliefs, we often fortify our expectations with tools. This is why good-luck charms, omens, and lucky underwear tend to enhance self-efficacy. Science demonstrates that this is not magic. When researchers look at the psychological impact of "tools" such as four-leaf clovers, horseshoes, dice, and lucky numbers, they realize that one of the reasons they are effective is because they reduce anxiety, and anxiety has a negative impact on performance. From this angle, lucky socks can indeed be helpful in a job interview.

Placebo pills are another example of how the brain turns expectations into self-fulfilling prophecy. Abundant research demonstrates how patients who take placebo pills report significant improvement when they need relief from pain, anxiety, depression, sexual dysfunction, digestive disorders, insomnia, and even tremors in Parkinson's disease. The common thread across these conditions is that they impact the brain regions that generate beliefs and expectations, interpret social cues, and anticipate rewards. Using MRI and EEG technology, scientists are able to pinpoint the neurological foundation of placebos. As we saw earlier, when faced with pain or fear or stress, the brain produces its own analgesic compounds called opiates, and placebos are known to activate them. These inert pills trigger areas of the brain that are responsible for assessing the significance of an event and potential threats. If you hear an alarm and you see smoke, you know something is about to happen and prepare for an escape. It is the same with pain. Placebo treatments hook into the brain's systems that dictate a course of action.

Placebos certainly have their limitations; for example, they can relieve pain from chemotherapy but will not stop the growth of tumors. Real medicine and placebos are not mutually exclusive. The placebo builds off real treatments, and real treatments rely on the power of expectations.

In any message you create, consider your audience's expectations. Tie your ideas or solutions to people's existing *beliefs* of hope, or create new beliefs of optimism for the future. In addition, provide *tools* that can act as a catalyst to help their brains release their natural power to foresee a better path. You will be surprised by how inexpensive tools can take people from Point A to Point B by igniting their expectations for a better future. Kleenex offered tissues. In other business contexts, we can offer checklists, brief how-to videos, free apps, or trial software to help your audience perform a simple task after they listen to you. The brain has many resources to take it to the finish line if you know how to tap them. After all, patients don't care so much whether their relief comes from sham pills or a kindhearted doctor. They want the *expectation* of getting better.

Expectations = beliefs + tools

It is also helpful to build strong associations between your content and something your audience truly enjoys. This is because enjoyment feeds the expectation of a desirable future. For example, when promoting pills, advertisers are brilliant in linking the benefit of taking a specific drug to a lifestyle that gives people satisfaction. When promoting acid reflux pills, marketers don't just show the product and say, "Take this; it will relieve your symptoms." In an ad from Saatchi & Saatchi, for instance, the intent is to associate an acid reflux pill with areas in someone's life that offer peace of mind: "Is it time with your children? Is it curling up with a good book on the couch? Is it your favorite television show? Is it a little purple pill that helps you get rid of acid reflux?" When interviewed, the Saatchi & Saatchi advertisers said that the uplifting associations have the potential to feed into people's expectations and activate the placebo effect. Viagra ads don't even show men. They feature a beautiful woman talking to us from a comfortable bed.

In a recent presentation for ESPN, I had the opportunity to work with Nathalie Bordes, an emerging platforms researcher who studies marketing and consumer insights. Bordes knew her audiences at a recent conference enjoyed hearing how data informs marketing decisions. For her presentation, we showed how the MediaScience lab she commissioned in Austin, Texas allows for a controlled test environment of various media and uses scientific tools and measurements, such as reaction time, eye tracking, facial coding, biometrics, surveys, and focus groups. She had an easy time getting her listeners' attention because she started with information they already enjoy: using data to measure marketing performance.

Link your content to uplifting associations.

CONTINUE TO ELEVATE YOUR CONTENT

Most of our actions are fueled by our desire to feel good. As we've seen in this chapter, a mixture of predictability and surprise provides your listeners with pleasure. However, each time you're surprising your audiences and the outcome is pleasant, you're helping them build a *new* set of expectations, a new set of possibilities for the next time they see you. This means that if you choose to offer surprises and elevate the familiar each time, they will start to expect it next time in order to stay satisfied.

In the 1920s, scientist Otto L. Tinklepaugh (what a delightful name!) carried out a series of experiments at UC Berkeley with rhesus monkeys. In one of his most famous experiments, Tinklepaugh trained monkeys to retrieve a hidden piece of lettuce. The experiment went like this. The monkey would sit on a chair and watch the researcher hide the lettuce under one of two cups. Then the monkey would be taken outside the room, and when it was brought back in, it would take the primate 3 to 4 seconds to go straight to the cup with the hidden lettuce and eat it. The experiment was then replicated, except this time, a banana would be hidden under one of the two cups. The researcher observed the increased enthusiasm of the monkey with the banana. Now that the monkeys expected the bananas, the researcher placed lettuce under the cup to watch the reaction. Here is what he noted: "Subject rushes to proper cup and picks it up. Extends hand toward lettuce. Stops. Looks around on floor. Looks in, under, around cup. Glances at other cup. Looks back at screen. Looks under and around self. Looks and shrieks at any observer present. Walks away, leaving lettuce untouched on floor."

Your listeners' expectations change constantly. Are you keeping up?

Once you get your audiences used to a specific set of experiences and expectations, be prepared to maintain and raise that level if you want to surprise them and if they are to remain satisfied. Don't give them lettuce if they expect bananas.

- Our audiences form expectations so that they can predict the next moment. When you give them something they expect, you satisfy a human need for accurate predictions, which generates pleasure.

- Audiences form expectations automatically and mostly unconsciously based on what they pay attention to, memories of past experiences, motivations, emotions, and beliefs they form along the way. To get attention, tie your content to existing beliefs for a better future and provide effective tools they can use after consuming your content, such as checklists, how-to videos, or free software trials.

- Too much predictability can lead to boredom. Offer your audiences something they expect (and can predict), as well as something that takes them by surprise. Use linguistic, perceptual, cultural, or social norms to break conventions.

- Juxtapose seemingly unrelated but existing schemas to create surprise.

- Continue elevating your content to ensure you are meeting your audiences' ever-evolving palate for satisfying experiences.

CHAPTER 6

SWEET ANTICIPATION

How to Build Excitement for What Happens Next

C arl Sandburg, the Pulitzer Prize–winning poet, spent the last years of his life on a farm in North Carolina. The distinguished journalist Edward Murrow (you may recognize him for his famous "Good night and good luck" sign-off) visited Sandburg for a stimulating conversation between two people in love with words. At the end of the interview, Murrow asked the poet:

"Mr. Sandburg, what is the ugliest word in the English language?"

"The ugliest word . . . ? The *ugliest* word . . . ? Uh . . . uh? The ugliest word . . . ?"

Most books and websites reporting this story relate it with a certain amount of detail before revealing Sandburg's answer. One says: "The poet frowned. He reflected awhile, face knotted in thought. After a long, pregnant pause, Sandburg's eyes brightened and returned to the reporter's." Another relates: "Sandburg pondered for a long minute and repeated the phrase slowly, 'the ugliest word in the English language. . . . the ugliest word . . . '" Yet another reads: "With characteristic playfulness and drama, the wise poet pondered the question at length, seemingly searching his vast vocabulary storehouse for the appropriate answer. With a quizzical expression on his face and stroking his chin, he mused, "The ugliest word? The *ugliest* word . . . ? The ugliest word in the English language is . . . 'exclusive.'"

However you come across this story, it is unlikely that you see the conclusion right away: "In an interview with a reporter, poet Carl Sandburg said that the ugliest English word is 'exclusive.'" The ellipses in the descriptions, the mental imagery, the qualifiers, the details that prolong the thinking process . . . all draw us in because they create a pleasant sense of anticipation. If we find the topic relevant and anticipate a good reward, we're motivated to linger with the text; the story turns the brain from passive to active by inviting it to think of what comes next. When we become active, we also feel more connected to what we see, and this connection brings pleasure.

There are many advantages associated with anticipation: it provides a cue that something interesting or important will happen, and it leads to improved attention, memory, and the decision to act. This is why it is worthwhile to understand anticipation and learn how to create it for your listeners in the quest to become impossible to ignore.

Something always happens next. Can you get others excited about it?

Anticipation provides a good lab for testing mental models or schemas so we know how to adjust behavior and make better choices or predictions in the future. Imagine you saw an article titled "Things You Thought Were French but Aren't." In the article, you learn that the croissant comes from Austria, the French press was patented in Italy, the French braid originated in Greece, and an American designer is credited for the French manicure. In another situation, you find out that Russian nesting dolls, the set of hollow figures that open up to reveal progressively smaller dolls within, originated in China, were copied by the Japanese, and *then* were brought to Russia. On another occasion, you hear how fortune cookies are not really Chinese. In time, you start forming a new schema related to "culturally misattributed objects." Next time you hear someone say, "This object originated in my country," you may question that statement and not believe it immediately.

Anticipation allows us to prepare our state of attention and arousal in order to use just the right amount of energy; after all, it's not useful to get excited if nothing worthwhile will happen, and it may not be advantageous to be fully surprised. During anticipation, the hippocampus gets a hit as well, which is why it facilitates learning and memory.

Anticipating well gives us not only a biological and cognitive advantage but a competitive advantage, too. For instance, experienced sports players in baseball, boxing, badminton, squash, tennis, or karate show superior performance compared with novices because they are good at anticipating an opponent's next move. Sports psychologists consider these athletes as able to literally "expand the present." The Romanian tennis star Ilie Nastase, one of the world's top players in the 1970s, was considered to operate on "manufactured time." This is the result of lots of practice, which turns skills into automated actions, and it allows real-time detection of relevant information about the opponent.

Based on these advantages of anticipation, let's look at practical ways to create it for our audiences to impact the way they notice cues, search their memories, and act on intention at Point B. First, let's distinguish in more detail the difference between expectation and anticipation.

WHAT'S THE DIFFERENCE BETWEEN EXPECTATION AND ANTICIPATION?

It is a bit of an exercise in hairsplitting because anticipation is part of expectation, and both are related to the brain's tendency to be on fast-forward. For this discussion, let's consider expectations as general beliefs about the world, which produce the tacit knowledge that something is going to happen. Anticipation is thinking consciously of what's going to happen and preparing for it. While expectations run in the background and may be generic, anticipation brings forward a specific moment. For example, let's say you're at a restaurant and have a sip of wine left in your glass. You're looking forward to finishing these last few drops when the waiter takes the glass away. That's interfering with your anticipation. However, if the waiter suddenly spills coffee on your lap, that's interfering with your expectations.

Let's apply the same definitions of anticipation versus expectations from your audience's perspective. When people listen to you, they hold in mind a wide range of possibilities, based on their previous knowledge, experiences, and memories of a similar context. With anticipation, you help them zoom in on a specific occurrence. And to achieve the biggest impact, as we will see in the rest of the chapter, add intrigue to the probable. After all, there is a reason for the popular term "sweet anticipation."

SWEET ANTICIPATION

INFLUENCING ACTION WITH ANTICIPATION AND EMOTION

One of the most important aspects of anticipation versus expectation is the emotion that anticipation can evoke. "I *expect* the plane to land at 10" is one thing. "I *anticipate* my lover's arrival on that plane" is another, and it is likely to get you to the airport. Anticipation invites others to imagine how the future unfolds, and that can impact the way they feel and make decisions.

Using the word "imagine" is a powerful way to create anticipation and emotion. Picture the messages below:

Imagine a world where every child owns a microscope.

Imagine getting rid of all the surveillance devices around you.

Imagine dragons.

While general expectations are about *seeing* the future (e.g., "Here is what to expect during business meetings"), anticipation is about *feeling* the future (e.g., "Here are three reasons to get excited about our next meeting."). Imaginative thought is aspirational, but it's imaginative emotions that push us into action. Anticipation is therefore a stronger expectation, a boost that gets us ready to act. Notice what happens in your brain when you read an introduction like this: "In October 2012, Jarrett Barrios, CEO of Red Cross of Eastern Massachusetts, decided to train for his first marathon. That race would be the tragic 2013 Boston Marathon, and Jarrett would be stopped at mile 25.8. This is Jarrett's story of that day." Would you pay attention to this unexpected cue and tune in and focus on what comes next? The anticipatory words not only include facts but also trigger emotions that make us focus on the content for a bit longer, despite possible distractions.

Anticipation is acting on expectations.

Why should we be concerned about including emotion when creating anticipation? Because people don't act on reason alone; they act on reason *and* emotion. Isn't a well-organized meeting agenda we share ahead of time worth showing up for? It is not, because people don't act on reason alone; they act on reason *and* emotion.

Emotion is instrumental in decision-making. Antonio Damasio, an acclaimed neurologist, describes the condition of patients who have experienced damage to the emotional processing areas of the brain. As a result, these patients are paralyzed when making decisions. Healthy people use emotions as markers at encoding, so that at retrieval they have an easier time choosing, whereas for the damaged brain, any option looks just as good as the next one. This makes even trivial tasks such as choosing what to eat or what to wear extremely agonizing. Part of the problem is that these patients cannot anticipate feeling future outcomes: "Will I feel good or bad if I choose the chicken?" Even though they are intellectually aware of negative outcomes and can pass IQ tests successfully, they are still not capable of making decisions because the feelings about the various outcomes are not palpable.

We don't just think about the future; we feel the future. While working with Victoria Guster-Hines, a vice president at McDonald's, I remember brainstorming on how we could incorporate anticipation in her presentation about several business drivers for the new year. It would have been tempting to dive right into the facts. Instead, we spent a few minutes building anticipation with emotion first, so her audience could *feel* the facts later.

She started by relating stories about her family, and she shared photos from family events, including one of a breakfast with 70 people. She remarked how looking at the pictures reminded her of the fact that "the family you came from is as important as the family you are going to have," and transitioned into speaking about the McFamily—the family she has at work, the family responsible for carrying out the new business drivers. This emotion-infused introduction took only 2 minutes, but those 2 minutes secured attention for 20 more afterward.

INFLUENCING THE AUDIENCE'S NEXT STEP WITH ANTICIPATION AND DOPAMINE

So far we've learned that anticipation has an impressive résumé: it leads to sharper focus (noticing cues), improved cognition, and faster reactions and decisions. Why does anticipation have so much power over our brains? The power stems from the "juice" that fuels it: dopamine. When we simulate the future, we are looking for rewards, and neuroscientists confirm that stimuli *predicting* the possibility of a reward invoke the same neuronal activity as the one triggered by the reward itself; this finding is valid in both human and animal research. Simply seeing the TV remote can get us excited in anticipation of all the fun things we get to see when we grab it.

Dopamine spikes in anticipation of rewards.

If we know how dopamine is released, we have the opportunity to impact not only the noticing of cues but also our listeners' motivation and momentum to act on what we say. Let's define motivation as the mental state in which we are willing to work to obtain a reward or avoid a punishment. Neuroscience research confirms that people feel more motivated to take action with a boost of dopamine.

Dopamine is transmitted from one brain region to another through a system of neurons, called the dopaminergic system. One branch of the system extends to the frontal cortex, where it impacts cognitive functions, such as thinking and short-term memory. Another branch goes to the striatum, which is responsible for motor control. Another goes to the limbic system, considered the emotional brain, which houses our reward center. Dopamine neurons signal the onset of important events and fuel the motivation to stay engaged, learn meaningful patterns, and ultimately obtain a predicted reward.

Many research findings related to dopamine mention its link to *positive experiences*. Neurobiological mechanisms associated with positive experiences typically include these components: *wanting, liking,* and *learning.* Consider chocolate. Wanting implies the motivation to go get it (that extra "oomph" we need to get on our feet and do something). Liking is the pleasure we get from eating it. And learning includes associations based on past experiences, which help us predict that the next experience with the same stimulus will feel just as good. Once we get a fix, we look back on the event to extract meaning and evaluate our predictive accuracy. Research has shown that even abstract pleasures, such as completing a project, admiring a painting, listening to music, or sharing opinions with others, can be as strong in generating a pleasant experience as basic sensory pleasures, such as eating something sweet.

Neuroscientists have dispelled the myth that dopamine mediates *liking* or the subjective pleasure we get from a reward. For example, researchers have observed that even patients with Parkinson's still like the sweet taste of foods even though they endure severe dopamine depletion. In other words, we don't need dopamine to like chocolate. We need dopamine to go get it.

Why should we be concerned with dopamine when we create content? It is because the presence of dopamine increases the likelihood that people have *enough motivation* to not only notice cues but come and get the rewards we're promising—and return to us again.

Help people convert the prediction of a reward into the motivation to go get it.

PRACTICAL AND REALISTIC WAYS TO GENERATE DOPAMINE

So far, we know two things: (1) if there is an anticipated reward, people notice and are willing to exert some effort to get it; and (2) dopamine is released in even higher doses when there is an *unexpected* but pleasant reward. Let's see how we can put these findings into practice.

Help Your Audience Anticipate a Pleasant Reward Accurately

When people anticipate a reward, dopamine neurons fire off. This is useful because you can rely on the audience exerting some effort—such as planning to attend your meeting, presentation, or training session or clicking to see your content—to get what you're promising.

What do people find so motivating that they are willing to act? To answer that, ask another question: What pushes *you* into action? And do you stay motivated with the same intensity all the time? Behavioral and neuroscience findings indicate that the strength of our motivations fluctuates according to our mood. Food is appealing when we're hungry and we're willing to go through great effort to get it, but it is not so relevant on a full stomach. To create anticipation, we must appeal to rewards that are linked to a *current* state of mind.

The degree of motivation that triggers behavior is also dependent on individual traits (some people are naturally the "go-getter" type), stress, sleep deprivation, and even the state of intoxication at the time of decision-making. For example, people who are already taking some drugs (e.g., amphetamine) find it easier to stay motivated to seek rewards because dopamine levels are already high. Learned rewards do not change in this case, but the intensity of the motivation *to do* something does. Overall, fluctuations in mood make it tough to predict what people want to do next.

Mere knowledge about a reward is not motivation.

Although it is possible that if we are hungry or stressed or sleep deprived, we may not be intensely motivated to do much, let's consider these states as exceptions rather than rules. And since we know the brain is constantly seeking rewards, let's look at practical ways to account for rewards and the value of those rewards in our approach to content. But what do people consider *rewarding*? And how do they assign *values* to rewards?

The values we assign to rewards come from the effort necessary to obtain rewards (physical, mental, or financial), from the risk, and from the delay before we receive those rewards; values also depend on the social impact we associate with those rewards. Even though studies remind us that food, sleep, sex, fun, entertainment, and leisure are strong motivators, business professionals immediately ask, "How will some of these drivers reflect in the content I create for work purposes?" Someone may say, "I can't really reference sex or food in my B2B content when I talk about Big Data."

Researchers Adrian Gostick and Chester Elton surveyed 850,000 adults from different countries to understand what drives people *at work* and what differentiates dedicated employees from those just going through the motions. Their list contains five main categories (Achievers, Builders, Caregivers, Reward-Driven, and Thinkers) with a total set of 23 drivers. *Achievers* find these aspects rewarding: challenge, excelling, ownership, pressure, and problem solving. *Builders* consider these elements rewarding: developing others, friendship, purpose, service, social responsibility, and teamwork. *Caregivers* are motivated by empathy, family, and fun. The *Reward-Driven* are excited about money, prestige, recognition, and autonomy. *Thinkers* are motivated by creativity, excitement, impact, learning, and variety. Consider using this list (for more details, visit thecultureworks.com) to create anticipation for any message. It is effective because the motivations plug into items that have different driving power for different kinds of people.

Let's say you are announcing a program on marketing automation, and you want to appeal to marketing professionals. You can customize the anticipatory messages depending on the type of participants you expect and what they consider rewarding. This technique enables them to anticipate rewards accurately:

> "Attend this program to learn 4 techniques for marketing automation." *(Thinkers motivated by learning)*

"Attend this program to be best-in-class for marketing automation." *(Reward-Driven motivated by recognition)*

"Challenge yourself to learn the latest marketing automation techniques." *(Achievers motivated by challenge)*

Business communicators sometimes wonder, "If I tell others what will happen during an upcoming conversation, meeting, or presentation, won't that spoil it?" Receiving ample information ahead of time is not a letdown. This is because the *proof* of what will happen influences people's feeling of power. For example, in a research study, people were asked to interact with each other; prior to the interaction, they were sent some information about their conversation partners, therefore creating anticipation about what this partner may be like (e.g., extroverted, friendly, energetic, outgoing). Some participants did not receive this information. Participants who had an informational advantage reported that they felt empowered. The reverse was also tested: having ambiguous information ahead of time led to the diffusion of power. People feel the need to control their environment, and the experience of power means having enough resources to take action.

Having information about someone else ahead of time is a source of power.

Reserve Room for Some Uncertainty

We've discussed helping others to anticipate *accurately* by looking at motivating functions related to reward. This perspective is useful because it reduces prediction error; in general, people want to feel in control and predict upcoming rewards if they are to exert any effort. However, neuroscience research reminds us that there is a functional and anatomical overlap between reward and *novelty*. The area of the brain that anticipates rewards is the same area that processes novelty.

Novelty has intrinsic rewarding qualities, and dopamine spikes even more in the face of uncertainty because of the magnitude of the prediction error.

The anticipation of novelty also activates the hippocampus, which means that those new items are more likely to enter long-term memory. For example, in an fMRI study, participants were shown cues that predicted novel or familiar pictures with 75% accuracy. Cues that helped participants anticipate novel pictures activated the reward center of the brain more than cues associated with familiar pictures. In other words, *anticipating novelty felt as good as anticipating a reward.* When novelty feels rewarding, we are more motivated to explore environments that contain novel stimuli. This exploratory behavior can have biological advantages, such as in animals exploring new territories for food or business professionals exploring new fields for entrepreneurship.

In a sense, we're dealing with a paradox: on one hand, we want to help people predict our communication accurately, but on the other, we want to provide novelty to trigger a larger spike in dopamine. Music composer and cognitive psychologist David Huron has practical recommendations for reconciling these two angles. Here is an adaptation of his views to general business communication: Let's imagine you're creating content that is based on a sequence of bits; these bits can be parts of a campaign, segments in a presentation, or multiple presentations in an event. Let's say you keep all the bits the same, and the sequence is like this: AAAAA. This would give your listeners a lot of predictability because after they detect the pattern, they will know what to anticipate next and are certain they will get it (hence dopamine release). However, after a while, boredom sets in. The opposite of this technique is an ABCDE sequence, where each component is different from the previous one. This means that the brain has to wait until the E bit is finished to see what happens next, and the lack of predictability is too unsettling.

A better approach is to start with the familiar, introduce a new component, allow greater familiarity to settle in with some repetition, and then move on to other new material. Dmitry Kormann, a musician from São Paulo, Brazil, observes how composer Igor Stravinsky creates momentum in his classic *The Rite of Spring*. Stravinsky uses *a few steps forward and one step back* to introduce new elements, returns to something familiar with a modification, and then reintroduces an older item. The rhythm continues between patterns that have emerged and novelty. Check out the image below: some of the shapes stay the same, some new ones are introduced, and then there is a return to older ones with a modification; note that each time there is novelty, there is also some familiarity.

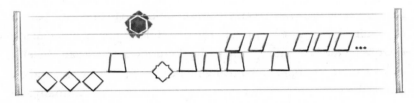

MIX PREDICTABILITY WITH NOVELTY

As you analyze your content, how does your sequence compare? Are you simply moving from one block to another in your content, or are you returning to a motif? Consider alternating between progressively larger blocks and smaller instances of familiar blocks.

We can learn about optimal content sequence based on accurate prediction and novelty from brand names. A brand name is a form of anticipation because we rely on feedback loops from the past to help us predict that our experience in the future will be similar when we use that brand again. Burberry, a brand widely known for its iconic checkered pattern (predictability at its best), is a good example of staying true to its history while allowing new designs to emerge. For example, you can still buy its signature beige trench coat, but Burberry has expanded its offerings beyond a full line of clothing to other products, such as cologne and cosmetics. Even if you can't afford a coat, you can still send "Burberry kisses" through digital media or listen to hip new artists when you browse in its stores. The brand constantly merges the old with the new.

Ration new material.

I once worked on a presentation with a CEO for a telecom company that produces session border controllers, multiservice security gateways, and session routing proxies. These are not the sexiest topics on the planet to discuss, but we managed to create anticipation and attract attention by announcing that the presentation was about disruption and how the company was best positioned to handle *new* trends in the telecom industry. Announcing key market trends had been done before in an executive presentation, so to break the pattern of predictable business content, the CEO interspersed personal stories of a recent visit with his son to the Roundhouse Railroad Museum in Savannah, Georgia. Juxtaposing pictures of his young son and old trains, the CEO pointed out the state of transition his company was undergoing and the fact that history never looks like history when you're living through it. Each time the CEO introduced new information (trends such as mobility, over-the-top applications, unified communications, cloud communication, and service diversity), he used personal stories to return to the same motif: being prepared to transition from old to new and stay relevant. This allowed his audience to enjoy a good mix of predictable and unexpected content.

TECHNIQUES FOR BUILDING ANTICIPATION WITH UNCERTAINTY

Providing a modicum of uncertainty in your communications is effective because dopamine spikes in the face of unexpected events. In general, uncertainty makes us uneasy, which is why it is often referred to as "tension." We can tolerate some tension as long as (1) we know its degree, (2) we are reminded about the importance of the final outcome, and (3) we can tolerate the amount of delay until that outcome is realized. Let's identify practical guidelines associated with each.

1. The Degree of Uncertainty

As a communicator, you must balance how much information to reveal (and allow listeners' brains to predict accurately) and how much information to withhold (and get listeners ready for action, even if the action only implies people showing up to listen to you). When the outcome is certain and of little consequence, the anticipation effect is minimal. This is why asking people to join you for a "status update meeting" is a fairly dull proposition, but it can be rescued with a little work.

Compare these two invitations: "Meeting update on Tuesday. We are on track for the first three tasks, but we need to discuss task 4." Versus "You won't believe what we found during our last task audit and the impact it will make on the final milestone of your project." Only use this tactic when it is truthful; avoid the click bait technique, marked by empty sensationalism.

Uncertainty can derive from the "what" or the "when" of a situation, which means you can manipulate these two variables when you create a message of anticipation. Notice what happens when you tell your partner, "I have a surprise for you tonight." You make the "when" known, but dopamine spikes because the "what" is uncertain. You also feel the power of anticipation if your employer says, "We have a small bonus for you, which you will receive this quarter." You know *what*, but you don't know specifically *when*.

2. The Importance of Possible Outcomes

When we anticipate events, the brain typically estimates the worst and best possible outcomes, consciously or subconsciously. For example, if you have elbow pain, you may be estimating the best outcome to be a bit of inflammation that will go down with some Advil; the worst outcome may be a torn ligament and surgery. Your decision to see a specialist depends on how important having a functional elbow is to you. If you're an avid tennis player, you will go through the extra effort to see a doctor even if you anticipate the diagnosis to be fairly benign. If walking or hiking is your main activity, the anticipation of elbow surgery may not bother you until it starts interfering with other outcomes that are important, such as brushing your teeth or picking up your child.

Reflect on your own messages. When you build anticipation for an upcoming event, ask from your listeners' perspective: What are some possible outcomes? How important are they? And is there a big difference between the best and worst outcome? For example, if you want to build anticipation to entice people to attend a conference, the possible outcomes are that they *fully* enjoy it; they somewhat enjoy it except some sessions may be boring; they may consider *all* sessions to be boring, but at least there is some beneficial *networking*; or they *totally* hate it and consider it a waste of time. To minimize the difference between best and worst outcomes ("loved it" versus "hated it"), conference organizers have a few options. For instance, they set up events in venues that go beyond a predictable conference center or hotel. Imagine a business event hosted in an old warehouse, aircraft hangar, museum, botanical garden, or restored nineteenth-century sailboat. These are creative backdrops. Even if the content doesn't appeal to them, people will likely remember the experience.

Business events sometimes showcase guests who have skills in fields other than what the event is actually about; this is another way organizers invite people to imagine optimal outcomes. For example, Orlando-based artist Rock Demarco can paint anything in 10 minutes. Picture the portrait of your CEO being done in record time to a rock 'n' roll soundtrack. For extra oomph, Demarco wears a glove with five finger-like paintbrushes that shoot lasers. Toronto-based street painter David Johnston uses chalk to make realistic drawings at live events. He creates those 3D scenes you may have seen that tease your mind, such as drawing stairs on a flat street that give you the sensation you can go down to another level, even if there is no other level. French artist Antonin Fourneau brings an installation made of thousands of LEDs set against a wall, which he lights up by using a damp sponge. The final result is a water light graffiti show. Some may consider these entertainments nothing more than marketing fluff, so be sure to tie them to a message you want to make memorable. Otherwise, they may seem superficial.

Unusual activities do not have to cost a lot of money. In some of my brain science workshops, I take participants to an area they have not visited before, where they can interview strangers on various topics important in their fields, including leadership, communication, conflict management, marketing, sales techniques, or artificial intelligence. We receive some of the most useful insights from Starbucks baristas, university students, tourists, and hotel staff.

What are some unusual activities happening in *your* area? Or what performers with skills different from your teams' can you invite to add a new take on your content or provide a break from it? Once you identify guests who can add insights, or an unexpected venue, link them to the value they provide and create anticipatory messages that make it easy for your audiences to answer, "What's the worst that can happen?"

3. The Delay Before the Outcome Is Realized

The third aspect that impacts tension is delay, meaning the time that elapses before an outcome is realized. When you create any sort of communication, you essentially take your audience from one state to another state. The time lapse between the starting point and the destination can be short (seconds, minutes) or long (weeks, months, even years). TV news programs are very good at creating tension via delay: "What will happen to the stock market in the next two weeks? And should you go away for the holidays? All of this and more at 11." Sometimes TV producers use *foreshadowing*, meaning constantly announcing what's been shown and what happens next. For example, in a *House Hunters* episode on the HGTV channel, a show where people search for a dream home in various parts of the world, we may hear something like: "Abby Gordon memorized maps of Paris before ever setting foot in France. So when a job transfer to the city of her dreams came up, she took the chance. Now, after five years of renting, Abby is ready to take her relationship with the City of Light to the next level. She wants to buy an apartment that reflects her personal style. See what happens when House Hunters International settles down in Paris, France." Then we see some commercials, and in the next scene, we hear a summary of the intro, and then view the first house that Abby visits. The formula of novelty + foreshadowing + brief summary of previous segment + novelty + foreshadowing . . . repeats a few times during the show.

If the topics are relevant, anticipation sustains the motivation to tune in to a program later; we appreciate it when programs release the tension with useful information, and we become disappointed when they don't ("We stayed up for *this*?"). Movie trailers provoke a similar reaction. They create anticipation and tension through delay, and sometimes they deliver. The trailer said just enough to get us interested, and the entire movie is a good experience. Sometimes they disappoint: the funniest moments portrayed in the trailer were the *only* funny moments in the movie.

A delay must keep the promise of the anticipated reward.

In business communication, the length of the delay depends on your audience. Sometimes business audiences are in such a rush that only a short delay is effective. Here are a couple of examples:

> "Do you know who is tracking your movements online? A plug-in for the Firefox browser called Lightbeam tells you which third parties want to grab hold of your data. It records every website your computer connects with, often more than the one you intended to visit. It then creates visualizations, ranging from a list to a clocklike design, to highlight who is requesting access to your data."

> "Are you sick of searching for a city parking spot? Let your phone do the work. An app can automatically determine when its user has parked, and can alert others when the spot comes open again, all without manual input. The app could also be

programmed to predict when a driver is heading back to his or her car and send out notice that a parking space is about to become free."

The tension and release happen quickly and are intended for busy professionals who only have a few seconds to listen or read brief segments. If you are working in a space where you know communication has to happen in very short bites, make sure the "reveals" that deliver on the promise of anticipation are satisfying and accurate.

If the delay is brief, find the right words for the reveal and practice them.

When your audience is fairly patient, you can create a slightly longer delay with longer sentences instead of just a few words; or if you're writing, using an attractive title, an intriguing image, and an interesting first paragraph motivates people to read on. For example, in an article in *Popular Science* titled "What My Mother Learned from Einstein," the author relates that in 1946, her mother was going to school in Cape Town, South Africa, and wrote a letter to Einstein to share her dream of becoming a scientist. The title and first paragraph invite us to read on to find out if Einstein replied. The delay is fairly brief. We find out that the writer's mother received a response from Einstein, full of encouragement. At the time, men and women were not seen as equal, especially in the sciences, so she was surprised to receive a second letter from Einstein, reminding her that she could achieve her dreams despite her gender. The quick tension is followed by an even more rewarding release. Not only did he reply, but he wrote her twice!

In other communications, such as comprehensive marketing campaigns, meetings, or conferences, you can stretch tension for hours, days, weeks, or months. Take, for instance, the prolonged tension generated by a campaign created by Grupo W, an agency in Mexico, for Rexona Power, a men's deodorant manufactured by

Unilever. The goal of the marketing campaign was to advertise the best attribute of the deodorant: 1 million active molecules, which means extra protection for extremely active men, aged 18 to 25. The agency built curiosity around the product by creating a website and advertising a national movement in Mexico to raise 1 million clicks to "save Fermin" (about whom nothing is known). The campaign reached its goal in a few weeks, after which it launched "Who Is Fermin?" on the site. Online visitors had to overcome various obstacles, which, when solved, provided information about Fermin and whether they shared his spirit. The long delay in showing the actual product, Rexona Power, was worthwhile, as sales increased once consumers related with the "Fermin spirit," which is living life to its fullest (and, of course, wearing the proper deodorant).

Even when an outcome is highly predictable, you can still use delay to generate that extra dose of dopamine to keep the brain engaged. We can learn from Hollywood how to do this. Imagine a highly predictable Hollywood plot in which you know the good guy will win. To delay predictability, directors:

1. Use slow motion.

2. Cut to a new scene in the middle of the predictable scene or just before the outcome is realized.

3. Turn what we thought would be a predictable shot and a decisive moment into a not-so-important one after all, with the real decisive moment happening later in the movie.

I was listening to a software executive who mentioned that he had previously worked at Apple as part of the team that developed Newton, an initial attempt at a tablet. He paused and allowed the people in the room to absorb the information. Everyone is impressed by anything related to Apple. Then he added, "Newton was the first product that Steve Jobs nixed when he came back to Apple." What we thought would be a predictable story of success turned out to be one of failure. Everyone smiled sympathetically and immediately connected with the speaker. He spoke about his successes later on in his presentation.

Provide sweet anticipation, not an agonizing wait.

I received some great advice from Jack Daly, an entrepreneur who has sold two multimillion-dollar businesses and is now inspiring audiences all over the world to grow their businesses. "Give people a valuable tool in the first five minutes of a presentation and announce five more for later on."

Ponder your communications right now. Can you delay gratification while sustaining attention? Are you making the reveal too soon? How long can you prolong anticipation without your audience getting discouraged or annoyed? Allow the answer to dictate the length of the delay. This mindset is important because anticipation triggers dopamine, which activates motivation and action.

KEEP IN MIND

- Use the word "imagine" to create anticipation and invite action. People don't just think about the future; they feel the future, and emotion influences decision-making.

- People feel more motivated to take action with a boost of dopamine. The presence of dopamine increases the likelihood that people have *enough motivation* to not only notice cues but come and get the rewards we're promising and return to us again.

- Dopamine is released when we help people anticipate a reward accurately, but also when we reserve room for *some* uncertainty. The area of the brain that predicts rewards is the same area that handles novelty.

- Dopamine spikes in the face of unexpected events. In general, uncertainty makes us uneasy, which is why it is often referred to as "tension." We can tolerate some tension as long as (1) we know its degree, (2) we are reminded about the importance of the final outcome, and (3) we can tolerate the amount of delay until that outcome is realized.

- Unusual activities or performers with skills different from your teams' are anticipation hooks and serve as strong cues that announce worthy outcomes.

- If the delay before realizing a promised reward is brief, find the right words for the reveal and practice them.

- Use foreshadowing, which means frequently giving signs of what will come next.

WE SHARE
CONTENT HERE A

THEY REMEMBER
B AND ACT HERE

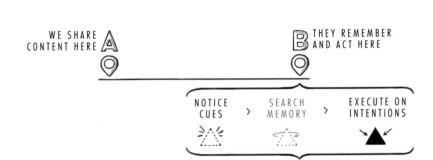

NOTICE
CUES > SEARCH
MEMORY > EXECUTE ON
INTENTIONS

CHAPTER 7

WHAT MAKES A MESSAGE REPEATABLE?

Techniques to Convince Others to Repeat Your Words

When we share information at Point A, we hope others will retain it and retrieve it at Point B to inform their next action. This means that at Point A we must create a memory strong enough that it endures long term. One technique for solidifying memory is repetition.

The impact of repetition on memory is rarely doubted. However, since we are looking at memory from the perspective of the future, this chapter is not so much about repeating the same message over and over at Point A. That's only part of the technique. The challenge is to make sure people can repeat that same message at Point B on their own. And *how* to create a message so it is repeatable in the long term is something that demands investigation.

Do you remember any movie lines someone may have dropped in casual or business conversation? Perhaps you heard, "Houston, we have a problem" during a work meeting? Or "You can't handle the truth" during an argument at home? Or "I'll have what she is having" during dinner with friends?

How about songs? Are there lyrics you can bring to memory and sing instantly? Maybe "Don't stop believin'," or "All you need is love," or "It's the end of the world as we know it . . ."

How about ads? If someone asked you the slogans for Nike or the U.S. Army, would you be able to state them quickly and accurately?

What makes lines from movies, songs, or marketing repeatable and therefore memorable for a long time? What attributes do these words have that make them get in our heads, stay there, and come to mind quickly? It's important to answer these questions, because if you want to influence people's memory, one of the most rewarding proofs of success is to hear others repeat your words.

Some answers may be intuitive; we tend to repeat what we hear or see frequently ("I'm lovin' it"), what carries strong emotions ("Frankly, my dear, I don't give a damn"), what is short ("I'll be back"), what easily rolls off the tongue ("Wax on. Wax off"), or what rhymes ("I feel the need . . . the need for speed"). But are there other properties of repeatable phrases that may not be so intuitive which you can use to craft your own repeatable content?

PORTABILITY

A team of scientists at Cornell University studied the attributes of a quotable movie line. The team built a computer program that analyzed thousands of quotes tagged by users on IMDb, or Internet Movie Database. The program compared quotable lines in a specific movie against other lines of the same length said by the same character in the same movie.

Their observation was that most memorable lines were applicable in various contexts. For instance, the famous line in *Jaws*, "You're gonna need a bigger boat," is portable; you can use it on or off the water to allude to the need for more resources. I recently used the phrase in a presentation about Big Data.

Other scientific studies confirm the importance of presenting a concept in various contexts to increase its recall. For example, when researchers wanted participants to remember the word "chocolate," they showed participants in one condition the word repeated by itself, and they showed participants in another condition the word repeated in various contexts: chocolate bar, chocolate cake, and chocolate milk. Participants in the latter condition remembered the word better, likely because the multiple contexts helped them build multiple retrieval cues.

Often we forget things because there are not enough cues or triggers in the environment to refresh our memory. If it's important to remember the word "chocolate," you may be reminded of it when you see the word "cake" or the word "milk." Most concepts you share with others have a habitat; they have a representation in a real context. Some objects or ideas can live in multiple habitats. For instance, if I say the word "flower," you may picture it in a field or in a shop or on someone's desk, or in someone's hair, or in someone's mouth if you imagine a sexy tango. But if I say the phrase "frozen-food aisle," you will pretty much imagine it in only one setting: at a grocery store.

You can see why a line such as "This is the beginning of a beautiful friendship" is portable: you can use it in a wide variety of contexts, and many contexts are likely to trigger it. Sometimes repeatable lines may mention a very specific context ("We will always have Paris" or "I have a feeling we're not in Kansas anymore"), but the meanings are so universal that they turn into portable lines.

Compare lines that are suited for multiple contexts and that can be triggered by multiple contexts with those that apply only to special situations, and therefore have fewer triggers. In the movie *The Social Network*, a potentially repeatable line is "A million dollars isn't cool. You know what's cool? A billion dollars." But how many of us could use that line in real situations? And how many environmental cues are there to trigger us to use that line?

What are some examples of repeatable messages from the business space? I remember a vice president of sales at Xerox Canada telling his team repeatedly to "Finish strong." It was a message rooted in personal experience, as he had just completed a cure-for-cancer 600-mile bike ride. I recall a marketing executive at Metaswitch who created a campaign in the telecom industry around the directive "Make the call," inviting partners to shift their technology and accommodate new consumer habits. I remember a vice president of operations at McDonald's, who had just received a promotion, motivating her new team with "The best is yet to come." We can use any of these messages in multiple contexts.

How do you craft something portable and cued by various environments? Start by creating generic statements, using few personal pronouns or indefinite articles, and keeping the statements in the present tense. The line in *Jaws* could have been, "You're gonna need *the* bigger boat," which would have applied only in that particular circumstance. Or the McDonald's VP could have said, "The best is yet to come in the food industry," which would have reduced its portability.

Any time you aspire to a repeatable message, ask whether your audience can carry your content from context to context. Can people repeat your favorite message at the supermarket, gym, dog-boarding facility, or new hair salon where a total stranger is approaching you with scissors? May the force be with you.

A message becomes repeatable when we can use it flexibly in many different contexts.

TIMELESS APPEAL

A message can be repeatable across *space* (context), but it can also endure through *time*. How long would you like to be remembered? Is it OK if others repeat your messages only for a few months until a project or a campaign is complete? Would you like your peers to repeat your content for years, even after you've moved on? Or would you want others to repeat your messages for a lifetime, perhaps even after you pass away?

If you want to craft a timeless message, then you aspire to create a "classic." But what is classic? To answer this, we look beyond quantitative studies in cognitive neuroscience and learn from qualitative insights provided by sociologists, historians, writers, and anthropologists. Unlike psychologists, interested mainly in the individual, other scientists study group dynamics. If your message endures through time, that means it becomes part of a larger collective memory.

A classic anything (book, movie, slogan, dress, gesture, one-liner) has lasting impact. For example, reflecting on the world's greatest works of literature, historian Richard J. Smith identifies what makes a book a classic by offering a three-point checklist. Any of us can benefit from this simple guide, regardless of the type of content we create: "First," Smith advises, "the work must focus on matters of great importance, identifying fundamental human problems and providing some sort of guidance for dealing with them. Second, it must address these fundamental issues in beautiful, moving, and memorable ways, with stimulating and inviting images. Third, it must be complex, nuanced, comprehensive, and profound, requiring careful and repeated study in order to yield its deepest secrets and greatest wisdom."

The checklist applies to short messages, too. Take the classic quote "My mama always said, 'Life was like a box of chocolates. You never know what you're gonna get.'" You can see how it meets the three criteria. It addresses a fundamental human problem: the inability to fully predict the future. It builds a mental picture in your mind. And the metaphor bears repeating.

When I analyze business messages, they typically falter on at least two of the three points on Smith's checklist. Most business communicators I hear are really good at identifying and addressing fundamental human problems. However, many fail to address them in beautiful, moving, stimulating ways, and they abuse complexity. Instead of creating a complex message that provides something profound each time you return to it, giving you a sense of discovery even if you've seen it before, you feel overwhelmed by it.

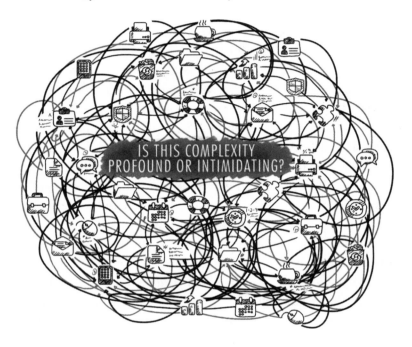

In his book *Why Read the Classics*, Italo Calvino reveals a longer list of characteristics for a classic. Here are a few extra points that complement Smith's checklist. In Calvino's view, a book is a classic when:

- It does not exhaust what it has to say to its readers.

- The more you think you know it by hearing about it, the more original, unexpected, and innovative you find it when you actually read it.

- You cannot remain indifferent to it; it helps you define yourself in relation to it or even in opposition to it.

A woman who reads Tolstoy's *Anna Karenina* every few years tells us why: "Each time, perhaps because I'm older and have experienced more, I find things I never noticed before. Not only is it a great source of pleasure, but I inevitably feel as if I'm getting a sort of pep talk from Tolstoy:

Go deeper. Try harder. Aim higher. Pay closer attention to the world."
A narrative does not have to make a mark with larger-than-life points.
Often, what is profound rests in the smallest details: "I've always loved
the scene in which Anna, having met the charming Vronsky, returns
home to her husband and is struck by how unattractive his ears are."

We can't all be Tolstoy, but in crafting your messages, use these
writers' checklists for guidance.

How much of your content meets the criteria for a classic?

CLASSICS, NOT CLICHÉS

A classic is always marked by something worth mentioning over and
over again, without the risk of becoming a cliché. Like a classic, a cliché
endures through time, but along the journey, it loses its original impact
and meaning, becoming worn and trivial. When the term "paradigm
shift" was first used in the 1960s, it was original. A lot of paradigms have
shifted in many fields since then, more than 7 million times according
to Google. The term is now considered one of the most dreaded clichés,
along with "breaking down the silos," "doing more with less," "it is what
it is," "move the needle," "think outside the box," "take it offline," or "take
it to the next level."

It is a shame that even highly innovative people who are finding solutions to clean drinking water, no-soil agriculture, urban tran-
sit, micronutrients, bionics, or orbital debris removal often speak in
trite phrases. Here is how an organization talks about methods for an
oil spill cleanup: "Clearly a paradigm shift is needed to address future
crises to minimize the potential disastrous effects on our ocean." The
statement could simply say, "We need better methods of cleaning
crude oil from the ocean surface."

We can't exclude clichés from communication entirely because
sometimes clichés are just pragmatic adaptations to new situa-

tions. Clichés can telegraph a specific idea very quickly. And repeating them can happen automatically, without thinking. After all, they come to mind so easily; they've been said so many times. The drawback, however, is that over time, a cliché can lose its meaning, and we may cease to pay attention to it altogether. How many of us are really attentive when flight attendants say, "For your safety and convenience, we ask that you do not move around the cabin"? Many people have great ideas to share, but when they use clichés, they drain their messages of their potency, rendering them common and forgettable.

As you aspire to repeatable messages, stay away from clichés as much as you can. These days we all want to be "the leader in every market" we serve and "benefit customers and stakeholders." These are phrases that are easy to repeat, but they have become empty words. Clichés have the allure of repeatable messages the same way cotton candy has the allure of food. As you use the techniques in this book and gain access to your audience's memory, plant messages that are wholesome, not processed.

In a study that analyzed 186 ads for linguistic and thematic content to see what made them memorable, the findings revealed that linguistic aspects such as alliteration, parallel construction, and metaphors correlated with brand recall, more so than frequency of exposure to that ad or the budget spent to create it. We don't have to be millionaires to be remembered. We just have to master our language.

DISTINCT WORDS TIED BY SIMPLE SYNTAX

"My name is Inigo Montoya. You killed my father. Prepare to die." If asked to quote anything from the movie *Princess Bride*, people who have seen it would most likely repeat this quote. Notice how the syntax, the order of words in the sentence, is simple and easy to understand. Yet the word choice attracts extra attention. The name "Inigo Montoya" is unusual. The word "prepare" is something we may expect in the context of preparing a meal or preparing for a meeting, not preparing to die.

In the list below, author Arthur Plotnik shows us how much harder it would be to repeat famous movie lines if they had been expressed with more convoluted syntax.

> Why not give me an excuse to shoot you legally, an act I would find satisfying.
> **"Go ahead, make my day."** (Clint Eastwood, *Sudden Impact*)

> I forgave you as soon as you said hello.
> **"You had me at hello."** (Renée Zellweger, *Jerry Maguire*)

> Make sure you work hard so I get paid more.
> **"Show me the money."** (Cuba Gooding Jr., *Jerry Maguire*)

> I favor a degree of intellectual weakness in men with whom I have a relationship.
> **"You're not too bright. I like that in a man."** (Kathleen Turner, *Body Heat*)

The impact of simple syntax on memory is backed by scientific studies. Research shows that people are able to reproduce sentence structures independent of meaning, words, or sounds, even when they have amnesia. For example, subjects in an experiment heard a sentence like "The governess made a pot of tea for the princess," and afterward they were more likely to describe other events using the same syntax: "The boy is handing the paintbrush to the man." However, if the subjects initially heard, "The governess made the princess a pot of tea," they were more likely to change their description of events to "The boy handed the man the paintbrush." This effect is called syntactic persistence and has been observed to work in natural conversation and in different languages.

The possible explanation is based on the difference between declarative and procedural memory. Declarative memory includes knowledge and facts (e.g., "Magnesium is to the right of sodium on the periodic table"), while procedural memory is based on perception and motor skills (e.g., your ability to swim even if you have not done so in the past 10 years). Simple syntax may be part of the procedural memory system, which is more resistant to forgetting.

When creating repeatable messages, ask: Can your audience repeat your statements easily? Psychologists call this processing fluency. Are your sentences simple enough, even for non-English speakers? This is not what I see in most business messages. For example, "In this meeting, we want to discuss how governance processes and the Omnichannel platform are inextricably intertwined, and in particular, focus on common corporate governance pitfalls by studying several real-life case studies to gain real-world application of best practices."

Simple syntax leads to repeatable messages.

Simple syntax is necessary but not sufficient for a repeatable message. Research shows that once the syntax is simple, providing a safe canvas, the foreground must be marked by distinct words, or *disfluency*. People are typically seduced by the opposite—fluency of words—and therefore tempted to process information superficially. In a classic experiment, researchers asked participants to answer these five questions sequentially:

What do we call a tree that grows from acorns? [Oak]

What do we call a funny story? [Joke]

What sound does a frog make? [Croak]

What is another word for a cape? [Cloak]

What do we call the white part of an egg? [???]

If you replied "albumen" to the fifth question, you're in the minority. Most people want to reply with "yolk," because it flows easily after the other answers, and they only reject that response upon conscious deliberation. The "yolk phenomenon" shows that people are cognitive misers, preferring to process information superficially.

Cognitive fluency certainly has benefits. Statements marked by fluency are perceived to be more likable, valuable, and accurate compared with statements that are perceived with difficulty. However, disfluency has benefits because it induces cognitive roadblocks, which, in a counterintuitive way, invite deeper processing. For example, in one study, professors assigned one group of students a set of worksheets and PowerPoint slides that were fluent to read, and they assigned materials that were disfluent to another group. The latter achieved higher test scores.

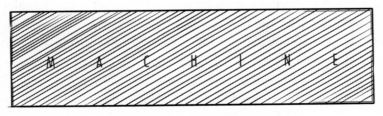

IT IS MORE LIKELY WE WILL REMEMBER
THIS WORD BECAUSE WE HAVE TO
PAY EXTRA ATTENTION TO READ IT

Another advantage of disfluency in messages is that it encourages us to ignore surface properties and focus on deeper meaning. This leads to the formation of abstract thoughts. Typically, when we process a stimulus, we have the capacity to represent it concretely or abstractly. For example, we might perceive Tolstoy's *Anna Karenina* as having 7 parts, 19 chapters, and 806 pages, or we might think of it in an abstract way as a tragic exploration of a married woman's passion for a younger man. Researchers contend that when we find it difficult to process stimuli, they seem farther away in space and time, and because of this fuzziness, we focus more on their global, abstract properties than their concrete features. The abstract properties invite us to process the message more deeply, and this contributes to recall.

Disfluency deepens information processing.

Should an entire message be filled with disfluency? Definitely not. Just like any other hardship, disfluency has physical consequences if sustained. It reduces cognitive resources over time. Use it sparingly. A burst of disfluency, when attention is likely to fade, is especially effective.

I remember a CEO from a technology company telling me that he would like his audience at the company's annual user conference to remember the sentence "Create a culture of transparency." While the syntax was simple, the words were not distinct enough, making the statement trite and predictable and giving the audience members the feeling they had seen it somewhere else before. Eyes and ears would brush right over it. If you Google "create a culture of transparency," you get about 90 million hits. He modified the statement to "Use technology to speak your mind." The syntax was still simple, but the dissonance created by an unexpected phrase ("speak your mind") combined with "technology" commanded extra attention in a corporate context.

Disfluency demands extra attention. And simple syntax makes a message memorable because it is encoded in procedural memory. Together, they make your message impossible to ignore.

ADAPTIVE COHERENCE

There are many paradoxes in the remembering process, one of which stems from the tension of going back to what happened in the past and trying to fit that into what the self requires in the present. From this angle, *memory is adaptive*. It helps us to survive another day.

Sometimes memory is random. You go about your day and suddenly something pops into your head, such as that week you had a fever or the lyrics to "Love Shack." Other times you retrieve what you need to complete a task, contribute to a conversation, emphasize a point, or bond with someone. From this angle, *memory is motivated.*

As we aspire to create repeatable messages, we must ask: What are some motivations that prompt the repetition of those messages? Sometimes we remember things and repeat them to please ourselves; other times we remember things and repeat them to please others. Let's look at internal motivations first.

Some scientists believe that memory is a database of the self. For this discussion, let's consider the self to represent a set of active goals and corresponding self-images. We retrieve from memory what fits coherently within our current goals, beliefs, and self-images. We self-regulate memories to give us stability. Research confirms that a coherent match between memories and the current self leads to high self-esteem and a sense of well-being. However, some scientists argue that from an evolutionary perspective, a memory system that does not keep close track of accurate experiences is not a memory system that survives. Hence, there are the contradictory demands and tension between retaining as many accurate realities as are experienced while, at the same time, satisfying a coherent self that is constantly evolving.

I once worked with the CEO of an e-commerce company to create a keynote about how top global corporations are restoring classic customer satisfaction. In this presentation, we balanced the need for maintaining coherence with the "self," meaning the need for any company to offer outstanding customer satisfaction, and figuring out how to do so in constantly evolving venues, such as online spaces, which can be impersonal. With this approach, we combined the adaptive and motivated nature of memory: give people a message that fits within existing schemas while teaching them how to evolve.

Most business content can be considered a reflection of what researchers call *adaptive coherence*, meaning that we retain from our experiences only that which optimizes survival. This is why, sometimes, remembering the gist of things is sufficient. You may remember a vacation from years ago or a time when you were sick without being able to recall the details. Your memory has reduced those experiences to a few conceptual tracks that ensure survival, such as "avoid Arizona in the summer" or "don't skip breakfast." Your brain achieves a trade-off between *coherence* and *accuracy*. Coherence is linked to long-term memory, while accuracy is often short term. Even though you go through your day experiencing a lot of things, many memories are forgotten unless they are integrated with a long-term goal needed for coherence.

Most repeatable messages are not concerned with petty goals, such as "Did I lock the house?" They point to long-term goals, such as health, beauty, and safety. A diamond is not just for an afternoon; a diamond is forever. If you want to create repeatable messages, tie them to your audience's long-term goals.

> ## Most short-term memories are fated to be forgotten unless they are tied to long-term goals.

STAY CONSISTENT WITH A DESIRED SELF

Scientific research finds that we often rely on what we remember to *realize a desired self.* Do a quick test. Let's say you want to perceive yourself as successful. Can you come up with four instances in the past year in which you were successful? Was this process of remembering easy for you? Numerous studies show that when subjects are told that specific traits lead to success (e.g., introversion or extroversion), they tend to recall more easily memories that exemplify how they possess those exact traits. *Memories consistent with a desired self* become more easily accessible, and the process of remembering is also perceived as easier.

Repeatable messages are aspirational.

Consider these slogans for a moment: Harley-Davidson's "American by birth. Rebel by choice." Or Visa's "It's everywhere you want to be." Or PlayStation's "Live in your world. Play in ours." Or Adidas's "Impossible is nothing." Or Marks & Spencer's "The customer is always and completely right!" Or Walmart's "Save money. Live better." These messages respond to people's aspirations, to the materialization of a desired self. As a result, they are highly repeatable messages.

Research also demonstrates that the types of memories that support a desired self are general, not specific. For example, when extroverted subjects in a study are made to believe that *introversion* leads to success, they recall general memories that substantiate their introverted personality (e.g., "I have often blushed when speaking in public"). The generality of the statement substantiates the trait. This explains why slogans such as "Just do it" or "Think different" or "Don't leave home without it" have such repeatable genius: they apply to all who aspire to many different goals in many different contexts. The generic quality also makes them portable.

Memory that reinforces a desired self thrives on generic statements.

When people repeat messages that support a desired self, those messages become *mantras*, often used for meditation or as inspiring guiding principles: "Make it happen," "Fortune favors the bold," "Look for the second right answer." For a while, I was so into the Insanity workouts by fitness trainer Shaun Thompson (or Shaun T), that I started telling myself to "dig deeper," which is his mantra. MRI studies show that mantras are like medicine. Those who meditate and use mantras display significant gray matter density growth in areas of the brain involved in memory, empathy, sense of self, and emotional regulation.

How do you create a good mantra for your listeners? Start where they are, not where you are. Listen to *their* vocabulary, to *their* way of talking. People often say the same things over and over without realizing it. Build a mantra based on what your audiences are already saying. It will make it easier to remember because those words already roll off their tongues easily.

SOCIAL DESIRABILITY (OR "WHAT WILL THE NEIGHBORS THINK?")

Do you ever repeat something just because it makes you look good in front of others? Your audience is no different. My parents always wanted me to get good grades for many reasons, chief of which was that they hated telling the neighbors otherwise.

A message often becomes repeatable if it confers status.

Harley-Davidson understands status. You don't buy a Harley to keep it hidden; you buy it to show it off and bond with others. This is why people pay $20,000+ for a Harley even though they could buy another motorcycle for half the price from another manufacturer. The company realized early on that it is not in the business of products; it is in the business of human behavior. One of its main selling points is "me in front of others." To make others repeat something relentlessly, you have to answer: How does your content make people look in front of others?

Which of the two messages below is more likely to be repeated after you talk to a group of people?

"Fulfillment Services Overview"

"How a burnt-out company doubled its customers with a new e-commerce tool"

The second example works better because it places the speaker in a storytelling position, and most people would rather come across as storytellers than mere distributors of data. If our audiences are likely to repeat messages to look good in front of others, it is useful to keep track of other people's desires, beliefs, and intentions. But how do we know what others find desirable?

Several previous chapters include information about people's motivations and drivers. Here is another angle. One source we use to analyze others' thinking and what they may find desirable is ourselves. Scientists are finding correlations between memories about ourselves (autobiographical memory) and our understanding about how others think (theory of mind). This type of social projection has been demonstrated in identifying others' moods, their motivational states, and the ease or difficulty of solving a task.

We tend to use self-knowledge more when we perceive others as similar to us. In this type of situation, if you want to create repeatable messages for an audience similar to you, reflect on what *you* are likely to repeat when you like to look good in front of others. For example, when Ken Schmidt, former director of communication for Harley-Davidson, speaks to other communication professionals, he generates buzz because those people are like him or want to become him. In many of his speeches, he is known for saying, "Customers who like us forgive us when we screw up." It is easy for his listeners to repeat this because they have found themselves in similar situations with their own customers and they easily relate to Schmidt.

When you're speaking to listeners who are different from you, developing repeatable messages is not as easy as self-reflection. When you perceive others to be different or you're speaking to mixed groups, you have to ask a different question: Are there universally accepted values that most people like to speak about because it will make them look good in front of others without fail? The most robust *theory of basic human values* has endured for almost five decades and contains the following values: achievement, hedonism, stimulation, self-direction, concern with nature, social concern, benevolence, conformity, personal security, and group security. Research based on 200 samples in more than 60 countries from every inhabited continent shows that these values are recognized across cultures. The values refer to openness to change, self-transcendence, conservation, and self-enhancement. As was the case with the human needs presented in Chapter 4, some are in conflict with each other, such as self-direction versus conformity. So when creating messages with repeatable value for mixed audiences, check to see if they match with at least one of the values from this universal set. To resolve conflict between values, zoom in on one that is a priority in the context you're addressing. For example, at a specific moment, conformity may be more important than self-direction.

Ultimately, getting our audience to repeat our words is not only about looking good in front of others; it is also about connection. Budweiser is expert at creating repeatable messages that emphasize connection. Check out its collection of ads that feature a yellow Labrador puppy. In one instance, we see the pup striking up a relationship with a Clydesdale. In another, the pooch loses his way and is rescued by his horse friends. And in another, we see the puppy waiting for his owner, who went to a party. "Next time you go out, be sure to make a plan to get home safely," the caption reads. "Your friends are counting on you. Enjoy Budweiser responsibly." Repeatable messages appeal to universal values and have the power to bind us. They enable stronger relationships, trust, and the opportunity for us to be best buds.

KEEP IN MIND

Criteria for repeatable messages:

- Portable

- Timeless

- Simple syntax

- Tied to long-term goals

- Aspirational

- Generic (no articulate prepositions or definite articles)

- Appeal to self-interest (make us look good to ourselves)

- Social currency (make us look good to others)

- Universal

CHAPTER 8

BECOME MEMORABLE WITH DISTINCTION

How to Stay on People's Minds
Long Enough to Spark Action

Who is your favorite superhero? Captain America, Batman, Superman, Wonder Woman, Wolverine, Jean Grey? The question may be tough to answer because these days there is superhero overload. At one point, Dash, from the *Incredibles*, is told by his mother, "Everyone is special, Dash." And he responds, "Which is another way of saying no one is." I am noticing a similar trend in content creation: when people treat every single piece of content as "special," none is. And the result is forgettable.

One way to avoid forgettable content is to make it distinct from what your audiences see elsewhere. We discussed distinctiveness in Chapters 1 and 4 to show how distinct cues draw *attention*. However, it is one thing to draw viewers' attention to a distinct stimulus and another for them to remember that stimulus long term. The purpose of this chapter is to explore that concept further, offer scientific explanations as to why distinctiveness works for long-term memory (not just attention), and provide practical guidelines on how to use it in your own messages.

WHY DISTINCTIVENESS WORKS FOR LONG-TERM MEMORY

Scientists consider memory to be ultimately a discrimination problem: when something stands out compared with neighboring items it commands a privileged spot in memory. This theoretical framework was introduced almost eight decades ago when Viennese psychologist Hedwig von Restorff completed a study in which she presented participants with either a list of nine numbers and one syllable or a list of nine syllables and one number. She reported higher recall of the isolated items. This is called the von Restorff effect, or isolation effect.

Ever since this classic experiment, many other researchers have investigated the isolation effect in different variations to test memory: presenting subjects with a list containing the same items and changing the physical property of one of the items (e.g., different color, size, weight, sound, or frequency); mixing materials by including an entirely different item in a list with the same items (e.g., a number inserted in a list of words); or making something incongruous at a semantic level, such as the meaningfulness of an item (e.g., mixing something irrelevant with what is relevant). In many of these experiments, subjects showed better recall for the distinctive item.

More recently, researchers have focused on not only what makes something distinctive but also *why* the isolation effect impacts memory. Researchers realized there is more to distinctiveness than isolation of physical properties. This can be demonstrated if the control element used for isolation in one experiment is placed on a list in which it is no longer considered an isolate. While the color red is distinct when it appears among words printed in black, it is no longer distinct when it appears near red words that hold the same physical characteristics.

While these observations may seem intuitive, what is not so obvious is why distinctiveness is memorable. Explanations are mixed. We've already read about isolates drawing more attention, therefore more rehearsal time, or provoking surprise, which in turn increases attention and therefore recall. Some researchers attribute the isolation effect to gestalt theory, according to which homogeneous items share the same memory trace and may lose their identity in the background, while the isolated items come to the foreground and are identified as distinctive.

It is possible that isolating items helps recall because it reduces interference from other elements that are too similar. Researchers suggest that when the brain detects differences between isolated and background items, encoding results in two categories: the isolated items and the background items. Since the isolated items represent a smaller category compared with the background items, recall is better for isolates. The probability of retrieving an item from one of the two categories is inversely proportional to the size of the category. This is why when we create content, it is useful to ask:

1. *How many items* do we want to isolate?

2. Do they represent the *most important* content we want others to remember?

It is practical to regard any messages you create as a set of items placed along a temporal continuum (e.g., a set of paragraphs in an e-mail or blog, a set of sounds in a meeting, a set of slides in a presentation, a set of campaigns in a marketing initiative). Audiences can discriminate between items depending on their position along this continuum. Similar items that crowd a psychological space are harder to discriminate compared with something that is distinct in a crowd or that does not have much in its close proximity. Cognitive psychologist Gordon Brown says, "The retrievability of an item is inversely proportional to its summed confusability with other items in memory." In other words, the more similar things are, the harder it will be to retrieve them later. This statement reminds us that distinctiveness is not only useful for drawing attention; it is useful for memory retrieval.

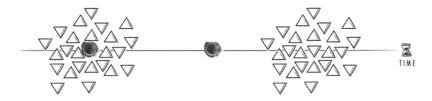

IT IS EASIER TO REMEMBER ITEMS THAT ARE DISTINCT IN A
CROWD OF SIMILAR ITEMS OR ITEMS WITH NO "NEIGHBORS"

Here is what happens in places filled with similarity. The following are excerpts from real value propositions created on the topic of predictive analytics and Big Data—an increasingly crowded space. I showed them to employees from one of the companies that created one of the statements, and removed the logos so they did not know which was part of their own messaging.

"We help uncover valuable insight from Big Data with the ability to access and combine unstructured or semi-structured data so you get improved predictions and optimal performance."

"We leverage business rules and predictive analytics to take the best action based on real-time context and maximize the value of every customer interaction."

"Using our tools, you can create a predictive modeling environment for both business analysts and data scientists, and give them the automated tools they need to build sophisticated predictive models for every data mining function."

Only 1 person out of 40 knew which message belonged to his company. When distinctiveness is absent, we end up creating content for our competition because two days from now, a prospect will find it difficult to remember who said what. It is possible to fix this.

Are you occupying a place that's already crowded in your audiences' minds?

Imagine if a company offering predictive analytics and Big Data tools said this instead: "Using our predictive algorithms, we prevented account closures at a bank and attrition dropped 30%." This remark comes from EMC data scientist Pedro Desouza, who adds that his company helped the same bank to "reduce the cost of Big Data analytics from $10 million to $100,000 per year." Another Big Data firm worked with a shipping company that handles 4 billion items per year and uses 100,000 vehicles. The Big Data firm created on-truck telematics and algorithms to identify and predict routes, engine idle time, and truck maintenance. Imagine if its message read, "Using our predictive analytic tools, we helped our shipping customer save 39 million gallons of fuel and avoid driving 364 million miles."

The brain is constantly looking for rewards. In business, when many messages are the same, we can create distinctiveness, and therefore improve recall, by being specific about these rewards, which we can frame as tangible results. Reflect on your own content: Can you *identify specific outcomes* of your work that help you differentiate your message from too much sameness in your field?

ABSOLUTE UNIFORMITY IS FORGETTABLE, BUT SO IS ABSOLUTE VARIETY

Neuroscientists remind us that an item will not be perceived as distinct if it is embedded in a series of varied items. The first red circle can be harder to recall when it is surrounded by too much variety. The second circle can be memorable when it is isolated.

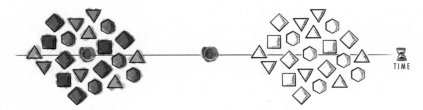

TOO MUCH VARIETY MAKES IT HARDER FOR
AN ITEM TO BE PERCEIVED AS DISTINCT

The irony is that similarity is mandatory for enabling distinctiveness. Think of it this way: after many formal meetings in an office, a meeting in a coffee shop is distinct. After many days of driving to the store, walking to the store is distinct. Something becomes distinct after periods of similarity. Reflect on your own content and approach to business: if you're not first to market, observe pockets of similarity in your domain and *then* strike with distinctiveness. Allow your audiences' brains to habituate to similarity; it will be easier for your message to stand out.

To perceive distinctiveness, we must perceive similarity.

DETERMINE THE DEGREE OF DRAMA

Isolating an item from its neighbors impacts memory for that item, but what does it take to make a stimulus distinct? And does the isolation effect happen at the expense of what comes *after* it? In other words, are we sacrificing some elements in our communication in favor of isolates? It is useful to consider the intensity we apply to distinct items because when something is too strong, neighboring items may be forgotten.

In most isolation experiments, the more an item differs from other items, the bigger the size of the effect. The largest effects have been obtained using size, color, and spacing manipulations, and in many of these cases, the degree of "intensity" from a nonisolate to an isolate was a minimum of 30%. In one study, researchers used items of four sizes, each being 70% of the next largest size. They reported that the isolation effect increased as the contrast between the isolate and the background items increased. Bigger is better to ensure the isolate is indeed distinct.

Many brands use exaggeration or hyperbole as a means of distinctiveness, which leads to long-lasting memory. Does America really "run on Dunkin'"? And if we buy Oscar Mayer, is it true that "it doesn't get better than this"? An Old Spice ad shows a handsome man in the bathroom, wearing 20 gold medals and carrying a chain saw over his right shoulder. Yet he's wrapped in a towel and standing between lit candles. The exaggeration goes in both directions: you will be manly and romantic if you use Old Spice.

In this slide, the presenter's message was that when we don't have the capability of targeted marketing, consumers receive ads for the wrong products. The presenter exemplified this with exaggerated associations: the bodybuilder receives products for the knitter and vice versa.

EXAGGERATION WORKS WHEN IT IS DRAMATIC

Cautious communication does not always stay on people's minds long term. Analyze your content and find opportunities to deviate from a reality that your viewers have learned to expect. Keep in mind, however, that in the process, neighboring items may be sacrificed. For example, one study found high rates of recall for distinct items in a slide presentation but also showed a *deficit* in recall of items following stress-provoking stimuli, such as a traumatic autopsy slide. The proportion of reality versus amplification results from how much we want the isolate to be remembered and whether it is acceptable for a few items that follow to be forgotten.

WHEN YOU DISREGARD ACCURACY,
YOU COMMAND ATTENTION AND IMPACT MEMORY

There is a paradox about elements that clash with their environ-ment and get attention and a memory slot. Some studies demonstrate that, initially, memory for what deviates from an expected pattern is better for something considered typical and expected. However, other findings remind us that if the deviant stimuli do not confirm the inter-nal beliefs or schemas we have, they eventually become filtered out because they are inconsistent with our core beliefs. Reflecting on your content, consider creating something that is distinctive yet fits in with what an audience considers rewarding. This way, you have the best of both worlds: a distinct element that attracts attention, is not filtered out, and stays on people's minds long term.

CREATE DISTINCTIVENESS
BY THINKING IN OPPOSITES

If distinctiveness is providing a stimulus that is different from neigh-boring items, we can create it by choosing the opposite of what an audience just saw. This idea may be easy to understand, but oppo-sites are not always easy to identify because not everything can be described in opposition. For example, science and philosophy remind us that black and white, hot and cold, or good and evil are not really opposites. They are part of a spectrum, not binary opposites.

It is useful to consider opposites from a contextual angle, with a fuzzy-trace approach. In underdeveloped nations, rich and poor consider themselves opposites, but an outsider from a well-developed nation may consider them both poor, and not opposites at all. What matters in your content creation is: What does *your* audience consider the opposite of what you presented for a while?

Some stimuli that our listeners experience may indeed be considered *binary* in a universal way. Elements such as on-off, entrance-exit, pass-fail, and dead-alive provide inspiration for opposites with little room for subjectivity. If your content has precision, this can be a starting point for creating distinctiveness with complementary opposites. For example, a lot of business content currently alludes to the dichotomy of dead versus alive. In discussing the concept of disruption, people speak about dead businesses, such as Circuit City, Borders, or Blockbuster, versus the ones that are alive and well, such as Amazon, Apple, Facebook, and Netflix. In a recent presentation, I heard Raj Verma, executive vice president of worldwide sales at TIBCO Software, use this binary contrast between dead and alive business models to ask the audience, "Are you on the right side of history?"

Relational opposites are another source of distinctiveness. In pairs such as above-below, doctor-patient, borrow-lend, take-give, and buy-sell, both items must exist to perceive contrast. For example, we typically associate brands having a goal to make money (*take*). When they act altruistically (*give*), they capture attention, such as a Giorgio Armani campaign that announced "Smell good, do good." The ad promised that for every bottle of perfume sold within a specific week, the company would donate $1 to the UNICEF Tap project, a nationwide campaign that provides children in impoverished nations with access to clean water.

If your content includes relational aspects, allow your audiences' brains to habituate to one dimension and then switch to the other to be perceived as distinct. I once worked with Chris Cabrera, CEO of Xactly, to create a presentation about the company's incentive compensation program. The theme of the presentation was that ideal incentives drive business. In order for this to happen, a company's goals must be exactly aligned with a sales team's goals, which is not always the case. To visualize the contrast in this lack of alignment, we started the presentation by showing the different goals of a house seller and his agent. "Imagine a homeowner who wants to sell his house for $1M," Cabrera said, "and hires a real estate agent for a 3% sales commission. The next day, the agent finds a buyer willing to pay $900K. So he can either push the owner to sell at $900K and cash his $27K check for one day of work or continue to look for another buyer for an indeterminate amount of time, for the extra $3K. What will the agent do? What would *you* do if you were the agent?" Using relational opposites, Cabrera made the point that "this is what happens when two entities have different goals. The same misalignment occurs in corporations." I remember this introduction vividly even though we worked on it seven years ago.

A third category of opposites is *graded*, meaning that there can be various levels of comparison on a scale. Pairs such as young-old, hard-soft, happy-sad, small-big, fat-skinny, early-late, and fast-slow are relative and can be interpreted in various ways by different people. This is where fuzzy-trace theory helps to distinguish, based on your audience and prior experiences and expectations, what level of contrast and distinctiveness will be perceived. For example, imagine seeing this ad from Haagen-Dazs: "Who says bigger isn't better? Introducing the new 14 oz." This will be seen as distinct to existing consumers who can contrast it against much smaller container sizes, but not to people who don't eat ice cream or are not aware of previous sizes.

HSBC is a master at creating content that plays off opposites. Imagine a picture showing several standing carrots and labeled "Order" and one with carrot soup, labeled "Chaos." The picture next to it shows the same pair of photos but with the labels reversed. In other ads, HSBC swaps the labels of "useful" and "useless" for pills and herbs, "pleasure" and "pain" for shoes and chili peppers, and "good" and "bad" for papaya and chocolate. The message is to be open to various points of view. The graded approach to contrast has made the campaign widely popular.

Including opposites in content design is helpful not only because it helps the brain distinguish some stimuli more strongly than others, but also because contrast is a shortcut to thinking and decision-making. For example, I helped someone with a presentation expressing the dichotomy "It was the best of times, it was the worst of times." We used Dickens's quote to describe the economy. If you are providing value, it is the best of times for a business; if you're not, then it is the worst of times. The presenter allowed the audience to habituate to a few examples of companies providing value (GE, Apple, and Facebook), and then switched to companies experiencing the worst of times, such as companies offering LAN lines. The contrast captured attention and evoked emotion, which result in long-term memory. The message and visuals are still on my mind, and I created this presentation three years ago.

ENABLE SELF-GENERATED DISTINCTIVENESS

Memory literature offers abundant evidence that in situations when listeners have the opportunity to generate content on their own, they are more likely to remember *that* content better compared with the same information given to them by someone else.

> It is easier to remember how you solved a problem than trying to memorize someone else's solution.

Anything related to the self leads to better memory because we implicitly pay more attention when we are invited to be active versus passive. We create better associations between new content and existing internal schemas and have better cues for later retrieval.

Imagine for a moment you're a runner. Which route would you remember more in a few days: one you just completed that someone else had recommended or one you just completed but generated yourself? Claire Wyckoff, an advertising copywriter in San Francisco, has been gaining in popularity as a "running-route artist." She generates her own running paths in order to create specific shapes. Currently, fitness trackers such as Strava, Garmin, and Nike+ allow you to record not only the distance you run but also the shape in which you run it. The company MapMyRun launched a contest in 2014, inviting people to submit images of their most creative running routes. The pictures included robots, guitars, and animals. A run around Golden Gate Park and some adjacent neighborhoods in San Francisco took the shape of a corgi. We can be sure Claire remembers these paths very well because they require extreme attention, repetition, self-generated cues, and tools that help along the way. So far, she's made more than 20 street drawings, including Slimer from *Ghostbusters*, a pilgrim's head, and a birdcage in honor of Robin Williams. And she laughs at the benefit. "Mapping a drawing, I'm way more engaged in the process of running it," she says. "I'll go an extra five miles if it means finishing a picture."

Neuroscientists confirm that self-reference improves long-term recall. For example, when subjects are given a list of traits (e.g., lazy, honest), they tend to remember those words better when they are asked "Are you lazy?" or "Are you honest?" versus "Is this a desirable word?" or "Does this word seem familiar?" or "Have you read, heard, or used the word recently?" Any encoding that leads to evaluative processing is linked to improved memory.

As you create content for others, invite them to answer the questions "How does this content represent you?" "Where does it fit within your reality?" and even "In what ways are you like this content?" For instance, returning to an earlier example on predictive analytics, the three Vs of Big Data are velocity, variety, and veracity. If we want our audiences to remember the three Vs, we could ask, "In what ways do these words describe you?" It will be much easier for them to remember these words in three days when applying a self-reference elaboration method versus simply seeing a list. The self-generated content will be active and distinct compared with viewing other content passively.

ACHIEVE DISTINCTIVENESS WITH A HUMAN TOUCH

If we consider distinctiveness "departure from the expected," a deviation that many will appreciate and find impossible to ignore is one with a human touch. We create our communication in the service of other people. Notice what happens when we shift from a formal, technology-oriented message to an informal, human-oriented language. "When I'm not deep into algorithm design, data modeling, or analytic visualizations, I really like to ski," says Pedro Desouza, the data scientist from EMC we met earlier.

Consider this excerpt from an interview with Robert Altman, the legendary director of *MASH*, in which he recalled his experience during World War II. Notice the transition from plain facts to remarks about human nature, which makes his response more distinct. What will you remember more? "I was a pilot. I flew a B-24 in the South Pacific. I did forty-six missions, something like that. We got shot at a lot. It was pretty scary, but you're so young; it's a different thing. I was nineteen, twenty, it was all about the girls."

Notice how former Russian president Mikhail Gorbachev, a recipient of the Nobel Peace Prize, distinguishes an otherwise detached message with a personal touch. In the 1990s, he founded Green Cross International, a global, nonprofit environmental organization. Given his serious approach to ecological issues, Mr. Gorbachev is often asked why he decided to star in a Louis Vuitton ad. He responds, "The proceeds go to Green Cross International and its American counterpart, Global Green." He adds, "Also, I travel a lot and a good bag comes in handy."

Patagonia's CEO Rose Marcario also achieves distinctiveness with a human touch. Recently, she embraced an environmental approach to business for her company. Patagonia advises consumers *not* to buy its clothes. By doing so, it sacrifices some of its earnings. The company also shares product breakthroughs with competitors—all in an effort to cause less wear and tear on the environment. The message in Patagonia's paradoxical campaign "Don't buy this jacket" is do not buy more than you need.

I remember a presentation by a pharmaceutical professional during a workshop I gave. Most of her presentation focused on critical and fairly technical matters. As she drew to a close, she left us with a video of a woman who, before getting double-mastectomy surgery, danced with the medical staff to Beyoncé. We were all compelled to get up and dance. I polled the class a week later, asking what everyone remembered. All 30 participants mentioned this moment. No exceptions.

Can you identify ways to create distinctive content using a human approach to business?

CREATE DISTINCTIVENESS (AND ACTION) WITH MEANING

Joshua Glenn and Rob Walker are two writers who collaborated on a literary and economic experiment between 2009 and 2010, to discover whether adding meaning to an object would draw attention *and* sway people to buy it for more money than it's worth. They bought knickknacks at thrift stores for a total of $129. They paid no more than $2 per object and asked various writers to compose a story for each object. Then they posted each item with its story on eBay and watched what happened.

A beat-up motel room key cost them $2. The story, written by novelist Laura Lippman, began with a wife putting away her husband's knickknacks. She asked him why he had kept the key for so many years. On the key was engraved Perkins Motel, Laconia, NH, Room 3. The husband replied that the key reminded him of the movie *Psycho* (the actor's name was Anthony Perkins, which he thought "was cool"). When the wife was unimpressed, he mentioned a trip to that motel with a "bunch of guys" in junior college and he forgot to return the key and has had it since. "Here's the moment where you choose to believe, or not to believe," the wife reflects. "A marriage is a kind of religion, defying rational thought." She realized that motel rooms no longer use traditional keys anymore, even in Laconia, New Hampshire. Whatever memory her husband treasured may have been beyond one shared with a "bunch of guys." She wondered if he wanted to keep the story to himself, for her sake or his, and not spoil what may have happened in Room 3.

The key sold for $45.01.

The writer Ben Ehrenreich tells the story about a jar of marbles and starts with an irresistible statement: "I pull a marble from your skull each time we kiss. 'Give it back,' you say, each time." The rest of the story is a surreal dialogue between two people during which we move from hunchbacks, to Noam Chomsky, to Beyoncé, to the narrator's lover arranging TV remotes attractively, to Vladimir Putin in the form of a crow, being the narrator's friend on Facebook. When we get to the final scene, we are left with this paragraph to ponder: "And I kiss your fingers and your dry lips and with my free hand I reach up and I stroke your hair and I poke about until I feel the bulge and then I dig in with my nails and pull another marble from your skull."

The jar of marbles was bought for $1 and sold for $50.

Overall, the Significant Object project made $8,000 and beautifully illustrates the impact of meaning in making decisions.

Reflecting on your own content, consider this: At any moment, the world is filled with sights and sounds that simultaneously compete for your listeners' attention. The human mind is limited in its ability to process information and selects only relevant stimuli that receive priority for further processing. In a world of constant data explosion, how do we create meaningful content that leads to recall and influences decisions?

Give your audiences the thrilling relevance of Room 3.

KEEP IN MIND

- Distinctiveness is important for long-term memory because isolated items draw more attention and rehearsal time. In addition, isolated items come to the foreground, reducing interference with other items, and also appear in smaller numbers, which makes them easier to recall long term.

- The more similar things are, the harder it will be to retrieve them later. However, similarity is important for the brain to detect distinctiveness.

- The brain is constantly looking for rewards. In business, when many messages are the same, we can create distinctiveness, and therefore improve recall, by being specific about these rewards, which we can frame as tangible results.

- If you're not first to market, observe pockets of similarity in your domain and *then* strike with distinctiveness. Allow your audiences' brains to habituate to similarity; it will be easier for your message to stand out.

- The more an item differs from other items, the bigger its effect. Select a property you want to isolate and increase its distinctiveness by at least 30% compared with neighboring items.

- Find opportunities to deviate from a reality your viewers have learned to expect.

- Create distinctiveness by thinking in opposites. This is helpful not only because it helps the brain distinguish some stimuli more strongly than others, but also because contrast is a shortcut to thinking and decision-making.

- Enable self-generated distinctiveness.

- Achieve distinctiveness with a human touch and deep meaning.

CHAPTER 9

"I WRITE THIS SITTING IN THE KITCHEN SINK"

The Science of Retrieving Memories Through Stories

W hat were you wearing two days ago? Take two seconds to think about it before you continue reading.

If you tried to answer, your mind calculated quickly which day was "two days ago," and from there it jumped to where you were (work, home, vacation), what you were doing (meeting with clients, spending time with family), and what other tangential thoughts, facts, and feelings were linked to that day. For instance, if you spent the day with someone you liked and you did something meaningful, some positive emotions came to mind, too. If the opposite happened, then negative emotions briefly became active. If these elements were easy to retrieve (visuals, actions, facts, meaning, and emotion), you found it easy to answer the question.

But maybe you found the question hard to answer, in which case there are several plausible reasons. One is *interference*, which means that too many memories in the same category are alike, and with enough repetition of similar stimuli, specifics turn into generics. For example, let's say you work in a formal office most days, doing similar things each day, and your outfits consist of business casual clothes, which are not that easily distinguishable from one another. It is difficult to answer the question "What were you wearing two days ago?" with precision, but you could answer it with gist. A typical response I get is, "I was wearing pants and a shirt."

We may also struggle with the question because there may be no deep or pragmatic *meaning* associated with what we were wearing two days ago. Someone may say, "Who cares?" The attitude changes if we had a job interview two days ago, or an important date, or an occasion where we wanted to impress someone. The meaning and, implicitly, the *emotion* attached to these visuals and actions serve as strong hooks to retrieve memories later.

Forgetting caused by interference or lack of meaning or emotion is not a problem when remembering attire. It becomes a problem when our audiences hear information from us that is not easily distinguishable from something they heard elsewhere. If someone were to ask our listeners "What content do you remember from two days ago?" they may not be able to remember because too many memories may compete with each other in the business content category. In the previous chapter, we learned how to be on people's minds in a *distinguishable* way so they can retrieve memories easily and accurately. In this chapter, we expand on that topic further by answering the question "How do people retrieve memories?" If we share information at Point A and expect them to remember it at Point B, how will they search their memories and bring to mind something we consider important?

In many cases, to retrieve a memory, we mentally travel to a specific place and time and then search for images and actions that took place, much like we did with the outfit exercise earlier. While on this mental travel, we may also extract meaning and factual information about the world. See how these elements are reflected in actor Al Pacino's interview in the book *The Meaning of Life*. Al Pacino remembers the first car he ever bought when he was in his early twenties, just as his movie career started blooming:

I went with my friend Charlie and got this white BMW right out of the dealership. We get in the car and drive to my apartment in Manhattan. As we're driving, I'm thinking, "Y'know, this just isn't me." It just didn't feel right. But I said to myself, "What the hell, you'll get used to it." I parked it in front of the apartment, and we went for a cup of coffee. When we came down to drive Charlie home, the car is gone. I remember looking at that space where the car used to be, looking at Charlie, and laughing.

Then Pacino has a flashback.

Years before, Charlie and I were riding bikes and we went into Katz's Deli on Houston Street. Now, the relationship I had with my bike was much different from the one I had with the car. I'd had that bike for a couple of years and used it to get from the Bronx to Manhattan. I didn't have money at the time, and it was not only my form of transportation but also a great source of fun and amusement. It was one of the few things I could do for free. Anyway, Charlie and I park our bikes on the street and go in the deli and get some hot dogs. Every other bite I would turn around to check on the bikes. I must have put mustard on the dog or something, because the next time I turn around, the bikes were gone. I remember running outside, and they were nowhere in sight. It wasn't funny that time.

It is fairly easy for Al Pacino to retrieve these memories—and for us to retell his story to someone else—because the brain has encoded a lot of information in a way that comes naturally. Consider these narrative elements:

1. *Sensory impressions in context.* We "saw" things: car, bikes, deli—and not just any deli, Katz's Deli—street, apartment, Bronx, Manhattan. We "tasted" coffee, hot dogs, and the mustard on those hot dogs.

2. *Actions across a timeline.* We visualized events happening in a sequence: getting into the car, driving, looking, parking bikes, laughing, and running.

3. *Facts.* We learned a few indisputable things, such as the existence of Katz's Deli, a BMW dealership, and a route from the Bronx to Manhattan.

4. *Abstract concepts.* We learned ideas that can be dissociated from a time and place, such as ownership of a car or a bike, or a statement such as "It was one of the few things I could do for free."

5. *Meaning.* We inferred conclusions we can use later on and in other circumstances: "Sometimes we feel more attachment to small things than big things" or "Things have relative value."

6. *Emotion.* We felt excitement at driving a new car, confusion when the car is stolen, resignation afterward, anxiety parking the bikes, and a strong sense of loss when the bikes are gone.

How many of these perceptive, cognitive, and affective elements are reflected in the content you share with others? It is an important question to answer because a combination of perceptive, cognitive, and affective elements is mandatory for encoding and retrieving memories. This combination is also important because it gives us a formula for storytelling.

MEMORABLE STORYTELLING

PERCEPTIVE	▷	SENSORY DETAILS IN CONTEXT	ACTION ACROSS A TIMELINE
COGNITIVE	▷	FACTS	ABSTRACT CONCEPTS	MEANING
AFFECTIVE	▷	EMOTION

Considering this model, it is easy to see why well-crafted stories are remembered; a good story invokes more senses and activates more parts of the brain: visual cortex, motor cortex, frontal cortex, amygdala, to name a few. As a result, when we tell a story well—especially if we lived the event ourselves—we can help *others* encode more memory traces. From this angle, the adage "Less is more" in creating content is a myth. It is the combination of perceptive, cognitive, and affective elements and the elaboration on them that helps an audience build *more* memory traces and connections in their minds.

Even though by some standards the Al Pacino story may be considered long, the length pays off in extra encoding. In addition, with elaboration, we're building more *cues* for retrieval. Seeing hot dogs, bikes, a deli, mustard—any of these later can trigger the memory of this story.

The absence or imbalance of perceptive, cognitive, and affective elements in a story is what makes it *forgettable*. Ineffective communicators tell stories that (1) stay too factual or too abstract (nothing wrong with facts or abstract ideas, but when the other components are missing, it leads to forgetting); (2) have no plot—nothing really happens across a timeline; and (3) lack emotional intensity.

Let's identify practical ways in which we can combine perceptive, cognitive, and affective elements to create memorable stories and influence other people's long-term memory.

BALANCE PERCEPTIVE AND COGNITIVE ELEMENTS

Learn the Difference Between "Abstract Versus Concrete" and "Generic Versus Specific"

When creating business content, we tend to stay more on the cognitive side (facts, abstract ideas, meaning—all of which are offered most frequently as words) than on the perceptive side (vivid visuals and actions). It is typical to hear statements such as "Our solutions drive

MEMORABLE STORYTELLING

| PERCEPTIVE | ▷ SENSORY DETAILS IN CONTEXT | ACTION ACROSS A TIMELINE |

| COGNITIVE | ▷ FACTS | ABSTRACT CONCEPTS | MEANING |

| AFFECTIVE | ▷ EMOTION |

the vital business process between the buyer's interest in a purchase and the realization of revenue. With our software, companies increase sales effectiveness while maximizing visibility of . . ." What does a statement like this mean to you? Can you picture what the speaker said? Will you remember any of it in the next few days?

It may be intuitive to believe that what is concrete and tangible, which appeals to our senses, is more memorable compared with abstract concepts, such as the ones in the statement above. The hot dogs and bikes we read about earlier may be more vivid in our minds than a "business process" or "maximizing visibility." Vivid sensory details are definitely memorable, but abstract and factual concepts can be, too, provided they meet some conditions. Several guidelines about the importance of abstract concepts were included in the chapter on repeatable messages. Here we explore the topic in more depth and provide additional guidelines on how to make facts and abstracts memorable, since they are prevalent in business communication. First, let's define two dichotomies: "abstract versus concrete" and "generic versus specific."

Although these words are used interchangeably (concrete = specific; generic = abstract), there are differences between them. Something is concrete if we can perceive it with our senses. Swiveling chairs, lavender, misty air, cherry pie, and text message tones on a smartphone—all of these ignite various senses. If we can't perceive something with our senses, we are talking about an idea or a concept

154

that is abstract (it appeals to our cognition). Autonomy, courage, and cynicism are examples of abstract concepts.

While abstract and concrete are opposites, generic and specific are subsets of each other, with generic being a large group and specific representing an individual item of that group. In Al Pacino's story, we did not read about a generic car (and possibly create only one memory trace); we read about a "white BMW right out of the dealership" (and could create multiple memory traces). Consider the difference between "he hit me" → "he decked me" → "he Steven Seagal'ed my butt." The more specific we are, the more memories we encode in our audiences' brains. Creative writing courses are a great way to learn how to produce deeper levels of specificity to impact our audience's memory.

Notice the mixture of abstract-generic and specific-concrete in the article "What I Learned from the Worst Guy I Ever Dated" by Genevieve Field, who quotes from readers' contributions. Lizzie, age 35, writes: "I met Bob when I was 22, and fell hard. He was a macho, messed-up guy: He ate raw eggs. He shot himself in the thigh with steroids. He drank Bud Light while lifting weights and wore his hat backward. But when two broken people get together, it's not a resurrection of *Jerry Maguire*—no one completes anyone. You both just tear each other apart in new and awful ways." The abstract ending is welcome after a series of concrete and specific sentences. If the specific examples went on, it would have felt like a dull list of facts. Lizzie's submission was titled "We Seek the Love We Think We Deserve," which is an abstract concept that represents an array of concrete thoughts.

There is a paradox regarding specific-generic and concrete-abstract and their impact on memory. We live every day in specific and concrete terms, but we tend to remember the generic and abstract, especially without reexposure or reflection.

Why is it sometimes easier to remember the generic and abstract? One interpretation is that these concepts are more interconnected, more networked, therefore increasing our chances for later retrieval. Another is that when we store items at a generic or abstract level, we can use them to interpret new events and plan for future action. We also tend to access these types of memories more frequently. And they take less mental effort to retrieve than the specific or concrete.

However, for our audiences to remember an abstract idea, we must still offer the specifics to help them encode information. The brain also needs to retain some of the original observational data to better adapt or reinforce generalizations or abstract concepts. Compare these two mission statements from organizations aiming to rebuild struggling communities in some urban areas. Which one may still be on your mind a few days from now?

> "In the spirit of volunteerism and community partnership, we aim to improve homes and neighborhoods so that people can live in warmth, safety, and comfort. We approach our mission with the understanding that home ownership is an important factor in the stabilization and preservation of neighborhoods."

> "We will build 150 affordable, green, storm-resistant homes for families living in the Lower 9th Ward."

The second message is the mission statement of the foundation established by Brad Pitt to help the displaced after Hurricane Katrina. To date, the foundation has completed 75 homes. A few days from now, we may not remember these exact numbers, but our initial exposure to them gives us a strong feeling of confidence, connection, and trust because of the specificity. If the second mission statement were merged with the first, we would have an even stronger package: specifics that draw us in and provoke an emotional reaction *and* abstract concepts we can retain for later use.

In business, too many content creators operate from one of two extremes. At one extreme, content is too abstract or generic, such as the statement earlier about "business process" and "maximizing visibility." At the other extreme, content is too specific: "Data Protection Manager (DPM) is a backup and recovery solution. DPM provides out-of-the-box protection for Files and Folders, Exchange Server, SQL Server, Virtual Machine Manager, SharePoint, Hyper-V, and client computers. For large-scale deployments, DPM also allows you to monitor your backups through a central console or remotely."

Why do we go to either extreme? The *pull toward the abstract* happens because we tend to speak in conclusions, rather than showing how we reached those conclusions. This is because we don't want to think about the details, we don't want to waste people's time with details, or we don't know the details. Here is an example.

Consider these statements: "Sometimes people drive as fast as they can, with the attitude that as taxpayers, they own the road." "People often cut in line." "Sometimes people feel underpaid and help themselves to a few 'souvenirs' from work to offset lower wages." "Clerks at the post office get snappy when you don't fill out the right forms." You may think these specific statements, but you don't say them. You simply say, "Everyone is so cranky these days," which is your conclusion. Notice how many sensory details the conclusion is missing.

The *pull toward the specific* is often driven by ego and the desire to make an impression. People want to show off their brilliance. During a brain science workshop with executives, I remember one man who said, "If I did not include all those details in my presentation, my boss would think I am lazy."

Neither extreme (content that is too perception-based or too cognitive-based) is favorable for memory. Too much of either is boring after a while because it becomes repetitive and predictable. Consider a balanced ratio of abstract-generic and specific-concrete. Here are two examples:

"She wasn't doing a thing that I could see, except standing there, leaning on the balcony railing, holding the universe together."
(J. D. Salinger, *A Girl I Knew*)

"I met in the street a very poor young man who was in love. His hat was old, his coat worn, his cloak was out at the elbows, the water passed through his shoes, and the stars through his soul."
(Victor Hugo, *Les Misérables*)

To make sure we don't err on either side of the spectrum, when our content becomes too abstract, we can ask, "Can I give an example of this?" "Can I include some facts?" Then, when the content is too concrete and specific, we can ask, "What is the bigger picture?" or "What is an idea that people can apply to other situations beyond this context?" The brain is constantly on fast-forward, and it will appreciate portable messages.

Here is a business example of the proper balance between the abstract and generic and the specific and concrete. This was the mission statement of the snowboard equipment company Burton at a time when snowboarding was a small niche and skiers considered it annoying. Jake Burton wanted to prove them wrong. The company's poetic vision comes from the rhythm between the abstract and concrete and the generic and specific. No PowerPoint slides are necessary when you achieve this type of balance.

We stand sideways.

We sleep on floors in cramped hotel rooms.

We get up early and go to sleep late.

We've been mocked.

We've been turned away from resorts that won't have us.

We are relentless.

We dream it, we make it, we break it, we fix it.

We create.

We destroy.

We wreck ourselves day in and day out and yet we stomp that one trick or find that one line that keeps us coming back.

We progress.

Burton's statement contains concrete words that appeal to our perception: "stand," "get up early," "sleep late," "floors," "resorts," "stomp." It also contains abstracts: "relentless," "create," "destroy," "mocked," "trick," "line," "progress." We also see generic words: "make it," "break it," "fix it," "day in and day out." And these are paired with some specifics. We don't just see hotel rooms; we see people sleeping on "floors in cramped hotel rooms."

When analyzing the content you're creating, ask yourself: What is the ratio between perceptual and cognitive elements? Is your language concrete and specific enough to cause a reaction, but abstract and generic enough to allow the audience to derive meaning that is easy to remember and use later in many other contexts?

Zoom In on Details Based on Your Audience's Expertise

Determining the ratio between perceptive and cognitive also depends on whether you're addressing experts or neophytes. Beginners tend to prefer the more specific and concrete, so for this type of audience, amplify the perceptive elements. More sophisticated listeners tolerate a higher level of the abstract and generic because they have more developed schemas for the content you're sharing. For this type of audience, amplify the cognitive side.

Here is an example of the ratio of details different people need as they listen to experts. The SR-71 was a famous U.S. spy plane, considered to be the world's fastest jet. The plane could go from Los Angeles to Washington, D.C., in 64 minutes, averaging 2,100 mph. Fewer than 500 pilots had the chance to fly it. When I asked Bert Garrison, a former SR-71 pilot, what he remembered about flying that plane, he mentioned a comment he heard repeatedly from his peers: "If you ever look out of the window, she will bite you in the ass."

This was an abstract conclusion. If you share just this conclusion with other pilots, regardless of what aircraft they fly, it's likely they will understand what that abstract sentence means, and you can move on with the conversation. Novices would need specifics to appreciate and understand the conclusion. An SR-71 pilot was a very busy pilot. What kept him so busy? "You're burning fuel at a high rate, 45,000 pounds per hour at Mach 3," Garrison explained, "so you have to manage your fuel balance. You're making sure the center of gravity of the airplane is

staying in trim. You're maintaining the inlets so they are running efficiently and you're burning the least amount of gas. You're constantly
checking the altitude to see if the fuel flow was correct for that altitude, and if it wasn't, you would have to climb." It is these details that
will keep neophytes interested in the conversation and enable them to
understand the meaning of the abstract statement.

Regardless of the audience expertise level, it is practical to lead
with the pattern your audience expects and deviate from that sequence
to break the pattern: {perceptual, perceptual, perceptual, *cognitive*} or
{cognitive, cognitive, cognitive, *perceptual*}. With this approach, we
avoid boredom, and we feed the brain's constant aim to mitigate two
processes: generalization and specialization. This dual process is how
the brain thinks.

Pictures Versus Text:
Which Is More Memorable?

We've discussed the importance of balancing perceptive and cognitive details, focusing mainly on verbal information. Since many business communicators err on the side of cognitive details (facts, abstract
ideas, and meanings), let's find ways to include perceptive elements in
our content, using visuals and actions. After all, sensory information is
at the basis of our memory.

Do we remember pictures more than text? Intuitively, people
believe that pictures are more memorable, but let's investigate more
deeply to see if this is always so. The analysis matters because it is not
always easy to create sophisticated visuals to include in our communication materials; or if we do have the budget to create amazing visuals,
under some conditions, they may still be forgettable. Words and numbers are often easier and cheaper to produce, but they have some conditions for recall.

Visuals seem to win memory space because we have a reflexive
preference for them. We are visual beings: we take the world in mainly
through visual receptors. Pictures are often more enjoyable and help
us arrive at meaning more quickly. They also tend to provoke stronger

emotions and provide a context. Which one would you be more likely to remember in a few days: the text or the image?

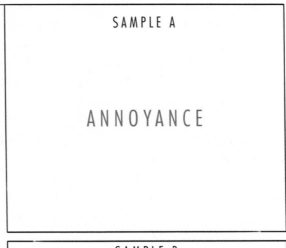

SAMPLE A

ANNOYANCE

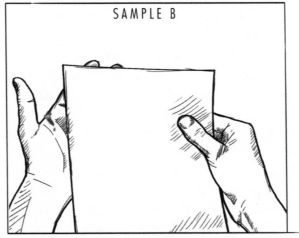

SAMPLE B

PICTURES ARE OFTEN MORE MEMORABLE THAN
TEXT BECAUSE THEY ARE GENERALLY MORE INTERESTING

Many businesses capitalize on the human propensity toward visuals, which is why the Facebook timeline is appealing and why Pinterest and Instagram are insanely popular. It is also why data visualization businesses have been booming: who wants to spend hours looking at

Excel spreadsheets instead of pretty charts that indicate trends and may lead to insights?

Processing visuals is often more efficient than processing text, especially when text is in a number format. In *Brain Bugs*, author Dean Buonomano says, "We can find a face in a crowd faster than we can come up with the answer to 8 × 7." He adds, "We have an inherent sense of the quantities 1 through 3, but beyond that things get hazy. We may be able to tell at a glance whether Homer Simpson has two or three strands of hair but you will probably have to count to find out whether he has four or five fingers."

Image processing efficiency means that a picture enables us to absorb a large amount of information quickly, hence the adage "A picture is worth 1,000 words." From a memory perspective, let's place this maxim under scrutiny. Two scientists from the University of North Carolina recently noted, "A picture is worth 1.5 words to be exact." They discovered that while simple line drawings resulted in superior recall compared with the printed word, this advantage disappeared when the words were *spoken*.

This suggests that there may be another way we can ask the question about memory for images versus memory for text: In what situations are pictures *not* superior? Surely there are circumstances for text supremacy. If someone asked us to picture the rainbow, we could do it effortlessly. If we were asked to name the colors in the right order, we would struggle . . . unless we remembered the mnemonic device we learned if we attended an English-speaking school: ROY G BIV.

When comparing the impact of words versus images on memory, cognitive scientists have offered a theory called dual coding: when we look at visuals or text, we have the opportunity to encode them twice, via a visual code and a verbal code. If we see a picture of a banana, it is easy to encode it twice: a code for the visual we see and a verbal code we generate quickly because the picture is easy to label. This is advantageous because generating two memory traces (dual coding) increases the likelihood of retrieval. The same holds if we see the text "banana." We can still encode it twice: the verbal code we see and its visual correspondent, which is easy to create because the item is easy to picture.

In studies where people are asked to generate a mental picture when they read words, findings suggest that subjects remember those words as accurately as if they were shown pictures.

A picture is memorable when it is easy to label, and text is memorable when it is easy to picture.

Text and graphics have the potential to be equals in memory. What this means to our content creation is that we don't have to create or buy a picture for everything we share. We can still impact others' memory with text, as long as the *text generates a mental picture* and this picture is easy to form. For example, "I write this sitting in the kitchen sink" is the first line in Dodie Smith's novel *I Capture the Castle*. She continues, "That is, my feet are in it; the rest of me is on the draining board, which I have padded with our dog's blanket and the tea cosy. I can't say that I am really comfortable, and there is a depressing smell of carbolic soap, but this is the only part of the kitchen where there is any daylight left." The words are strong enough to generate dual memory traces. We don't need actual photographs to see her context.

When we don't have enough time to generate a label for a picture, visuals lose the dual coding advantage. In a study where participants viewed approximately five items per second (text and visuals), people did not remember pictures more than words. Scientists suspect it is more time consuming to come up with a label for a picture than to read words.

Based on the evidence so far, we can infer it is possible for some text to be memorable and for pictures to be forgotten. Ultimately, images and text are both graphical elements. Each comes with its own set of conditions for impacting memory. Artist Bert Dodson offers a strong metaphor to use words and pictures for maximum memory impact. He asks us to imagine two ladders, one labeled "Words" and one labeled "Pictures." You start climbing one of them until at some point, he says, "the climbing gets difficult." Dodson advises that instead of getting stuck, "You simply cross over to the other ladder. Suddenly the climbing gets easy again." So it's not one or the other; it's *moving* from one to the other. In the case of Dodie Smith's novel, after she builds a mental picture of writing from the kitchen sink, she switches to something more abstract: ". . . I have found that sitting in a place where you have never sat before can be inspiring. . ."

Pictures don't always have a memory advantage. We often place text at a *disadvantage*, which is why it is easily forgotten. In the next few pages, let's answer the questions "What makes text memorable?" and "How do we avoid forgettable pictures?" The answers will help us improve storytelling and enhance memory.

Link Abstract Words to Concrete Pictures

Business content tends to contain more abstract than concrete or specific words. We hear messages such as "Corporations realize that they must provide differentiation through higher-value experiences, cost efficiency, and agility. These ultimately lead to other higher goals, such as leveraging of core assets, revenue generation, and brand loyalty." Notice all the abstract words: "differentiation," "value," "efficiency," "agility," and "loyalty." Also notice the generic (and still abstract) words: "experiences," "assets," and "goals." There is nothing wrong with this type of message as long as listeners extract the same meaning from the statement as intended by the speaker. When content is abstract, it is important to ask: Do the abstract concepts mean the same to you as they do to your audiences?

Different people have different images of abstract words, depending on various contexts, life experiences, beliefs, and current intentions. Take the word "value," for instance. If you're an accountant, you may understand it as the monetary worth of a specific good or service. If you're an economist, you may see it as the benefits and rights of ownership, such as utility or the possibility to exchange those goods or services for something else. If you're in marketing, you may consider the perceptive value of a good or service and whether people are willing to pay for it because it meets a need. If you're a mathematician, value is simply a quantity represented by a number.

When we communicate in abstract concepts and leave it to an audience to come up with a mental picture for what we said, we run into a couple of problems:

1. People may find it hard to imagine some abstractions and give up. For instance, how do you visualize these words: "Our virtualization products deliver a complete and optimized solution for your entire computing environment"? Unless you work in cloud computing, it is difficult to picture much. Your audience is likely to zone you out and focus on other stimuli that take less cognitive effort.

2. When people don't understand what we mean, we have to speak to them multiple times, which is ineffective. And what happens if we don't have the opportunity to clarify our message multiple times?

One way to ensure that others extract the *same* meaning we do about a concept is to pair abstract words with concrete pictures. Check out the pictures that follow related to the abstract concept of "socializing." The mental picture someone has in mind may be different from someone else's, which is fine, but if we picked one or the other, at least an audience knows what we mean by "socializing" in more specific and concrete terms.

The advantage of combining abstract words with concrete pictures to control for meaning is that our visual system is able to extract conceptual information from a visual stimulus three or four times a second. In an MIT study, researchers found that the minimum time needed for visual comprehension is 13 milliseconds. That's fast. And it is possible because we have perfected our visual system throughout our lifetime to categorize pictures and scenes after *one* visual pass. Mary Potter, MIT researcher, concludes, "The fact that you can do that at these high speeds indicates to us that what vision does is find concepts . . . that's

SOCIALIZING

DO YOU AND YOUR AUDIENCE HAVE THE SAME
PICTURE OF AN ABSTRACT CONCEPT?

what the brain is doing all day long . . . trying to understand what we're looking at . . ." Pairing abstract words with concrete images gives us the advantage of controlling for meaning in a quick and efficient way.

Another advantage to linking abstract words with images is that when we process images, we store not only the meaning of the picture but also visual details, such as color, size, shape, and texture, which means we help others form multiple memory traces, increasing the likelihood of retrieval.

Often communicators use visual *metaphors* to link abstract concepts to something concrete or specific, especially in an effort to make complexity easier to understand. Imagine something complex, such as an aircraft. Remember Bert Garrison, the SR-71 pilot? He also flew the B-52, which is a long-range, subsonic, jet-powered strategic bomber. He remembers a metaphor he was taught, which changed his flying style forever. "I was flying kind of rough, and one of my first aircraft commanders said to 'fly like you're chauffeuring people holding champagne glasses.'" It is a metaphor that he's retained for decades. The commander could have said, "Fly it in a steadier way," or "Ease up a bit." When we use *visual* language and place *concrete* images in people's minds, we have better chances at creating stronger memories.

Why metaphors have such a strong effect is a matter of debate. Marketing scholar Martin Reimann of the University of Arizona maintains that metaphors are rooted in our subconscious: they help us interpret our surroundings as we age; in other words, metaphors help us convert abstract environments or situations into more relevant terms. "We, as humans, try to understand the world, in part, by metaphors," Reimann says.

Use metaphors to explain complex and abstract ideas, not simple ones. I saw someone recently use an image of a lion and its pride to explain the concept of being a supervisor. We don't need a metaphor to understand that. Supervising has a clear meaning, and that meaning is fairly consistent among listeners. With the increasing popularity of stock photography websites, too many content creators use metaphorical images too often, rendering communication unnecessarily trite. Pictures of business professionals on a racetrack, attractive people in staged group encounters, or a dart in the bull's-eye of a target are not additive to memory, especially when they are paired with simple concepts that are easy to understand. Metaphors linked to football, golf, sports cars, and mountaineering are often overused and may be too clichéd to still have impact.

Let's say you have a complex concept you want to explain using a metaphor. There are two ways to go about it. One technique is to use an old metaphor but add a fresh meaning. For example, imagine someone speaking about tennis player Serena Williams not in a sports-related way, but rather focusing on her entrepreneurial skills.

Or create new metaphors. Any book on creativity will steer our brains away from habitual metaphors. In *SoulPancake*, author Rainn Wilson offers a good list of sources of inspiration to move away from the cliché. "Go to a costume store," he advocates. "Look inside a grand piano. Watch a pastry chef decorate a cake. Watch a bartender mix drinks. Watch a salsa lesson." Any of these experiences—and many more you have the courage to explore based on your own interests and comfort level—can help you create new metaphors for abstract content. Make the first place you reach for metaphors *your own* experiences before going outside your world and borrowing from others' stories.

The advantage of pairing abstract concepts with concrete pictures is that we are better able to control the meaning people take away from our communication. Burton, the company whose mission statement we read earlier, ends it with "Burton Snowboards is a rider-driven company, solely dedicated to creating the best snowboarding equipment on the planet." The company wanted us to enjoy the original poetics but did not want us to lose sight of its meaning.

When referring to concrete elements (even when some are generic), their meaning stays fairly unchanged. For example, the meaning of a chair (a concrete and fairly generic object) is the same when we are 10, 20, 40, or 80 years old. Whether we talk about the generic category of chairs or we get specific, such as "a walnut and ebony rocking chair, handmade by renowned craftsman Sam Maloof, that sold for $80,500," we can rely on the fact that most people will retrieve the same meaning. The way we *value* a chair may change: we may need it more when we are older, or we may not appreciate one selling for a high price.

However, we understand the concept of a chair in a fairly consistent way. In contrast, the meaning of abstract concepts tends to change over time, from context to context, and from person to person. Hope at the age of 4 and hope at the age of 40 do not hold the same meaning.

When others extract a different meaning from what we intend, they may act in ways that do not serve us. When we control meaning, we are more likely to impact subsequent action. The easiest negotiations are the ones in which everyone in the room shares the same picture that means the same thing.

Wrap Abstract Words in a Concrete Context

Which will you remember better in this image: the picture of the Santa Ana winds or author Raymond Chandler's text description?

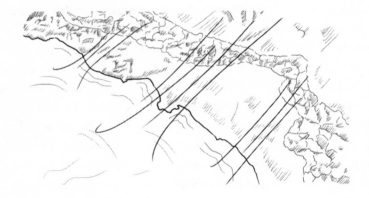

DESERT WIND

There was a desert wind blowing that
night. It was one of those hot dry
Santa Anas that come down through
the mountain passes and curl your
hair and make your nerves jump and
your skin itch. On nights like that
every booze party ends in a fight.

Even numbers are memorable when they are presented in a concrete context. I am sure we can remember numbers that are linked to our cholesterol level, a new lover's address, the completion time of a race, or a quota achieved at the last minute. It is possible for people to hate math but to love numbers.

The impact of context on memory has been demonstrated since the 1970s, when psychologists D. R. Godden and A. D. Baddeley designed a classic experiment in which divers learned a list of words under water and were later tested on dry land. The experiment showed reduced recall when the context changed and the initial environment was not reinstated. Scientists have extended the notion of context from environmental factors to the *mood* we're in at the time we learn new information or to the *time* at which we learn it.

More recently, in an EEG study, participants were shown a series of pictures (e.g., dog, tree, car) and asked to identify whether the picture displayed an animate object, whether the object could be used indoors, and if it could fit in a shoebox. Half of the 42 pictures required a positive response. Some participants saw pictures only once and some three times. In the repetitive condition, researchers also varied whether people saw the pictures multiple times in the same context or in multiple contexts. When their memory was tested, participants were shown old pictures along with new pictures and asked to recognize the ones they had seen before. The obvious finding was that people showed more accurate and faster recognition for items that had been presented three times, not just once, and this recognition was based on recollection (memory for details). However, people also showed a greater degree of familiarity for items that had been seen in multiple contexts. The study also confirmed that deep encoding (e.g., asking participants to comment on animacy, size, and usage) also increased recollection.

Repeated exposure to the same information in the same context leads to item-context binding, which supports verbatim information (recollection). But in real life, things aren't so simple. We encounter events in multiple contexts. In this situation, we must ask: Do we want people to recollect things precisely, or will simple familiarity be sufficient for their next move in your favor? If we want precision, it helps to present the same information in the same context repeatedly. If familiarity is sufficient, varying the context is better.

When creating content, it is also practical to ask: Will this context be replicated later to offer cues to retrieve memories? For example, have you visited your old high school as an adult? You may have thought that you had forgotten a lot, but being there brings a flood of memories that are activated by simply revisiting the context. What context will your audiences be in when you expect them to remember certain things? And do you want them to remember verbatim information (rely on recollection), or will gist memory do (rely on familiarity)?

Recently I was working on a presentation for Lyra, a company that helps enterprises manage their behavioral healthcare. The purpose of the presentation was to show how data-driven technology enables corporations to approach behavioral health in a way that improves productivity and reduces costs. In one segment, we were making the point that data-driven technology helps users find mental healthcare with precision. To visualize this, we showed a map of an area in San Francisco and simulated a search engine in which someone typed various terms: "psychological care in San Francisco, CA," "medication management," "experts in high-quality depression care," "accepting new patients and in my network," "near my office." With each of these searches, icons disappeared on the map to represent the idea of eliminating unnecessary hits. When the presenter delivered the speech to an audience in Richmond, Washington, we switched the maps so that listeners could relate to the context better and seeing the map later would act as a cue for memory.

EMBRACE THE PERCEPTIVE

MEMORABLE STORYTELLING

PERCEPTIVE	▷	SENSORY DETAILS IN CONTEXT		ACTION ACROSS A TIMELINE	
COGNITIVE	▷	FACTS	ABSTRACT CONCEPTS		MEANING
AFFECTIVE	▷	EMOTION			

Create a Symphony of the Senses

Earlier, we discussed the notion that a memorable story has the presence and proper proportions of perceptive, cognitive, and affective components. Most business communicators feel comfortable elaborating on the cognitive, presenting facts, abstract concepts, and meanings. It is a safe technique that makes them feel like they are bringing value with metrics, charts, and graphs.

There are two drawbacks to focusing mainly on facts, abstract concepts, and meanings. The first is that memories will be weaker. It is difficult for our audiences to remember many facts, unless we repeat them regularly, and repetition is often hard in business contexts. Sometimes we have only one chance to leave a mark. The second drawback is that when we present facts, abstract ideas, and meanings—essentially conclusions—it is difficult to control those conclusions. People are more inclined to act if they believe *they* reached a conclusion. And it's harder to reach a conclusion when they don't see what you saw. This is why we need sensory details in our content.

A good example with abundant sensory details placed in context comes from speaker and author John Vaillant's TED talk about what humans and tigers have in common. He relates his studies of tiger attacks in the Russian Far East, which he describes as a "rough and remote place, bordering North Korea and China, where temperatures drop to –40F," adding that "it rains a lot in the summer, the bugs are brutal . . ." In 2007, when he started his studies, he noted the story of one man who shot and wounded a full-grown male Siberian tiger. "These are big animals," Vaillant observes. "They can weigh 500–600 pounds, they can jump across this stage . . . and have been known to eat the Russian equivalent of grizzly bears." He continues, saying the tiger went to his enemy's cabin, found the belongings that had his scent on them, and "chewed them to pieces." The tiger waited by the cabin until his shooter came home and killed him by his front door.

After talking to the villagers, Vaillant found that this attack was an exception. Humans and tigers have many commonalities: both species are adaptable, apex predators with good memories, a capacity for vengeance, and the ability to problem-solve. The rest of his speech focuses on lessons that tigers can teach us about long-term success and mutual survival, including sustainability. His speech has influential power because we are better persuaded when we can reach a conclusion on our own, and we can do that more easily when given sensory details of an experience. Vaillant manages to sustain attention for his 20-minute TED talk with abundant details that appeal to all our senses. I saw his TED video years ago, and some of the visual details are still on my mind.

One of the best and easiest ways to include perceptive details and activate our audiences' senses is to share personal experiences.

Kevin Kregel was a NASA astronaut from 1990 to 2003. I had the opportunity to speak with him, and no interview with an astronaut is complete without a story about seeing our planet from an exclusive vantage point. Here is what Kregel remembers from one of his missions, after being in space for eight days: "The flight deck on the space shuttle is not that much bigger than a 737. A bit wider, a bit deeper, but not by much. There are six windows and two overhead windows. We turned off all the displays on the flight deck and blocked off the access to the mid-deck because there are lights there that cannot be shut off. It was pitch black. Even though there was not much room, we all had good body control, and floated, and put our faces in front of a window so you could not see anybody else. You could see the Earth below, and the stars, and we floated that way for 45 minutes, listening to Pink Floyd, *The Dark*

Side of the Moon. It felt like you were just flying and you weren't really in the shuttle. Nobody said a word. Nobody moved. Nobody touched anything. We were all floating in our separate window and the sun finally came up, and it was gorgeous." He concluded humbly, "I guess that's what it must have been like to be on LSD in the '60s."

Personal stories influence others' memory not only because of the abundant sensory details and actions across a timeline, but also because (1) they are easier for *you* to remember, so you're more likely to share those sensory details, and (2) you have the backstory, which may provide additional sensory details. If people have questions, you will find them easier to answer. If anyone asks you details about the Al Pacino story earlier, you won't know unless you're Al Pacino. If anyone asks you details about what it's like to write from the kitchen sink, you won't know unless you're Dodie Smith. Or . . . unless you dare try it yourself. What if you created your next pitch with your feet in the kitchen sink?

AVOID FORGETTABLE PICTURES

Pictures have the ability to ignite the senses, but not all pictures impact memory equally. Here are some ways to avoid forgettable visuals.

Escape the Cliché

Despite their physical distinctiveness compared with text, it is still possible to forget images because they are dull. Check any stock photo site that offers pictures of business professionals in awkward contexts, such as doing yoga, holding megaphones, or using laptops on mountaintops and wheat fields. Sometimes communicators are in such a rush that they don't bother to purchase the images, and we still see the copyright holder's watermark in the corner of the photo or even right in the middle. Many media outlets such as BuzzFeed, Mental Floss, Reddit, The Hairpin, or the *Huffington Post* beautifully capture the ridiculousness of some stock photos. A 2011 article on The Hairpin website, titled "Women Laughing Alone with Salad," went viral and captured attention for months.

Why do people use clichés? To answer, we look at variables that tend to block our creative thinking, which include stress, time constraints, worries, fears, unsolved problems, and other peoples' opinions. Some content creators also tend to be lazy observers. Who has the time to look for an unusual reflection, the light hitting the floor just the right way, or an object seen from a different angle? We are too busy to notice the authentic around us because we focus on more pragmatic concerns, such as another meeting that day or the next e-mail. The more distracted we are, the more shallow our reflections, and the more trivial and clichéd our content. When we slow down and focus, we are able to improve our content.

It is hard to find memorable pictures on stock photography sites. It is easier to create memorable photos when we are in our neighborhoods, at work, or while traveling. We can find them looking at real people. Henri Cartier-Bresson, the master of candid photography, reminds us that we just "have to live and life will give you pictures."

Use Vivid Images

Why does looking at vivid images help us remember? And what does "vivid" really mean? Neuroscientific studies confirm that the amygdala is more active when looking at images that are rated as vivid. Given that the amygdala plays a critical role in memory formation, it helps us to learn *how* to create vivid pictures.

One dimension of vividness is emotion. Rebecca Todd, a researcher in the cognitive science department at the University of British Columbia, has completed several studies on the concept of "emotionally enhanced vividness." Using MRI scans, Todd and her colleagues have observed that how vividly we perceive something "predicts how vividly we will remember it later on." When we look at images we consider vivid, we augment activity in the visual cortex and in the posterior insula, the part of the brain that integrates bodily sensations. Todd says, "The experience of more vivid perception of emotionally important images seems to come from a combination of enhanced seeing and gut feeling driven by amygdala calculations of how emotionally arousing an event is."

In several experiments, Todd and her colleagues asked participants to look at pictures that were neutral or pictures that were emotionally arousing in positive and negative ways. The researchers then superimposed a level of noise on these pictures, much like the dots we used to see on old TV channels. Participants were asked to evaluate whether each picture had more, less, or the same amount of noise compared with the original. Participants considered the emotionally enhanced pictures—both negative and positive—to show less noise than the benchmark. When their memory was tested 45 minutes afterward and also one week later, participants showed improved memory for vivid pictures. The measure of vividness was based on how much detail participants used to describe the pictures they remembered. "Both studies found that pictures rated higher in emotionally enhanced vividness were remembered better," Todd remarks.

Using brain imaging, she discovered that the amygdala, visual cortex, and interoceptive cortex activity increased the more vividness was perceived. "We know now why people perceive emotional events so vividly—and thus how vividly they will remember them—and what regions of the brain are involved," Todd says.

Besides emotion, are there any other variables that make information more vivid? We can find a more detailed answer when we investigate how memory champions perform feats of memory, such as memorizing strings of more than 1,000 randomized digits or several decks of cards. When interviewed, these mental athletes confess they convert abstract information such as numbers or names and faces into vivid visuals with one or several of these attributes: funny, unreal, offensive, unusual, ridiculous, and definitely captured in motion. For example, the number 476 may be an image of Howard Stern bouncing on a barrel of grapes.

Vividness means adding an extra layer of tension, drama, or mystery that intensifies an emotion in our listeners. In earlier chapters, we defined emotion as a state elicited by obtaining a reward or avoiding a punishment. If we know what the reward is, we have more chances of intensifying a stimulus. For example, a few years ago, my friend and graphic artist Mark Damiano created a picture of a camel. If we were to see the camel in the desert, in its natural habitat, it might not make that much of an impression. A camel dressed up in an outfit is less expected. A camel in a winter outfit visiting the Antarctic is less expected yet. The more we perceive a familiar entity in dramatic, unreal, funny, or unusual contexts, the more vivid it is in our minds, and the more easily retrievable later on.

EXPLORE NEW HABITATS

HOW TO APPEAL TO THE FEELING BRAIN

MEMORABLE STORYTELLING

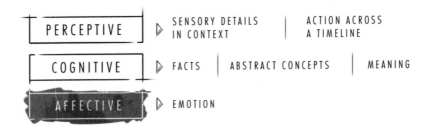

PERCEPTIVE	▷ SENSORY DETAILS IN CONTEXT	ACTION ACROSS A TIMELINE	
COGNITIVE	▷ FACTS	ABSTRACT CONCEPTS	MEANING
AFFECTIVE	▷ EMOTION		

What Are You Making an Audience Feel?

In the finale of the show *Mad Men*, the main protagonist and advertising guru Don Draper, one of the most compelling lead characters in modern TV, ends up at a hippie commune on the California coast. During a morning therapy session, people are sitting in a circle and sharing their problems, and it looks as if Don is about to take the hot seat. However, another participant, Leonard, unexpectedly gets up, takes the hot seat instead, and tells his story: "I work in an office. People walk right by me. I know they don't see me," he laments. "And I go home and I watch my wife and my kids; they don't look up when I sit down." He continues his tear-filled confessional: "I had a dream I was on the shelf in the refrigerator. Someone closes the door and the light goes off, and I know everybody's out there eating. And they open the door and you see everyone smiling and they are happy to see you, but maybe they don't look right at you and maybe they don't pick you. And then the door closes again, the light goes off."

His words are so emotionally vivid, we can picture them and feel them, without the need for real images or PowerPoint slides. There were 3.3 million viewers who tuned in for this final episode of *Mad Men*, and after three days' worth of DVR playback, that number jumped to 4.6 million, making it the show's highest-rated episode. Twitter activity after the final episode reached an all-time high with nearly 50 million impressions. The episode was also considered "the most engaging program on Facebook that Sunday night."

The refrigerator scene was one of many moments that triggered emotion during the show. There are many other scenes like these throughout the 94 episodes, which have found their way into casual conversations, even of those who did not watch the series. Emotions solidify memory. Think of your romantic partner. Do you remember your first kiss? Now compare the strength of that memory with remembering the first load of laundry you did when you moved into your current place.

Repetition aside, emotion is the most widely discussed variable in relation to memory. Emotional stimuli lead to neurochemical activity in the areas of the brain responsible for encoding, storing, and recalling memories. The amygdala modulates the visual cortex to ensure priority is given to the perception and attention of the event, which helps with encoding. At the storing stage, during sleep, emotion-based memories are given preferential consolidation treatment, and they lead to a relatively permanent trace compared with nonarousing items. Because emotion-based memories may be distinct from neutral ones experienced in the same context, they are easier to retrieve.

The stigma of emotion, especially in business, may come from the perception that emotion is the weak cousin of reason, or according to an old metaphor, emotion is the slave of reason. Emotion may also be seen as inferior and primitive, something that needs to be suppressed because it is dangerous and unreliable. This is far from true where memorable content is concerned.

Sensory perceptions are coded based on their cognitive properties (soft, delicious, strong) as well as their emotional properties (pleasant, unpleasant, exciting, calm). This dual coding of experience helps us understand why some items are forgotten: they may be encoded only once, without an emotional marker. Given that we are exposed to so much stimulation, we constantly have to decide which things to pay attention to. Stored emotional markers help us to discriminate, so that when we are confronted with a similar stimulus, we don't have to think about how to react—we already know what to do.

Just as our eyes perceive light and our ears hear sounds, our emotional system perceives the emotional significance of a stimulus.

How do we include emotion in our messages, especially when content is dry, technical, and complex, and audiences increasingly cynical? Here are a few guidelines.

Clarify What Emotion Means and What Kind You're Using

Let's consider this definition: emotions are states we feel when we obtain rewards or avoid punishments. When we look at various stimuli around us, we evaluate and decode their value in terms of predicting what happens next. For example, we see food (reward), and if we can get it, we feel elated. Or we see food, and we want it but can't get it; therefore we feel frustrated. We feel positive emotions when we advance toward rewards and negative emotions when we deviate from them. We also feel positive emotions when we avoid punishments and negative emotions when we approach them. So to the extent that the nature of the content we create is linked to receiving rewards or avoiding punishments, it can elicit an emotional reaction.

Cognitive psychologist Edmund Rolls has identified and studied emotions that cover the spectrum of four dimensions, which we feel when we:

1. Move toward rewards: pleasure, happiness, elation, ecstasy, love, sexual arousal, trust, empathy, beauty

2. Move away from rewards: frustration, indignation, disbelief, sadness, anger, rage

3. Move away from punishments: relief, liberation

4. Move toward punishments: apprehension, disgust, aversion, fear, terror, unfairness, inequity, uncertainty, social exclusion

When speaking of emotion and its impact on memory, we can also distinguish between (1) the emotional *content* of the materials we create and (2) the emotional *state* of the people who receive those materials. Research findings confirm that emotions activate two networks: the "executive control" network (including the dorsolateral prefrontal cortex and parietal areas) and the emotional "salience" network (including the anterior insular cortex, anterior cingulate cortex, amygdala, and hypothalamus). Our audiences may comprehend when we present emotional content, such as showing how someone got hurt. However, if the emotional state we provoke is not intense enough, they may be aware of the emotion but not feel it deeply or be moved by it.

Reflecting on your own content, ask this: Which of the four dimensions for emotion could you address without making an audience feel skeptical or cynical?

In general, people adopt a cynical attitude when there is an obligation for reciprocity and that obligation is broken (e.g., employees versus organization). Typically, in business settings, we become cynical in these circumstances:

- Expected outcomes created by an organization are unevenly distributed (e.g., high executive compensation and low raises for the staff).

- People with lesser skills are promoted.

- There are harsh layoffs.

- Expectations are unrealistically high.

- Communication is inadequate.

- Management is characterized by mediocrity.

- Role ambiguity and conflict are prevalent in the workplace.

- People are suffering from work overload.

If this is the context in which your listeners operate, the context must be addressed first before any other piece of communication has the chance to leave an impression. The most effective piece of content, soaked in the proper emotion (from your view) will fall flat if your listeners are experiencing any of these variables. On the other hand, it is not beneficial to meet audiences in an entirely negative space either. Each time you speak to such audiences, consider lessening the emotion they feel just by a few levels on the same scale, without adopting an entirely different emotion. For cynical audiences that feel anger, by including emotions related to frustration, you still meet them on the same emotional scale but in a way that is toned down. This technique will make them less suspicious of your content.

Of course, cynicism, much like boredom, is not always situational. There are dispositional traits that can lead to cynicism, such as self-esteem, the belief we can control outcomes, reactions to equity (how fair we believe some transactions are), a tendency to view life events as negative, heightened sensitivity, Machiavellianism (viewing others as self-serving), work ethic, or demographic characteristics.

Reflecting on your own content and the emotional state of your audiences, ask: Is the emotion in the content you include appropriate for the emotional state that your audiences are likely to be in when they listen to you?

Let's see how taking into account the four emotion tracks and an audience's emotional state plays out in real life. *Shark Tank* is a TV show in which five investors listen to pitches for various products and services. We can learn from this show when crafting content because it provides abundant examples of persuasive scenarios: people have something to sell, and investors need to be convinced to buy. Kevin O'Leary, one of the investors, is known for caustic criticism but also for metaphors and stories he links to business concepts. In one episode, O'Leary is talking to a couple pitching a kids' clothing line. He is appalled that the entrepreneurs had 2,700 SKUs, which they felt were needed to keep the line fresh and modern. After several business-related questions, O'Leary tells a story from Greek mythology that expresses his *fear* of a dangerous business tactic.

O'Leary's story is about the goddess Persephone, daughter of Zeus and Demeter. "One day she was picking flowers, and she was always tempted to go for more colors. The earth opened, and she fell into the bowels of hell. Here we are in hell." Fellow investor Mark Cuban pretended to be asleep after the second sentence. Even investor Lori

Greiner, who is typically sweet and polite, said to the entrepreneurs in reference to O'Leary, "Hell is *his* home."

This is an example in which the speaker's emotion (O'Leary's) does not match the emotional state of the others around him. "Fear" means we are moving toward a punishment, and that's not where the others were. If anything, the high number of SKUs may cause some apprehension, which is on the other emotional scale, moving away from a reward. To avoid the raised eyebrows, a story expressing apprehension would have been better received.

O'Leary knows when he is pushing buttons, so he cut the story short and made the point that too many choices have bad consequences. As we discussed earlier, there are memory trade-offs. You can take the chance and use a different emotional scale than where your audience may be and generate negative emotions. This still results in memory. A negative emotion may be a good place to start, but it is not a good place to end.

Gradually move your audiences to a place that feels optimal for them. Decades of positive psychology research remind us that positive emotions lead to growth and well-being and widen people's thought-to-action capabilities.

Use Nostalgia

Nostalgia is an emotion that helps to abstract and extract meaning. It is especially effective with cynical audiences because it levels the knowledge in the room. Romancing the past has the potential to strengthen the bond with others. When everyone feels like an equal, people are more likely to trust each other and are more likely to allow themselves to be swayed in a certain direction by others. This is why messages that start with "Remember when . . ." are so effective. Remember when we only had a few channels on TV? Remember when there were no cell phones? Remember when there was no Facebook?

Nostalgia is associated with persuasion because it has the potential to impact our senses, our preferences, and our loyalty toward an object or a person. Advertisers take advantage of this. I remember a

KFM radio station ad that showed a cassette tape with a callout box that said, "iPod, I am your father." Marketers often invite us to re-create the past through nostalgic consumption. Can you do the same with your audiences? When they are disenchanted by something in the present, can you meet them in an idealized place in the past and build from there?

The formal definition of nostalgia is a "bittersweet longing for home." During this emotional state, we yearn for an idealized or sanitized version of the past. I can immediately relate to the definition of nostalgia because I grew up in Romania, in the 1980s, under the Communist regime. I often long for our small apartment, eating polenta after a day of unsupervised play in the streets, and not being tempted into prolonged TV watching because we only had two channels. In reminiscing about the "good old days," we ignore many negative traces.

If my own recollection of that tiny home in Romania were to include an accurate description, I would also mention how we had hot water only once a week, how the electricity would go out at random times for no apparent reason, and how you could hear all your neighbors' arguments through the thin walls. The two hours of television a day were mostly filled with patriotic poems, sterile Communist propaganda, and censored films. These were times of scarcity and restrictions placed on almost everything, including heat, food, travel, and information. If we were to be accurate about nostalgia, we would define it as a utopian version of the past.

Nostalgia seems to work best when we are torn between the past and the future—whenever there is some anxiety between two worlds, one that used to be and one that is emerging without much direction. Some would call this "disruption." We've heard that word too much in the past few years. If we understand such states of transition, we can appreciate that many of us tend to look back for emotional security. What's less threatening and more comforting will feel good. The unknown (initially) provokes anxiety.

Rose Ballesteros works for Husky, a company that produces plastic injection molding systems (the preforms that give bottles and jars their shapes). Ballesteros is a business manager in the Mexico and Central

America region and recently attended one of my workshops. I still remember one of her presentations, in which she used nostalgia to show the evolution of milk packaging. Depending on your age and where you're from, you may have seen only some of the options in the slide below on TV or in magazines. Nostalgia works well because it evokes the familiarity and security of the past. (PET stands for polyethylene terephthalate, the breakthrough molding material Husky uses.)

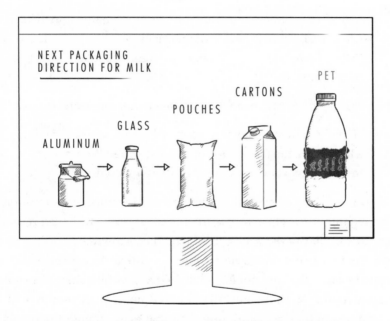

NOSTALGIA FEEDS OUR NEED FOR EMOTIONAL SECURITY

Use Wabi-Sabi

One of the most touching exercises I conduct in brain science workshops is asking people to take pictures of their shoes and to type a brief story that their shoes might tell. Notice the authentic emotions attached to these entries:

- "These shoes have taken my son to college and allowed me to walk away with confidence!"

- "These shoes match every pair of pants I own. So they simplified my life every day by reclaiming 60 seconds of indecision. I get back seven minutes per week for the rest of my life."

- "With these shoes, I finished the NYC Marathon and Camino de Santiago. They mean victory."

- "My friend owed me money and gave me her shoes instead of payment."

- "These shoes have gone from the start of a relationship to its unfortunate conclusion. From no laces to unbreakable laces. From pop music to black metal. They are a collection of my immediate life."

- "These shoes have been through cancer treatment and survived."

- "I really wanted to buy some cooler-looking shoes. Something a little more hip like some pointy suede ones. But I'm too indecisive. So here they are in all their uncoolness."

The authenticity of these entries makes them impossible to ignore. One technique to help us stay authentic is wabi-sabi, which represents a Japanese view of the world, in which objects are seen as imperfect, impermanent, and incomplete. Objects invite us to get close and to relate because they are not fully polished and predictable. Wabi-sabi is an invitation to simplicity but not boredom. A quick search online for wabi-sabi images will remind you that even though the objects they capture are stripped down to their essence, they are emotionally warm. They are simple but not sterile.

Reflect on your own content. Are you staying close to reality in a warm, approachable, modest, and humble way? Can you bring your content down to its essence, without stripping its poetry, even if that implies some imperfections?

In some of my workshops, I ask participants to create or find a picture that is understated and unassuming, yet explains a complex message they want to share with their audience. These are some of my favorites:

- A rusted bike stuck in an overgrown tree with the message "How you run your business should adjust to provide customer value and not morph around the legacy systems that are in place."

- A dead flower with the message "Many platforms send alerts days after something happens, so we must use technology that enables real-time reporting."

- A vintage picture of a corner store with the message "Even the most modern infrastructure will eventually be outdated."

These unpretentious entries provoke emotions, even in the most cynical audiences.

Use Intense Emotions

I remember an old Nike ad with a lot of attitude: "If you're serious about sports, buy Nike shoes. If you want to dance, buy Reebok." This works for memory because it adds tension, which generates emotion. It is not a flat statement such as "Buy these shoes to enjoy running." This would generate an emotion, too, but not a strong one. You don't need to bash the competition, but it is important to ask, "How intense is the emotion I include in my content?"

Research on psychological arousal finds that high arousal (versus low arousal) leads to better memory. For example, highly intense positive emotions, such as awe, excitement, and amusement, and highly intense negative emotions, such as anger and anxiety, leave a stronger impression compared with their low-arousal counterparts, such as contentment on the positive side and sadness on the negative side.

The more emotionally intense and crisp your statements are, the more likely they are to be repeated. Lines such as "Come with me if you want to live" from *Terminator 2*, or "I just shot Marvin in the face" from *Pulp Fiction*, or the pun "I am having an old friend for dinner" from *The Silence of the Lambs* all express strong emotions.

Messages such as "Here is how to gain access to tools and resources for your job" or "Efficiency of value generation must be quantified and evaluated" are fated to be forgotten if they are not associated with emotional intensity. How do we add emotional intensity? Think of current events, and tie the stories behind them to business messages. David Purdie, PhD, head of Patient Access and Quality of Care at Genentech, told me about a presentation he had to give to some senior managers to convince them to form a new group of analysts. They were suspicious that analytics would really benefit their decision-making processes. Purdie said, "I knew that a traditional presentation with plans and timelines was not going to have the kind of impact I needed to move them to action." Purdie saved the logistics for a later meeting. During the initial interaction, he shared how the Boston Red Sox used analytics to win the 2004 World Championship and the strong emotion behind a team winning its first World Championship in 85 years. Purdie was excited at the impact of his speech. This was before *Moneyball* was published or made into a movie, so his story included novelty and surprise for his business audience. Purdie remembers, "My presentation that day started a groundswell of support for the new group, and for the acceptance and adoption of using analytics to inform decision-making. Within a few short years, the group grew to 45 statisticians informing critical decisions all across the company."

Any content that has a high-arousal characteristic, such as awe, anger, amusement, or anxiety, tends to be more viral, so if we create emotion-based messages, we have the opportunity not only to influence memory but to influence *more* people's memory. For example, a study analyzed all *New York Times* articles published online over a period of three months and discovered that those articles that contained high-arousal emotions were more likely to be e-mailed compared with articles that evoked low-level emotions, such as sadness.

Emotion seems to influence not only whether a message will become repeatable but also how much and how quickly it will be repeated. A German study using SentiStrength—which analyzes emotions in tweets by looking at emotional terms, amplifications (haaaaapy), emoticons, and spelling corrections—examined 165,000 tweets and found that the more positive or negative emotions a tweet expressed, the more quickly and frequently it was retweeted.

LONG STORY SHORT

MEMORABLE STORYTELLING

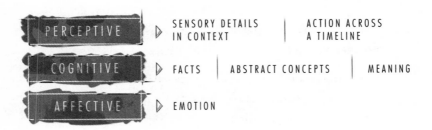

PERCEPTIVE ▷ SENSORY DETAILS IN CONTEXT | ACTION ACROSS A TIMELINE

COGNITIVE ▷ FACTS | ABSTRACT CONCEPTS | MEANING

AFFECTIVE ▷ EMOTION

In this chapter, we addressed the components mandatory for creating content in such a way that it becomes easy for people to search and retrieve it days, weeks, or even years later. When we look at the combination of these elements, they provide the formula for memorable storytelling. Ultimately, all memories include some combination of sensory elements, contextual details, cognitive processes involved when that memory was formed, abstract concepts, and meaning. To make the search for memories easier at Point B, appealing to emotion ensures retrieval because of an additional marker in memory.

I remember an ad from a company called Blanco Attika. It advertised a faucet. The text boldly asked, "Is there emotion in steel? We think so." A picture showed a close-up of a beautiful faucet, and the description told us how the company "embraced an exclusive blend of artisan craftsmanship and German precision. From the dramatic architecture of the raised rim to the enchanting beauty of the lustrous finish, this unique work of art brilliantly captures light as it captures attention." I never thought it was possible to have an emotional reaction to faucets. If this company can add emotion to steel, I am convinced you will be able to tap into the emotions of any audience in a way that leaves a lasting impression.

KEEP IN MIND

- Memorable stories contain the following components: perceptive (sensory impressions in context and action across a timeline), cognitive (facts, abstract concepts, and meaning), and affective (emotion).

- Something is concrete if we can perceive it with our senses. If we can't perceive it with our senses, we are talking about an idea or a concept, which is abstract. Balance both in your communication and, to avoid habituation, break the pattern an audience learns to expect.

- While abstract and concrete are opposites, generic and specific are subsets of each other, with generic being a large group and specific representing an individual item within that group. Zoom in on specific details based on your audience's level of expertise (advanced audiences can handle abstracts better).

- Text and graphics have the potential to be equals in memory. Make pictures easy to label and text easy to picture.

- Pair abstract words with concrete pictures to ensure that your audience extracts a uniform meaning from your message.

- Use visual metaphors to explain abstract concepts. Steer away from clichéd metaphors by either giving an old metaphor a fresh meaning or using unexpected metaphors.

- Wrap abstract words in concrete contexts. Repeat information in the same context for verbatim memory. Vary the context for gist memory.

- Appeal to the senses to activate multiple parts of the brain and create more memory traces. The more personal experiences you share, the more opportunities to include sensory details.

- Avoid clichéd images. Instead, use vivid images to evoke tension, mystery, wabi-sabi, or nostalgia.

- Use strong emotions by showing an audience how to:
  - Move toward rewards: pleasure, happiness, elation, ecstasy, love, sexual arousal, trust, empathy, beauty.
  - Move away from rewards: frustration, indignation, disbelief, sadness, anger, rage.
  - Move toward punishments: apprehension, disgust, aversion, fear, terror, unfairness, inequity, uncertainty, social exclusion.
  - Move away from punishments: relief, liberation.

CHAPTER 10

HOW MUCH CONTENT IS TOO MUCH?

How to Handle Content Sacrifice

S*mith Magazine*, an online publication, firmly believes that people should have a place to share their life stories, and their staff invite anyone with a good narrative to submit it to their website. There is a caveat: users have to limit their life story to six words. Here are some examples:

New house. New closets. Same skeletons.

Siri, delete Mom from my contacts.

Brought roses home. Keys didn't fit.

Head in books, feet in flowers.

A few days from now, will we remember these stories better than longer stories? Brevity is advantageous because it gets attention and sustains it since there is not much to absorb. It also creates a feeling of mastery and completion, which generates positive emotions. Message miniaturization is increasingly popular and appeals to modern audiences. But what happens when we can't bow to the rhetoric of the micromessage? And how short is too short and how long is too long where memory is concerned?

Let's start with the assumption that you have a message that will move your audience toward a reward or away from a punishment. If this condition is not met, the discussion about optimal length does not apply because no amount of content will be memorable if it's not linked to obtaining relevant rewards or avoiding pain. If this condition is met, consider the steps below when determining the length of your message.

CLARIFY WHAT THE AUDIENCE MUST REMEMBER

In an earlier chapter, we discussed verbatim versus gist memory. When we want others to remember precise information, to recollect it with details, we aim for verbatim. If we are satisfied when others are familiar with what we said, without recalling many details, or use some of their own words to describe what they remember, we are aiming for gist.

Considering the ratio between verbatim and gist has immediate impact on content length. If we aim for *verbatim*, we have to leave some room for repetition and elaboration to make sure those concepts stick in a precise way. In other words, simply sharing some key words in a brief message will not make them memorable just because they are short.

For example, let's say we want an audience to remember three steps for creating a successful e-commerce platform. Let's summarize these steps as "enable," "engage," and "execute." To make these words stick, we have to link them to what we discussed in the previous chapter: perceptive, cognitive, and affective elements (e.g., concrete scenarios, testimonials, abstract ideas, facts, and emotions). We would also have to repeat those three words multiple times. These techniques add up in time and content length.

On the surface, the presentation is about three words, and it may seem that we can keep it short. But those three words run the risk of being similar to other words people will encounter after that presentation. Type "the three Es of . . ." in a search engine and you will find that others describe their content using three Es, too. It will be difficult for an audience to remember who said what, unless we have strong anchors and distinctive hooks for that content.

Less is not necessarily more if we aspire to memorable content. We sometimes need more content, and the intent is not to create more memories. It's to create a few precise memories.

Short feels good but is not always memorable.

If we aim for *gist* memory, the standards for length are looser. We can get away with more content, as long as at least one main message is clear and we draw attention to it often. And if the content is complex, we don't need to sacrifice all the complexity; we just need to ensure that we return frequently to that one main message we would like our audience to retain. When we use the guidelines for noticing cues, repetition, and distinctiveness, we have a good balance between the gist and one verbatim message that ties everything together.

At any given time that people are listening to us, their working memory has capacity limitations. At any specific moment, they can keep in their working memory up to four items, and items that are in focus all at once may be associated with each other in listeners' minds. When we present more content, those associations are no longer formed. If associations are not important and people can get the gist, then lengthy content is acceptable.

DETERMINE WHAT THE AUDIENCE MUST ACT ON NEXT

If our intent for a communication effort is to have others simply "like" the content, leave a comment, or share it with others, these intentions are better achieved with shorter content. On the other hand, if the audience needs to make a difficult decision, such as awarding us a significant amount of money, effort, or time, then longer content is necessary to be convincing.

Listerine can get away with a message such as "We fight bad breath" because the company is asking for little money, time, and effort. It's harder to convince someone to buy a new marketing platform worth $50,000 after an elevator pitch or even a 30-minute presentation. If 30 minutes is all we have initially, then the main intent for the conversation changes to "Can we schedule another meeting to explain more?" In this case, the only item for the audience to act on is to grant us more time. With each exposure to information, we can aspire to a bigger decision. One of the mistakes we sometimes make is that we are too ambitious about what others should be acting on next. Because of this ambition, content is unnecessarily long: we feel the need to express everything all at once so that our listeners can make a buying decision when what we should really be after, at least initially, is sharing enough content for them to make a "time allowance" decision.

BALANCE EASE OF RETRIEVAL WITH QUALITY OF INFORMATION

In a research study, participants were asked to recall either 6 or 12 examples of when they showed assertive behavior (e.g., asked the boss for a raise). Then they were asked to rate how assertive they considered themselves to be. If participants based their judgment on the *quantity* of the content that came to mind, they should rate themselves more assertively when they could recall 12 examples instead of 6. If they based their judgment on the *ease* with which information came to mind, then they should rate themselves as more assertive if they could recall 6 easy examples rather than struggle recalling 12. The study confirmed the latter hypothesis. People scanned their personal histories, and the memories that could be pulled easily were considered diagnostic of a *specific trait*. People thought they were more assertive when 6 easy examples came to mind.

The situation is reversed when we make *judgments* about others. We rely more on the *amount* of content we retrieve rather than how easily the information comes to mind.

In one study, when participants read either a small list or a large list of arguments made by other people, they tended to be more influenced by the *larger* list. The more reasons people can think of for hiring you, the more likely it is that they will make that recommendation. In these situations, people link the number of items to frequency or probability. For example, people tend to be more easily persuaded by an appeal when they are told it contains nine rather than three favorable arguments.

When you analyze your content, determine this: Are you offering pieces of information that describe traits of a specific audience? For example, are you asking listeners if they are keeping up with the new economy of increasingly demanding customers and operating in an increasingly mobile world? If you expect an audience to identify with specific traits, keep the content short. However, if you're presenting on a subject about which your listeners don't have much information or context, and they must make an important decision, then longer content is beneficial.

MEET TIME CONSTRAINTS IMPOSED BY OTHERS

Sometimes our audiences are in charge of how much time they allow us to speak. A client says, "You have an hour for this presentation." Someone may be a bit thriftier: "We can give you only 30 minutes." In an investor presentation, you may have 10 minutes. Someone may just want your elevator pitch.

Adjust to any of these situations by starting with two questions: "What do I want the audiences to remember?" and "What do I want them to act on?" If these are clear—and knowing that we speak at a rate of about 140 to 160 words per minute—you have a metric for how much you can say in 30 seconds, 10 minutes, or 1 hour. Treat each of these segments as a stepping-stone for the audience to get closer to a reward. Antonio Bertone, global director for brand management at Puma in Boston, looks at 15-second commercials as "flirtations." He considers them teasers, and if you treat them as such, they must be short. "You don't want to be like a joke that goes on too long," he reminds us.

There can be advantages to time limits. Research shows that when limitations are imposed on us, we end up being more innovative. Look at Yves Klein who painted using only blue. Or photographers who create just in black and white. Check out "ukulele weeps" by Jake Shimabukuro: he produces moving music on a tiny, four-string, two-octave instrument. Treat a limited amount of time as an opportunity to clarify your main message.

It is also practical to ask: Have we earned the right to more time? I remember being at a store and rushing to pay at the register, when the cashier started a story. Imagine my reaction: we expect a cashier to be fast and efficient. Storytelling is not something we picture at the cash register. "I had a dream last night," she began. I thought selfishly, "She has 20 seconds to finish this." She did it in less. She said, "Yesterday, I took a cab and forgot my keys in it. That really happened. Then last night, I dreamed that the cab driver brought my keys and was standing by my bed, watching me sleep." Her brief story was so potent that another shopper joined us to empathize and recognize how creepy that must have been. The store clerk intuitively knew she had a short time to appeal to someone, and she did it masterfully. We can all learn from her: take only the time granted by a specific context, and if you push the limits, don't go for too much. When we do it well, we earn the right to more time on the next occasion.

THE AUDACITY OF GOING BEYOND 140 CHARACTERS

Another way to mitigate complexity and the need for longer time is to consider the question: Under what circumstances does exposure to content *feel* short? Scientific experiments confirm that we feel time is flying by when:

> *Something is visibly progressing.* At stoplights, seeing the number of seconds we have to wait reduces the perception of wait time. Reflect on ways in which you can show your audiences how much progress they've made toward the completion of something they find rewarding. Showing progress through a presentation, setting specific times for conversation ("I will spend 10 minutes discussing X"), and providing progress bars for content download are just a few examples of how you can positively impact the perception of time.
>
> For written online content, reading position indicators—in the shape of color progress bars, a display with the number of words left, or even "minutes left"—helps us manage our expectations of time better. In formal presentations, seeing "slide 3 out of 12" puts us at ease. The same is true of meetings or conversations for which we set a specific time ("the meeting is from 11:00 to 11.30") and refer to the duration that remains ("we have only 10 minutes left").
>
> *Attention shifts.* When our attention shifts constantly, we experience the passage of time less keenly. I know a college in Edmonton, Alberta, that could not immediately fix the problem of slow elevators, so the administrators placed mirrors next to the elevator doors—and received fewer complaints. Consider directing your audiences' attention toward rewarding stimuli and vary the stimuli frequently to avoid boredom.
>
> *An experience is considered aesthetic.* Abundant literature demonstrates that aesthetics is not just a subjective matter. Things that look and feel beautiful alter our perception of time; we want to stay longer and return more frequently to what we consider aesthetically pleasing.

How do we cater to aesthetics in business content? We can start by ensuring content is well organized. Business content is often consid-

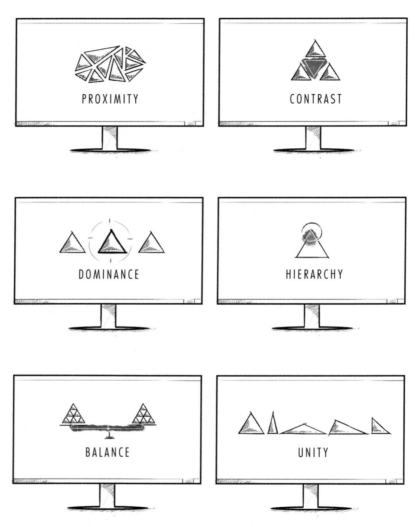

EASE OF PROCESSING LEADS TO THE IMPRESSION
OF AN AESTHETIC EXPERIENCE

ered complex because it is chaotically displayed, not because it really is complex. Guidelines such as proximity, contrast, dominance, hierarchy, balance, and unity are just a few of the techniques that give an audience the *feeling* of organization, which influences the perception of time and memory. *Proximity* indicates a connection between close elements. *Contrast* distinguishes items by emphasizing differences in physical or semantic properties. *Dominance* helps us focus on only one element out of many. *Hierarchy* shows a difference in the importance of message components. *Balance* implies equal distribution of these components. *Unity* means that all components of your message appear to belong together. Any of these elements influences how the brain processes information. For example, in one study, participants were shown four fictitious molecules along with their names and were asked to remember the pairing of molecule and name, as well as how many "spokes" it had. Participants had better recall in the group in which the molecules and their names were in close proximity because the brain organized them rapidly, leaving more time for encoding.

Consider providing your listeners with a proper mix of fact-based content and aesthetics so they too can have, as one of the six-word life stories described earlier, "head in books, feet in flowers."

KEEP IN MIND

- Clarifying what an audience must remember and do helps to filter unnecessary content.

- Keep it brief when an audience must identify with the content. Offer more when your listeners don't have much information or context, and they must make an important decision.

- Earn the right to provide more information by offering value.

- If your content is long, alter your audience's perception of time by offering visible signs of progress, shifting the audience's focus frequently, and making the content aesthetically pleasing.

WE SHARE
CONTENT HERE A

B THEY REMEMBER
AND ACT HERE

NOTICE CUES	>	SEARCH MEMORY	>	EXECUTE ON INTENTIONS

CHAPTER 11

HOW DOES THE BRAIN DECIDE?

The Neurobiology and Neuroeconomics of Choice

D espite the best of intentions, many actions go unfulfilled. Think of your friends, family, or coworkers. In the past week, how many of them said they would do something and did not do it? There is often a gap between what people say they will do and what they actually do, and that gap has negative influences on relationships and business.

In our communication efforts, we create content and share it at Point A, and we hope people remember it and act on it later at Point B. From this angle, it is practical to study the concept of prospective memory—enabling others to remember to act on future intentions—because it keeps us viable. When our audiences do what they say they will do, we stay in business. When they say they will meet with us again and they do, we have the opportunity to move forward. When they say they want to hire us and they do, we have the opportunity to grow. Memory has evolved to help us keep track of the future. This means that for communicators, it is useful to consider techniques that *make us part of our audience's future*, especially at critical decision points.

How do we complete the cycle of prospective memory? At Point B, people may notice cues related to something we mentioned at Point A, search their memories for appropriate actions, and decide to act on an intention. Or not. Use these guidelines to make it easier for your audiences' brains to decide in your favor:

1. Design cues that are hard to miss, and link them to something rewarding.

2. Create anticipation, which releases dopamine and sparks action.

3. Make important messages easy to repeat and recall later.

4. Ensure that important content comes to mind easily by making it distinct from other content.

5. Use effective storytelling with a proper combination of perceptive, cognitive, and affective components.

6. Offer an optimal amount of information.

Despite following these guidelines, it is possible our audiences need even more convincing to act. This chapter will equip us with additional persuasive power.

Much has been published on the concept of neuroeconomics and the neurobiology of decision-making. The difference between the two fields is that neuroeconomics offers models that aim to predict or explain our observable choices. Neurobiology aims to explain the mechanisms in our nervous system that mediate behavior and generate choices. We can use insights from both fields. This chapter presents research-based guidelines to influence decision-making that have not been widely discussed beyond academic circles.

HOW DOES THE BRAIN DECIDE?

At the beginning of the book, we discussed three angles for understanding how the brain makes decisions. We make choices in a *reflexive* kind of way: we instinctively and subconsciously react to tastes, sounds, sex, novelty, altruism, or control over our environment and decide what to do next quickly and subconsciously. Reflexes require few resources. As I was writing this, an ad from Pinterest popped up on my computer saying, "Access these photos so you never miss anything on the latest fashion." A message such as "never miss anything" is effective because it appeals to our instinct to control. It takes more energy to ignore that message than it does to indulge it.

We also make choices based on *habits*, which we develop when we explore our external environments and inner states. Habits are conscious at first, become automatic in time, and tend to stick when they are rewarding and not costly in cognitive energy. We also decide according to *goals*. Depending on what we consider rewarding (public image, financial wealth, or health), we are willing to make deliberate decisions. Unlike reflexes and habits, goals require willpower, which implies more cognitive resources.

As our lives unfold in a series of decisions, ranging from fully *automatic* to fully *strategic*, we may experience some tension balancing them. An instinctual voice in your head may say, "I am craving something sweet." The automatic voice adds, "A KitKat bar would be really good." And the strategic voice asks, "Can I afford the calories?"

Reflecting on your own content, ask this: What gives your own audiences a rush? What do they crave? What lights their fire naturally? Can you divide your content approaches so as to appeal to something automatic and strategic in balanced proportions? For example, in a current antismoking campaign, we see a young girl, Amanda Green, writing a "contract" in which she agrees to relinquish part of her freedom to a cigarette. The voiceover bluntly states, "There is a contract in every cigarette; when you light up, you sign up." The commercial appeals to all three decision drivers: a reflex, our automatic desire to be in control; an existing habit, smoking; and a goal, quitting. The ad ends with "Know the real cost," which appeals to a strategic approach for quitting.

WHAT IS AUTOMATIC?

When analyzing decision-making, it is practical to understand what *automatic* decisions really mean. Psychologists agree that in order for a mental process to be automatic, it must be related to one or more of these four: awareness, intentionality, efficiency, and controllability. A process is automatic if we are not aware of it, in the sense that we may not notice a stimulus, such as an air-conditioning unit running in the background at a comfortable temperature. Sometimes we are not aware of how we interpret a stimulus (such as when we engage in stereotyping) or believe that something is the cause of an event when it isn't (such as believing that a new type of music is corrupting kids). A process is also automatic if we don't intentionally start it (e.g., feeling hungry) and if it is efficient, meaning it does not require cognitive resources (e.g., you don't have to think to realize you're hungry). A mental process is also automatic if it is uncontrollable, meaning we cannot stop it; it will run until completion (e.g., salivating to digest food).

Consider creating some of your content with the concept of automatic processes in mind, because when you appeal to instincts and existing habits in particular, which are automatic, decisions are easier. You may not meet all four of the criteria described for automatic processes, but even one or two dimensions are helpful. We can learn from marketers at Oreo, who generated a lot of buzz for the cookie in 2012 when the company turned 100 years old. Marketers created a 100-day *Daily Twist*, which included pictures of the Oreo cookie linked to something that happened in the news on a specific day during the 100 days. For instance, one cookie had an orange filling with tire tracks to celebrate the Mars Rover landing. Another showed an Oreo doing the Gangnam-style dance. A cookie with rainbow-color filling celebrated gay pride. The campaign invited action because it hooked into elements people already knew and did not require extra processing power. One might say it was a cognitively efficient campaign. The campaign led to 5 million likes and a 110% increase in consumer engagement.

I remember working with Mike Ray, a vice president at McDonald's. He needed to deliver a presentation with the intent to improve the revenue of a region by generating more sales through effective operations. What would it take for his audience to listen and decide to act on what Ray said? Cash flow. With that clarity, the message we created was based on automatic *and* strategic thinking. The concept of cash flow comes to mind automatically, so we titled the presentation "You Profit Most When You Serve Best," and we linked profit (automatic thought) with operations (strategic thought). In another segment, he urged his audience to "create a customer who creates customers," which combines automatic thinking (creating customers) and strategic thinking (those customers will later bring their friends). Toward the end of the presentation, Ray asked, "If your last customer interaction were posted on Facebook, would you feel proud of your performance?" This also appealed to something automatic (Facebook posts) and strategic (the more satisfied customers are, the bigger the cash flow).

When we are communicating new information to people, we are asking their brains to incorporate the new information while maintaining old information. This is not always easy to do. The problem is called the stability-plasticity dilemma. Researchers are now looking more seriously at the question: Does learning new things incrementally decrease the memories of old things? If people are only learning something once, the answer is a strong yes. This is why an important first step in deciding what we would like others to remember and act on is this: hook into what they already know and have practiced for a long time so the memory has longevity.

HOW DO WE KNOW IF THE BRAIN IS DECIDING BASED ON HABITS OR GOALS?

The way to test the difference between habits and goal-oriented choices is to notice whether an organism changes behavior in light of new information. To show this, studies have been performed on both humans and animals. For instance, hungry rats are trained to press a lever to receive a specific type of food. After a while, the food is "devalued," in the sense that either the rats can have access to as much as they want or the food is injected with drugs to make it unappetizing. Then the rats are offered the opportunity to press the lever again for food. Do they act based on past satisfaction, or do they act based on consequences?

A key factor that differentiates habits from goal-oriented behavior is the *amount of exposure or training* the organism receives. Rats who complete training in lever pressing to receive food for five half-hour sessions prior to devaluation stop pressing the lever when food is devalued. Rats who complete 20 sessions of lever pressing continue to act out of habit. This is why highly practiced actions such as driving to work can become automatic even when they are detrimental, such as ignoring construction signs and still taking the usual route.

Recently, scientists replicated the devaluation experiment with humans to see what it would take to get people to act based on habits or based on goals. Thirty-two healthy participants who were not dieting were trained to associate different actions (button presses) with obtaining either Fritos or M&Ms. One group received six times more training than the other, after which the food was devalued (i.e., participants could eat as many Fritos or M&Ms as they wanted). Later when they were asked to press buttons again to receive rewards, participants who had received more training continued to act based on habits, even though the reward had been devalued.

Thinking about your own content, ask this: How long has your audience been performing a task that you would like them to change? If they have not been doing it for long, present goal-oriented information (e.g., "reduce Facebook time to be more productive at work"). If they've been doing it for a long time, tie the change you want to see to an existing habit (e.g., "every time a Facebook notification pops up, write a sentence for work before opening it").

If your content is aimed at convincing people to change an existing habit, it's important to remember that habits are formed by doing, not by *not* doing. Frame your messages in a positive way. Imagine if the famous slogan "Just do it" was "Don't procrastinate."

HOW DOES THE BRAIN KNOW WHAT TO VALUE?

To ensure biological fitness, the brain has evolved to pay attention to internal or external cues, quickly determine their predictive value, compute the optimal choice to obtain rewards, and act. With this in mind, we can list the steps that are part of any decision:

1. Identify sensory stimuli: What is it?

2. Select an action that will maximize a reward: What is it worth?

3. Act on the intention.

4. Evaluate the results: Did you predict the outcome well?

Notice that the first step in making choices is paying attention to stimuli. This means we have to draw people's attention to what we consider important in order for them to act on an intention. For example, I was browsing through a magazine and was compelled to read the story about Dimitry Morozov's tattoo. An artist and self-taught engineer from Moscow, Morozov has tattooed on his left forearm an 8- × 3-inch barcode. When he scans it with the right gadget, he gets . . . music. Morozov created the barcode in Photoshop and molded a scanner with two black-line sensors, a stepper motor, and a Nintendo Wii remote. As the motor guides the sensors along his tattoo, the length of each bar dictates the duration of the sound. If he moves his arm, the Wii's accelerometer detects the shift and changes the tone. The story had enough familiar and new stimuli that made my decision to look and engage with it easier compared to other articles in the magazine.

Once we have people's attention, they select an action to maximize a reward, and this reward depends on the value they attach to it. MRI studies confirm that the brain integrates sensory and reward information to make choices, and it weighs costs against benefits into a single representation of net value. Neuroeconomists Joseph Kable and Paul Glimcher call this abstract measure of value a "common currency of choice."

We learn values through experience and reinforcement. The brain encodes a "teaching" signal each time we learn the subjective value of our actions. Each time we go through the same action and experience an outcome, we update the value estimate by using the old value and a reward prediction error, which represents the difference between the experienced outcome and expected outcome.

At the time of choice, we retrieve stored values, taking into consideration the magnitude of expected reward and the likelihood the reward will happen. A phrase that neuroeconomists use frequently is "predicted utility," which means the expected value of a predicted outcome, typically learned and remembered from the past. If you enjoy going to the website TED.com and generally get good information from it, you expect that if you go there today, you will be rewarded with good information again.

When faced with choices, we tend to remember the total pleasure or displeasure associated with an outcome. The stimulus properties of the outcome are part of our experienced utility and are state dependent. For example, we remember food differently based on whether we are hungry or satiated. So when we have specific goals for the future, we combine the knowledge of the outcome values from the past and calculate *decision utility.*

We generally expect future rewards to be as good as the ones we remember from the past. What if we need to make decisions when we have not experienced something in the past? We can still compute future value by estimating its similarity with something we do remember, using knowledge acquired from observing others or through inferences or instructions from others.

It is not sufficient to simply encode values and store them. We still need to act on a choice. Once the brain notices something has high value, it makes a choice from a set of alternatives and passes it to the motor system for implementation.

After we make choices, we evaluate the outcomes. This process can depend on higher cognitive processes, and it is independent from the original stimulus. For instance, if someone uses the word "expensive" or "healthy" to describe food or drinks, you will evaluate your experience differently—the same way you would if you are made to believe that you are smelling cheddar cheese or stinky feet. Or whether you believe that a picture you're looking at is a museum piece or the product of a computer program. This means it is possible to influence the memory of value even *after* you have exposed your audiences to a specific communication experience. Words such as "worthwhile," "helpful," or "relevant" to describe their inter-action with you can help solidify the value code needed for the next interaction.

HOW DO WE KNOW WHAT PEOPLE VALUE?

Given that rewards drive decisions, when we create content, one of the biggest challenges we have is to figure out what our audiences con-sider rewarding. Clarifying rewards is challenging because what peo-ple value differs. An ad from HSBC bank demonstrates this well. The ad shows pictures of three people's bald heads, viewed from the back, and they are labeled "Style," "Soldier," and "Survivor." The tag line reminds us that "Only by understanding what people value can we better meet their needs."

What do people value?

This question is important because too many companies talk past their customers, without paying attention to what they value. In a 2014 survey of 1,408 companies by McKinsey, executives were convinced that customers would most appreciate a brand that "promotes and practices sustainability in its products or services," "has global reach," "is a driver for innovation," or "promotes diversity and equal oppor-tunity." When customers were asked what they really cared about, the factors considered important by companies were not statistically sig-nificant. Instead, what customers really wanted were brands that "care about honest and open dialogue with its customers," "act responsi-bly across its supply chain," "have a high level of specialist expertise," and "fit in well with my values and beliefs." You can imagine how you would get bored if what you cared about was expertise and instead lis-tened to a pitch about product sustainability.

A positive example of putting effort into what people value is *Alice's Adventures in Wonderland*. The real accomplishment of this book is not that it has been translated into every major language but that it has been translated at all. The story is filled with so many puns and cultural references that translators had to be very creative in offering readers something they considered rewarding and valuable. For example, here is the parody that Lewis Carroll offers for "Twinkle, Twinkle, Little Star" in the original version:

> *Twinkle, twinkle, little bat!*
> *How I wonder what you're at!*
> *Up above the world you fly*
> *Like a tea-tray in the sky.*

In an effort to make the translation relevant and meaningful to German readers, the translator converted the parody to one deriding the German Christmas carol "O Tannenbaum." Here is the gist of that translation:

> *Oh parrot, oh parrot!*
> *How green are your feathers!*
> *You're not only green in times of peace,*
> *But also when it snows plates and pots.*

As *Smithsonian* writer Andrea Appleton puts it, we sometimes have to "sacrifice a literal interpretation" in order to offer what is linguistically and culturally relevant. Emer O'Sullivan, an expert in children's literature, remarks that "all translations are adaptations," and being able to tell how much of the original story was kept "is a matter of degree." And here we have arrived full circle from the initial conversation at the beginning of the book, advocating content creation from the lens of proportions rather than absolutes. Be prepared to sacrifice some accuracy, not to diminish the truth but to adjust content to a specific population to provide something audiences find rewarding.

There are several technologies that help us remove guesswork from what people value. I asked Kevin Lindsay, product marketing director at Adobe, about optimal ways to help customers make decisions, based on what they value, especially when shopping online. Lindsay mentioned conversion rate optimization (CRO), which is concerned with understanding the decisions that shoppers have to make at different points during their buying journey. He recommends making incremental improvements at each step and testing constantly. He points out, "If, as a result of testing, you discover that more shoppers add items with at least 10 user reviews, you may start directing all shoppers to the most reviewed products. If buy-one–get-one-free entices more people to explore your store than 15%-off-site-wide, pay attention. Testing gives us a statistically reliable way to validate what people value."

Does knowing what customers value work in practice? Lindsay mentioned working with a retailer to help it implement CRO. At that time, the retailer had a unique visitor count of around 13 million, and the conversion rate hovered at about 2.8%. Lindsay noted, "As a result of applying rigorous CRO practices, in just three months we saw conversions increase to 3.1%. If you don't think that sounds like much, reconsider: the result was an annualized revenue gain of more than $33 million!"

The values we assign to different objects, people, and experiences can range from functional and concrete to something more abstract. For example, we buy things because we value their tangible attributes, such as a dishwasher, a type of detergent, or even insurance. But we also buy things for their *emotional* value: think of the last time you used your GoPro or enjoyed food, drinks, or a film with friends.

Much has been studied about the impact of emotion on attention, memory, and decision-making—the three main pillars of this book. When we are faced with emotional events, the amygdala modulates the visual cortex to make sure we direct attention to these events. While the hippocampus is necessary in memory storage, the amygdala modulates memory in the face of a highly emotional event and ensures the event is retained. Emotions act as markers for important information, which is why at a decision point, we are likely to recall an emotional event versus a neutral one.

Studies show how emotions such as happiness, sadness, stress, or anxiety impact decisions. Take stress, for instance. Under stressful circumstances, we tend to be more risk averse in the gain domain and more risk seeking in the loss domain. A sad mood also pushes us into taking more risks for greater rewards. Anxiety biases us the other direction, toward low risks and low rewards. Some of us are generally more anxious or cheerful than others, which is why our choices are different.

You can change value by changing emotion.

We may also choose things or people or experiences for their *epistemological* value: this includes products or experiences that give us the opportunity for *knowledge* development and intellectual stimulation, such as books and seminars. We value things for their *aesthetics*, such as clothes and decorations. We also seek *hedonistic* values because they evoke sensory pleasure, which is why we enjoy good hotels and fun nightclubs. Sometimes we choose because of *situational* value, such as selecting champagne versus wine because of a special occasion. And if we're lucky enough, we may be exposed to things of *holistic* value: choosing a vacation in Paris with a new lover is likely to appeal to a range of values from emotional to epistemological, aesthetic to hedonistic.

Which of these values do your customers appreciate, and are those values coming across clearly in your communication? If so, then there is a greater likelihood of action.

DO WE ASSIGN VALUE TO STIMULI ONLY WHEN WE HAVE TO MAKE A CHOICE?

The brain automatically assigns values to elements in our surroundings, from the very first presentation of a stimulus, even in a choice-free context. Neuroimaging evidence suggests there is an automatic valuation system that encodes values for preferences under all circumstances. This system is personal, generic, and automatic.

In an MRI study, participants were shown pictures of faces, houses, and paintings and asked to rate their pleasantness and guess their age. The brain value system was activated even when the value was not necessary for the task at hand. Even if subjects were simply asked to guess the age of the house or the face or the painting, activity in the brain value system was higher for the pictures that were later identified as preferred. *We constantly judge.* This could be because the brain value system evolved before money was invented and values come first, potentially providing a basis for when we may have to make choices later. Such anchors influence subsequent decisions and sometimes unrelated decisions, too.

We assign values even when we don't have to choose.

We don't even need to pay attention for a long time to assign value. In one MRI study, participants in one condition (high attention) were shown a set of cars and asked to rate their attractiveness; in the other condition (low attention), participants were asked to fixate on a target, while some car pictures were displayed in the background. After scanning, participants were asked to rate their intention to purchase one of the cars. Results showed that the brain areas that predicted preferences were activated even in the low-attention group. *Unattended stimuli can still influence choice.* Participants did not know that later they would be asked about their intention, so the study was set up to show that it is possible to have unconscious environmental triggers and automatic processes in decision-making. Even in the absence of explicit deliberation, the brain regions associated with expected reward value were activated. It is no wonder cultural stimuli, such as cars and logos of cars that indicate wealth and status, have been shown to activate the reward network in the brain. We can still make complex economic decisions without fully deliberating and even without paying much attention.

Using eye-tracking devices, we know we can make value-based decisions without having access to our full cognitive resources, in about a third of a second. For example, if we are hungry and we prefer Snickers to Doritos, and someone shows us pictures of the two options very quickly, we will look toward our preferred option in 404 milliseconds. Perceptual decision-making is even faster. We can pick out which natural scene has an animal in it in about 140 to 160 milliseconds, and we can tell if a facial expression or body posture is fearful or neutral in 350 milliseconds.

What does this information mean to our content? Even when we are not asking others to make a selection in our favor, we must still offer quality content. Our audiences' brains are constantly encoding value for what we show them. *There is no break from greatness if you want to become impossible to ignore.*

Research informs us that once people assign values to choices, it is possible they forget those values particularly for products with longer sales cycles, products that are more complex, and products that do not imply too much consumer involvement. Consider your content with this finding in mind. Do you operate in any of these categories: complexity, long sales cycles, and sparse consumer engagement? If yes, consider constant activation of what people value, via more frequent communication and social media. With these messages, it is important not to insist on features, but rather to remind people of how much they value that product or service.

RISK AND REWARD IN DECISION-MAKING

In addition to studying *rewards* and *values* as they relate to decisions, neuroscientists are noticing other variables that have an impact on our choices: *effort* to get the reward (physical, financial, or mental), *time delay* until we get the reward, perception of *risk* in getting the reward, and *social impact* in relation to that reward. Some of these variables have been addressed previously in the book. In the next few sections, let's look at additional research studies that help us gain practical insights from understanding how a combination of these variables influences decision-making.

When analyzing decisions made on automatic or strategic processes, scientists are noticing that decisions tend to be automatic when we are depleted of mental energy or when we perceive a situation as stable. We rely on more strategic decisions when we perceive risk. We can choose toothpaste without thinking but not a stock investment or a partnership with a new vendor. Consider your own perception of risk toward money, job, health, safety, ethical behavior, a vacation in a foreign country, or even just interactions with other people. You may be willing to take bigger risks with your vacation than with your career.

When we ask anything of our listeners, especially if they don't know us, they may be sensitive to risk, which typically arises from two sources: *ambiguity* and *uncertainty*. We can address ambiguity by offering clear content. Uncertainty is harder to handle but not impossible. We are aware that uncertainty is unavoidable in our daily lives, and yet we are capable of making decisions even in uncertain situations.

For example, to reduce uncertainty, we would have to identify all possible outcomes in a situation, list all possible actions, determine the consequences of these actions, attach a value to each consequence, and select the action that maximizes the outcome. American statistician Leonard Savage gives this example of uncertainty as it relates to the decision made by a person cooking an omelet. Picture someone who "has already broken five good eggs into a bowl, but is uncertain whether the sixth egg is good or rotten." This person needs to decide whether "to break the sixth egg into the bowl containing the first five eggs, to break it into a separate saucer, or to throw it away." This situation is easy to handle because even though there is uncertainty, there are a finite number of outcomes, and the person knows the three possible actions, along with their consequences, and the value for each outcome.

Unfortunately, real life is not always so straightforward. There is scientific consensus on three types of uncertainty: (1) state space uncertainty, which means we are not aware of all the consequences of our actions, such as when a company reorganization is focused on cost but overlooks employee morale; (2) option uncertainty, which means we cannot predict the consequences of our actions in detail, such as taking an umbrella because it is raining, but not knowing if it will help because the rain may be too heavy and the umbrella too small; and (3) value uncertainty, which means we don't always know the value we will place on the consequences of our actions—such as when we switch jobs, we may not know the impact of the new boss's personality on our productivity or how much importance we may have placed on the availability of a subsidized company cafeteria.

There is abundant research on handling uncertainty, ranging from fast and frugal heuristics to more formal tools. Heuristics are "quick-and-dirty" means for people to make decisions in uncertain situations, such as the scarcity heuristic, in which we decide that if something is scarce, it must be desirable and therefore we make more of an effort to get it. Formal tools include prospect theory. According to this theory, we would rather get $1,000 now if the amount is certain than $1,500 later if there is a 20% chance we may get nothing. If you won $1,000 and lost $800, you would focus more on the large loss than on the $200 gain. And if you receive a 10% raise and your coworkers do, too, you will not feel any sense of gain. But if you get a 10% raise and no one else does, you will feel better off.

What can we apply from prospect theory when we create persuasive content? We can frame messages to emphasize gains or losses. Research in the health industry, for example, looks at gain-framed versus loss-framed messages and concludes that for prevention medicine where the *risk is low*, gain-framed messages are more likely to lead to behavior change. For instance, "Join us to find out how an increase in your walking regimen helps to prevent heart disease" works well because there is little risk in walking. This may also work because it promotes self-efficacy and positive emotions. Gain-framed messages also appear to have a bigger impact on how they are processed and therefore remembered later.

Another modern tool for handling uncertainty is the fuzzy logic approach, in which we can still analyze risks despite insufficient knowledge or imprecise data. This is because fuzzy logic models allow an object to be categorized in different sets with different levels of truth.

If your audiences perceive a high amount of uncertainty in their interactions with you, consider heuristics to help them make quick decisions. For example, the *availability heuristic* helps someone make a judgment based on examples that come to mind. Where your content is concerned, invoke people's existing experiences or allude to the experiences of others who are like them. Research confirms that we tend to view something with greater certainty if we have lived through it ourselves or if we've observed it through others, especially if they share similar demographics with us and if it comes to mind easily.

I interviewed Nicolas Rivollet, director of business development at Husky. He once gave a speech about motivating others and mentioned his philosophy of never telling people "I want you to do this or that." Rivollet said that when we make people "want what you want" not "do what you want," then you don't need to manage them anymore. He then shared how this approach helped him when he managed 5, 50, and 150 people. He considered his speech effective because he spoke from experience (he was not sharing something he had read in a leadership book) and he is very approachable (others can identify with him easily).

In addition to the availability heuristic, the *familiarity heuristic* also lowers the perception of risk. For example, people are more likely to take bigger risks when investing in stocks in their own company or in their own country because of familiarity. When you expose an audience to completely new things (your content, you, or both), their brains have to organize that information in ways that make sense to them. This process will seem longer because it requires more effort. On the other hand, if they are familiar with you or your content, this familiarity and cognitive ease reduces the perceived passage of time. When we ask people to act on something in our favor, we must ask: Are they familiar enough with us? Often, communicators are too ambitious and ask for a decision before familiarity is assured and risk is addressed.

Audiences also respond to the *authority heuristic* when they believe the content they see comes from an authority figure. Ensure your content is well researched, and include third-party confirmation of your credibility.

David Hill, senior director at Hewlett Packard, has had to lead large organizations to meet large sales goals, manage a great deal of risk while implementing new e-commerce platforms, and negotiate through large corporate actions such as a spin-off or a split. I had the opportunity to ask him about his approach to convincing others to act on future intentions in uncertain situations. "By and large, people act in their own self-interest," he states. "Even if that interest is improving the life of a child through education or the outcome of a patient through improved healthcare, it is still deeply personal. If you want to influence others, you have to address people on an individual level." He advises starting with the fundamentals that tone down the perception of risk. Answering questions such as "Will I get laid off?" "Will I reach my goal?" and "How will my job change?" helps with risk management. "Fear clouds judgment and the ability to make rational decisions," Hill observes, and he reminds us that in mitigating risk, "you must show you care for their well-being."

When you manage the degree of uncertainty, the importance of possible outcomes, and the delay before the outcome is realized, you are in a position to turn something considered negative (e.g., risk) into something positive: anticipation and action.

TEMPORAL EXPECTATIONS

The way your audiences view time impacts their decision-making. How do we know this? We know temporal judgment takes place in the same brain regions as decision-making. People who seek immediate gratification tend to have larger neural responses when judging short delays than when judging long delays, while those who are patient in terms of gratification show the opposite. In fact, scientists can predict simply by looking at brain activity whether someone will place value on something that will happen in the future (and is willing to wait for it) or simply discount it and look elsewhere.

Temporal discounting means that we tend to prefer smaller-now versus larger-later rewards. This could be because the future seems more abstract and uncertain, while closer events are more vivid and concrete. So if you are offering content and promises that will materialize at some point in the future, make them vivid and concrete to increase the affective impact. To test this hypothesis, researchers asked participants while in an MRI scanner, "Would you prefer $20 now or $40 in one month?" They also gave participants a concrete context in which they could spend either choice they selected (e.g., a pub). In some conditions, participants were asked to describe what a delayed reward could buy them, while in others, they were asked to imagine how the money could be spent in the future. Participants were also asked to rate the vividness of the emotional intensity associated with what they described or imagined. The results showed that imagining *specific* ways in which to spend the money led to more vivid imagination and higher emotional intensity. These dimensions impacted their choice of rewards. Participants who scored higher for vividness and emotional intensity opted for the longer-term payoffs.

The ability to imagine future events shapes their affective value, which influences current decisions.

Expectations also shape patient or impatient behavior. Let's say you expect a meeting to last one hour. You know that this type of meeting hardly ever goes over, and if it were to be slightly longer, this predicted delay does not feel too bad. On the other hand, let's say you call the customer service department of your cable company, and you're put on hold. Sometimes in this situation, you're on hold forever, and sometimes you're not. It is generally a random process. The more hold time has elapsed, the more the predicted delay *increases* and you start to lose patience. As communicators, we must be cautious about how much we delay gratification, particularly in circumstances in which our audiences *don't have prior experiences* or prior knowledge of interacting with us.

Many are familiar with the classic marshmallow test in which researchers at Stanford worked with over 600 kids to study delayed gratification. Children were told they could have one marshmallow at the time of the study or two marshmallows if they waited 15 minutes. There has been a recent twist on this test. Researchers wanted to see whether waiting for a larger reward was simply a sign of self-control or whether the environment played a role as well. Celeste Kidd, the lead author of the new study, stated, "Delaying gratification is only the rational choice if the child believes a second marshmallow is likely to be delivered after a reasonably short delay."

In her experiment, she told kids they would receive supplies to complete an art project. In one of the groups, the promise for better supplies was not kept, and kids were made to feel that the environment in which they were working was not "stable." Then the same kids were invited to complete the marshmallow test. Only 1 out of the 14 kids who had been in the "unstable environment" group waited for 15 minutes to receive the second marshmallow. Kidd was inspired to create the study after volunteering at a homeless shelter, where she observed how kids were fighting for resources. "When one child got a toy or treat, there was a real risk of a bigger, faster kid taking it away," she said. "I read about these studies and I thought, 'All of these kids would eat the marshmallow right away.'"

Reflecting on your content and the decisions you're asking others to make, ask this: How stable do they perceive the environment to be? In gauging the time delay before they receive a reward for making a decision, are you able to help them perceive a stable environment? For example, if a new software platform will be implemented, showing how many other systems (financial, operational) will stay in place until one major change is completed helps ease the tension of uncertainty.

DECISION-MAKING IS SOCIAL

Even when others are not physically present, we are often influenced by social factors in the decisions we make. This means decision-making is influenced by norms and the expectations of others. For example, in a study with randomized samples, researchers found that when patrons at a restaurant were shown the five most popular dishes, the demand for those same dishes increased by 13 to 20%. In another study, participants looked at a list of 48 songs arranged randomly or arranged by the number of downloads. The list of previous downloads had a bigger influence on the songs they downloaded.

We often choose on the basis of what others have chosen or what others would want us to choose. If you're looking for a new book to read, the *New York Times* bestseller list may guide your choice. If you're expecting guests and Miller is a popular beer, then that's the beer you reach for at the store without thinking too much. This type of heuristic (the bandwagon effect) pushes us to choose what others would choose in order to avoid embarrassment and stand out in the wrong way.

Of course, there is a threshold for social decisions. When something becomes *too* popular and everyone jumps on that option, it degrades its currency. Something is so liked that at some point it's hated. The more mainstream something becomes, the more criticized it becomes, too. How do we handle this situation? Researchers at University Park, Pennsylvania, found that popularity is shaped like a wave. At first, members of a subculture like a product; then the product goes mainstream, and the popularity subsides. They did a study to investigate if coolness was related to design and originality. More than 1,000 participants answered various questions on existing products. The researchers discovered that the utility of a product was not so much a part of "coolness." Products such as a USB drive or a GPS were ranked as highly useful but not necessarily cool. Products such as Wii and Xbox Kinect were cool but not entirely useful. MacBook Air, Instagram, and Pandora were seen as useful, but utility was not a determining factor when judging how cool they were.

Scientists concluded that if we are after cool, we must be after something that is novel and attractive and has subculture-building capabilities, all of which involve a constant need to innovate around something that many people like. This is how these insights play out in real life. Leah van Zelm, vice president of digital strategy at Merkle, discussed her company's use of proprietary research and advanced analytics to find out in what areas hotel chains could innovate in order to stay competitive. The research revealed five key decision chains that consumers use when they choose a hotel brand: good amenities (ability to relax), good amenities (easy choice), consistent positive experience, having status, and accruing rewards. She noted that the top three brands—Hilton, Marriott, and SPG—are very close in scores in the five categories, so they must seek opportunities to innovate in each in order to differentiate. For example, Marriott's strength is in its rewards program, so according to this research, it should build on this category. Hilton received the highest scores in the "consistent positive experience" category, so it is advised to create differentiation from the other chains by emphasizing this message in its positioning. The lesson for all of us is to offer something novel that is built on what people already like.

In social decision-making, we must consider the thinking of others. Psychologists have labeled this phenomenon "theory of mind," which means thinking of how others think. When we try to understand others' way of thinking, it is typical that we go back into our autobiographical memory and draw from past experiences. Scientists are finding correlations between the strength of our own memory and the ability to understand others' thinking.

A company we can learn from in terms of adjusting messaging to how other people think and what they consider rewarding is Domino's Pizza. Recently, the company has had great success in India because it tapped into several social dimensions that impact decisions: it hooked into existing cultural keystones (sharing food and eating with your hands); it did not impose fully Western menus but rather included local options; and it recognized that people like to make an impression by being seen appreciating "Western anything."

For example, in northern India, Domino's offered the Taco Indiana, a combination of kebabs, parathas, and pizza. In a Domino's ad, a woman tells a man that he is like a Taco Indiana: "Western-looking on the outside, but Indian on the inside." In southern India, where pizza is not so popular, instead of forcing something new, Domino's provided ingredients that locals appreciate. That's how the spicy, raw-banana pizza was born. Writer Saritha Rai called Domino's Subwich, a burger with a pizza filling, a "Western slice that tastes just Indian enough."

Are you able to consider others' thinking and create your message from where they are sitting? Can you phrase your message in such a way that if people acted on it, they would look good in front of others? Are you offering a slice of content that is "[*socially desirable concept*] enough and [*socially desirable concept*] enough"? The repetition is intended to prompt us to include seemingly contradictory values. For instance, we may like to project an image of authority but also one of humility, both of which are socially desirable.

IS WHAT YOU DECIDE FOR YOURSELF THE SAME AS WHAT YOU DECIDE FOR OTHERS?

Research reminds us there is a difference between individual and social decisions, and this difference has associated benefits.

When we make decisions, we tend to picture distant events in a high-level, abstract, generalized, and decontextualized way. When we make decisions about close events, we tend to picture them in a more concrete and contextual kind of way. The advantage of this difference is that abstract thoughts are known to activate creative problem solving and generate new ideas.

For instance, imagine the following scenario: "A prisoner was attempting to escape from a tower. He found a rope in his cell that was half as long as it needed to be to permit him to reach the ground safely. He divided the rope in half, tied the two parts together, and escaped. How could he have done this?" Research has demonstrated that people are more creative solving this problem if they are asked to imagine this situation a year from now, compared with tomorrow. They are also more creative when subjects are asked to imagine *someone else* in the prison tower instead of themselves.

In another study, when participants were asked to draw an alien for a story they would write versus a story that someone else would write, the latter alien was drawn more creatively. Creativity in this

225

study was measured by the amount of unusual features in each drawing (e.g., not earthlike or more than two eyes). We tend to perceive our current selves in a concrete, contextual way, but we tend to perceive our future selves and the behavior of others in an abstract way. In other words, the decisions we make for our future selves mimic the decisions we make on behalf of others. And since these images are abstract, we have the opportunity to be more creative.

It is important to consider creativity in relation to decision-making because we want to inspire others not just to make decisions but to make *creative decisions* that lead to innovation. For example, consider the company Aobiome, a biotech startup that breeds bacteria and puts them in cosmetic products. The company created AO+ Refreshing Cosmetic Mist, a spray that "looks, smells, and tastes like water, but is bacteria-loaded." Someone on the Aobiome team decided to make bacteria seem appealing. The product has been successful since 2012, capturing interest from young urban professionals, known to seek nontraditional ways to stay healthy. How many of you would like to have this type of person on your team? To arrive at this kind of creative decision-making, we have to invite others to imagine decisions they would make in the future or decisions they would make on behalf of other people.

Creative decisions are also a function of being prosocially motivated. Research has found that people report enjoyment when associating decisions with outcomes that help others, and they are willing to exert more effort because making decisions for others brings meaning and fulfillment. When we are intrinsically motivated, we are focused on the present, and when we are prosocially motivated, we are focused on the future—and this results in greater creativity.

Not all decisions are inspired by prosocial motivations. In the classic psychology experiment called the *ultimatum game*, subjects tend to forgo a material payoff to decrease the other person's payoff when they believe a deal is unfair (e.g., people refuse $1 if they know someone else gets $9). More recently, neuroscience research on this game has found the situation is even worse when participants' serotonin levels are low. High serotonin leads to social cooperation and affiliation, while low serotonin leads to aggression.

This means our content must communicate very clearly the concept of fairness and trust: two factors that can impact serotonin level. If the serotonin level is high, then prosocial motivations are stronger, which can result in more creative decisions.

DECIDING BASED ON DESIRABILITY VERSUS FEASIBILITY

When we analyze variables such as rewards, values, effort, time delay, risk, and social impact, we can also ask whether people decide based on desirability or feasibility. And do these factors differ when we make decisions for others versus ourselves? When we decide for others, we tend to focus more on desirability, defined as the *value of an end state*. When we decide for ourselves, we focus more on feasibility, which is the *means of achieving that end state*. Going on vacation somewhere beautiful is desirable. Going on vacation somewhere cheap is feasible. It is of course optimal to select something that is highly desirable and highly feasible, but that's not always possible. This is why we look to strike a balance when either one is low: we desire something badly, but it's not feasible; or we don't really desire something that much, but it is feasible to get it.

When do we give more weight to desirability versus feasibility? To answer that question, we must understand the difference in their mental representations. Desirability is abstract and reflects a high-level mental construct. Feasibility is concrete, reflecting a low-level mental construct. To differentiate between the two, we must also consider psychological distance, in that we tend to activate abstract concepts for psychologically distant actions and concrete concepts for psychologically close actions. When we make decisions about something in the distant future, we choose based on desirability. And when we make choices for something near, we choose based on feasibility. For example, in a study where subjects hypothetically had to buy a software program "tomorrow" or "a year from now," their desirability for the *quality* of the program strengthened when they chose the delayed option.

Do all these change when the decision target changes? Looking at how we decide for ourselves versus how we decide for others can be interpreted through the lens of psychological distance. In one study, participants were asked to choose a job for themselves, for a best friend, or for an acquaintance. They had the opportunity to select from two jobs. Job A offered better pay but lower self-fulfillment, and job B the opposite. In this case, salary was viewed as feasibility and self-fulfillment as desirability. More people chose job A for themselves and job B for friends or acquaintances. These results were replicated when choosing a restaurant, course for enrollment, or vacation spot for oneself versus others.

People tend to focus mainly on prominent and desirable attributes when deciding for others, whereas they tend to focus on a wider range of attributes, including less important ones, when deciding for themselves. We also tend to tolerate greater risk when selecting for others than for ourselves. Some researchers equate utility with desirability (because it describes the value of an end state), and probability with feasibility (because it describes the ease of attaining that end state). So if we consider risk a combination of subjective utility and probability, then when we choose for others, we tend to focus more on utility.

What does this all mean for your content? Reflecting on your own messages, ask: When do people welcome advice to act on something? Your audiences typically come to you and listen to a message in order to gain more information that they can share with others or in order to improve their own decision-making. In that regard, a *balance* between desirability and feasibility leads to more persuasive content. This is because feasibility will help with their own decisions, and desirability will help them in their transactions with others.

FUZZY LOGIC IN A REAL-LIFE CASE STUDY

We've seen the reflection of various variables impacting decision-making in research studies: rewards, values, effort, time delay, risk, and social impact. Let's see how these variables are reflected in real business examples. The following is a case study we can learn from because the executives and sales teams involved were able to achieve something outstanding: stay on people's minds long enough to reach a favorable decision. When we witness success in business, defined as "getting others to act in your favor," we want to know: How did they do it?

Using the fuzzy logic theory, we can determine the "degree of truth" with which these variables apply to a given decision-making process, especially in situations where there is uncertainty but we still want to rely on science. Experts in any field can assign a score between 0 and 1 for each variable (the closer to 1, the higher the impact of the variable) and cumulatively observe its impact on decisions. When the scores are closer to 0, decisions are easy.

To simplify the exercise, let's consider these four variables: effort, time delay, risk, and social obscurity. Think of doing laundry: little effort (let's say .2), little time delay (.2, we see results quickly), no risk (0), and no social obscurity (0, people appreciate us when we wear clean clothes and smell good). In this example, {.2, .2, 0, 0} leads to action.

If one variable is high but three are low, it's not too bad. If two are high and two are low, it is harder to make a decision, but not impossible. If three variables are high and only one is low, the scales begin to tip. If all four are high, forget it. If we had to go to Colombia each time we craved chocolate, work in the cocoa fields while hearing gunshots, harvest cocoa only once a year, and no one would appreciate our efforts, we would never eat chocolate. A set of {1, 1, 1, 1} in this scenario does not lead to action.

Let's see how these four variables that impact decision-making played out for a software company. For most technology companies, the end of a quarter is not just a date on the calendar on which numbers are summed up and reported. Some executives are nervous by default at this time because forecasts usually come in at the last minute. That was the case for TIBCO, a technology company headquartered in Palo Alto, California, with a presence in America, Europe, Asia, and Australia. With less than a day to go before quarter end, the decision maker of a top prospect said "Not now" to TIBCO. This was a large opportunity TIBCO had been trying to close for two months.

Erich Gerber, TIBCO's vice president of global sales, remembers: "We were all ready to end the quarter, and it would have been fantastic to start relaxing and celebrate. However, the customer did not see any reason why the deal needed to be closed now versus later." Yet Erich and his sales team managed to persuade the customer to act now. The customer engaged six resources in legal, finance, and procurement to work at least 10 hours each to successfully meet the end-of-quarter deadline. Just in time.

How did Erich and his team do it? Reflecting on the effort, Erich observes, "It's like flying a helicopter; we had to keep our hands on the joystick at all times." Let's analyze the situation using the variables. First, it is important to clarify the overall *reward* for both parties because action without reward is unlikely.

- *Reward for sales.* In sales, the expected reward may be money, but this is not always so. In TIBCO's case, the reps who went the extra mile would not benefit from their bonus the next day. Their reward was different: the opportunity *to look good in front of the organization.* Prominence is often a stronger motivational driver than money.

- *Reward for the customer.* On the surface, it may appear that the main reward was to get the best price possible. However, as Erich mentions, "At some point in our interactions, another reward emerges: the opportunity *to accomplish a team effort on good terms.* This is what we often observe."

Clarifying the reward is helpful because in many conversations during a sales cycle, we can use key words and phrases that emphasize the reward and lead to action. For example, phrases that highlight prominence may include "making an impression," "time to shine," and even "wait till everyone hears this" said in a positive tone. Words that emphasize team effort include "collaboration," "cooperation," "partnership," and "relationship." If we know someone is motivated by teamwork, a message such as "We appreciate the close relationship we've formed in these past few days" will be more rewarding than "You will be receiving a discount."

Let's assign each variable a score between 0 and 1, for both sales and the customer.

Decision-making on the *sales side*:

1. *Effort.* Let's assign this a .6. A sales team at quarter end expects the extra effort, and the extra effort did not extend for many days, just a few.

2. *Time delay.* The time delay before all the individuals would see the rewards of their work was short. Everyone knew the quarter would be over soon. After a short time delay, others in the organization would appreciate the effort. Let's assign this a .2.

3. *Risk.* The perception of risk was high. If we consider the reward "prominence in front of the organization," its opposite would be risky. If the deal did not go through, many would know about it. Let's give this a .9.

4. *Social obscurity.* This is definitely a 0 because everyone in the organization would know quickly about the implications of outstanding effort.

Decision-making on the *customer side*:

1. *Effort.* The effort on the customer's part was huge because it was not a one-person transaction. A larger team had to be involved. Let's assign this a .9.

2. *Time delay.* Considering the reward to be "accomplishing team effort on good terms," the effects of this reward would be noticed immediately. Let's give this a .2.

3. *Risk.* The perception of risk was moderate because the customer was working with a company it could trust. Let's assign this a .4.

4. *Social obscurity.* Customers like to act on decisions that make them look good in front of their own organizations. A big decision like this for buying applications that impact many parts of the company comes with big social impact. Let's give this a .2.

Looking at these scores helps us realize how people make decisions on both sides. Some variables were really high but others were really low for both sales and customer. A short time delay before rewards, coupled with huge social impact and low perception of risk on the client side, makes it easier to get things done. If we know the reward and anticipate the scores for each variable ahead of time, we can calibrate our interactions better. This is important because what we perceive as risky may not be that risky for others, or what we perceive as having high social impact may not be so for others. One of the best ways to determine the scores is to simply ask others: "What organizational impact will this deal have?" "What level of risk would you associate with this process?" "How much effort are people willing to put in?" And most important, "What do you consider rewarding?"

The brain is searching constantly for the next and biggest reward. In the process, it balances *exploitation* and *exploration*. Through exploitation, it goes back to habits that proved rewarding in the past. Through exploration, it seeks new sources for rewards. Are you going to be part of the next reward your audience seeks? When you develop content that hooks into rewards from the past but also provides new sources of rewards, you become impossible to ignore.

KEEP IN MIND

- If your audience has been performing a task for a long time, link your content to an existing habit. If there are no habits related to your products or ideas, present goal-oriented information. When you do it repeatedly, you help an audience form new habits.

- Habits are formed by doing, not by *not* doing. Frame your messages in a positive way.

- Decisions typically include four steps:
    1. Identify sensory stimuli: What are they?

2. Select an action that will maximize a reward: What is it worth?

3. Act on the intention.

4. Evaluate the results: Did you predict the outcome well?

- The values our audiences assign to different objects, people, and experiences can range from functional and concrete to something more abstract. People buy things because of emotional, epistemological, aesthetic, hedonistic, or situational value. Clarify these values for your audiences.

- Even unattended stimuli influence choice. There is no break from greatness for the communicator who aspires to be influential, because everything you share has the potential to influence decisions.

- Variables that have an impact on our choices include effort to get the reward (physical, financial, or mental), time delay until we get the reward, perception of risk in getting the reward, and social impact in relation to that reward.

- If your audiences perceive a high amount of uncertainty in their interactions with you, consider heuristics, such as availability, familiarity, or authority, to help them make quick decisions.

- Fast decision-making is also based on the perception of a stable environment and social factors.

- A balance between desirability and feasibility leads to more persuasive content. This is because feasibility will help people with their own decisions, and desirability will help them in their transactions with others.

- Develop content that hooks into rewards from the past but also provides sources for new rewards.

CHAPTER 12

THE RIGHT TO BE FORGOTTEN AND THE INTENT TO BE REMEMBERED

How to Balance Accidental and Purposeful Forgetting

I n 2012, a lawyer named Mario Costeja González got really mad at Google. It all started 12 years earlier, in Spain, where Costeja was in financial trouble and a newspaper in Spain published information on his finances. Even though his issues were eventually resolved, Google still linked to that content years later, reflecting negatively on the lawyer's reputation. Costeja contacted the Spanish authorities, demanding that Google remove the links. In the spring of 2014, the European Court of Justice asked Google to do just that: stop showing the links as part of the search results related to Costeja's name. The European regulators also affirmed that any person from a European Union country had the right to request "inadequate, or no longer relevant," information to be removed from searches. In a sense, Europeans now have what Americans don't, for the time being: the right to be forgotten.

In the United States things are different. If you did irresponsible things during your college years and documented those unfortunate events online and you now want to be taken seriously, it may be tough because search engines have perfected the sedimentation of old and sometimes irrelevant information, which anybody can access. In a poignant *New Yorker* article, journalist Jeffrey Toobin describes the efforts of Christos Catsouras, who tried to do something close to impossible: delete information from the Internet. Unlike Costeja, who was worried about his reputation, Catsouras was devastated by the emotional impact of graphic images showing his 18-year-old daughter who was decapitated during a traffic accident. It took Catsouras five years to receive some compensation from the police officers who leaked the pictures, but he received nothing from Google.

Ever since the European ruling, Google has tended to more than 174,000 requests for removal of information, covering more than 600,000 URLs. But this only applies in EU countries. You may not be able to find something in Germany on Google.de, but if you search on Google.com, you may find it. Yahoo and Microsoft are joining the effort to remove search results and are expecting that, at some point, regulators may impose rules that require these links be removed outside of Europe, too.

Consider the possibility that your content, once made public, may never disappear. It is useful to stay humble and mindful of the possibility that what we want to place in our audiences' memories today may change tomorrow.

Does the memory for your content have an expiration date?

The ability of your audiences to remember will influence their decisions, but their ability to forget may be equally important to your cause. Think of it this way: forgetting is accidental or purposeful. *Accidental* forgetting happens when people fail to encode new information we provide them or when existing knowledge we've given them decays over time because of a lack of reactivation. Forgetting is *purposeful* when we want to convince people to give up old routines in favor of new thinking. In this case, it is preferable that audiences forget the old and remember the new.

Reflecting on your own content, consider catering to both types of forgetting: reactivate your most important message often to avoid accidental forgetting and purposefully direct your audiences' attention toward new things when the old does not serve them any longer. Keep in mind that the type of content and experiences you create can live in social memory potentially forever. Will they still do justice to your image and your cause in a few weeks, months, or decades?

KEEP PLANTING FLAGS IN THE FUTURE

Bill Besselman, vice president of integration and digital strategy at Under Armour, told me about an ad they aired a few years ago, showcasing how computers and clothing could merge. The ad portrayed a woman wearing a shirt that conformed to her body, changed color and temperature when she touched it, and displayed these metrics on her wrist. This sounds wonderful. The only problem is the shirt did not exist. However, that did not stop Under Armour CEO Kevin Plank from releasing that vision into the world. Besselman is impressed with Plank, who reinforces a "done, done, done" culture in their company. Plank is convinced that in the near future, retail items will have a connected chip. "We will create that shirt," he claims.

If our audiences' brains are constantly on fast-forward, then to be on people's minds, we have to be part of their future. Reflect on your messages and ask, "Where will my content be a year or two from now?" Then create it from that point of imagining.

ACCOUNT FOR BLACK SWANS

When we share information at Point A and plan for people to remember and act on it at Point B, the trajectory is not always a straight line. Portions of their lives often unfold like S shapes. Our audiences may plan to do something and may start off slowly at first, settling into routines or "best practices," until something happens. An updated technology, a market crash, or a company restructure provides enough disruption, and a new S shape emerges. When we plan to influence other people's memories and decisions, we must anticipate that these moments may occur in their lives, so we must be ready to generate new content and to associate it with new cues, memories, and decisions when disruption hits.

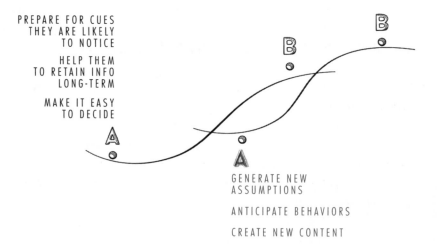

Analyzing your content and your audiences' context, consider studying literature on "black swans," unexpected events that can have an extreme impact on your goals and generate the start of a new S shape. Practical guidelines in this domain remind us that even though by definition, we cannot predict these kinds of events, we can prepare for them. Some steps include mapping out the space in which we operate and considering second-order and even third-order relationships between factors that have major implications for business success. For example, at one point, Apple had run out of lithium-ion batteries, which it needed for its iPods. Its suppliers sourced the polymer used to make the batteries from Kureha Corporation, a company that had been badly affected by the 2011 earthquake in Japan. Kureha held 70% of the global market for the polymer used in lithium-ion batteries.

Considering a list of possible disrupters in our audiences' contexts, asking what-if questions, and determining contingencies will help us be prepared for the emergence of new S shapes.

STAY CAUTIOUS ABOUT BRAIN SCIENCE MYTHS

The advantage of using brain science in creating content is that we can place memories in people's minds and guide them toward action. When science-based principles are a result of empirical studies, we can enjoy valid and reliable results. Be cautious, however, of unfounded sources that advocate "the science of . . ." This is why we see myths such as "We only use 10% of our brain." fMRI scans perpetuate this myth when interpreted by nonscientists. The colored areas we see on brain scans don't indicate that *only* specific areas are active; they simply show higher activity in those areas. This does not mean the brain is idle in other areas. Other myths such as "Dopamine is responsible for pleasure," "The amygdala produces fear," or "Pictures are more memorable than text" capture the interest of nonscientists who are more eager to get attention than question scientific merit.

Using guidelines rooted in solid science allows us to influence what we want others to remember instead of leaving the process to chance. Using valid brain science in content creation is also important because our audiences' brains don't always receive messages with the intent to remember; there is a great deal of external noise and stimulation. Most of the time, people consume content in a state of partial attention and with the intent to multitask. And their own internal chatter often takes the spotlight of attention.

———

One of the most important memory lessons I remember from graduate school came from Steve Joordens, a professor of psychology at the University of Toronto Scarborough. In one of his lectures, Joordens discusses Dante's *Inferno*, in which Dante travels to various circles of hell and meets horribly tormented souls. When they realize Dante will eventually return to the land of the living, the most pressing wish of these tormented souls is to be remembered by those who are still alive. At some point, we all desire to be in other people's memories and to impact them in some way.

Being on someone's mind and influencing decisions is a position of honor and responsibility. UNESCO, the United Nations Educational, Scientific and Cultural Organization, reminds us that "wars begin in the minds of people" and "that's where peace can be constructed too." Using the guidelines in this book, consider placing in people's minds thoughts and ideas that are enduring enough and rewarding enough to take us on fulfilling paths.

After all, if people remember you, you are still alive.

CHECKLIST FOR MEMORABLE CONTENT

magine your content as a sequence of segments (e.g., slides in a sales deck, paragraphs in a blog, messages in a marketing campaign, or sections in a training program—each of which has a strong meaning if viewed in isolation). At a macro level (e.g., deck, campaign, or training session), include, on average, 9 of the variables from the checklist in at least half of your segments. This will help with gist memory (people will retain the general meaning of your communication). To ensure that a variable is present in your content, use the checklist to score its level of intensity on a scale from 1 to 5, where 5 is the highest.

To create precise memories and compel action, at a micro level, 40% of the segments in your content need to be intense, meaning you must include at least 7 of the variables in the *same* segment. For example, you might create a slide that establishes context, is distinct from other slides, offers facts that are new and relevant, provokes an emotion, and makes you look good in front of others.

For an electronic version of the checklist, e-mail your request to info@carmensimon.com.

	Description	
1	**Context**	1 2 3 4 5

Definition: the setting in which the encoding of information takes place.

For this checklist, let's consider context to represent both space and time. The more vivid the place and action at Point A, the more accurate and easier the recall at Point B. We can influence this for others in two ways: We can create the context in their minds in a *conceptual* way, so it's clear for people where to pull a memory from. For example, "There are three pillars of our company: people, processes, and products."

We can also ensure that the *physical* context in which we show people new information matches the context they are likely to see when they retrieve memories. Think of pilots who learn specific tasks at Point A, in the cockpit, instead of a classroom. How much does the context you present at Point A match what your listeners will see at Point B?

	Description	
2	**Cues**	1 2 3 4 5

Definition: internal or external triggers about important content, once we are no longer exposed to it.

Cues are reminders that help with recall, depending on how strongly they are related to the initial content, how many connections there are with other similar content, and how salient they are to draw attention at the time of remembering. For example, in an effort for sustainability, some stores have recently displayed giant signs in their parking lots that read, "Bring your shopping bag." That's a great cue to remind us what to do.

Analyzing content, ask yourself: "Will there be cues later on that will remind my listeners of a particular piece of content? Or will they have to expend more effort to remember things on their own?"

	Description	
3	**Distinctiveness** *Definition: the ability of a stimulus to stand out compared to its neighbors.* If we have a sequence of text-text-text-graphic-text-text, the graphic in the middle stands out compared to the middle graphic in a sequence of graphic-graphic-graphic-graphic-graphic. The transition from one stimulus to another must be dramatic enough (at least 30 to 40% of the intensity of the previous stimulus, if it can be quantified) for us to detect that something is distinct from the pattern. Viewed from this perspective (items analyzed in a sequence), distinctiveness is not only a physical property but also a psychological process, which underscores the importance of temporal distinctiveness. When scoring distinctiveness, start with a 5 at the beginning of a set and inspect whether the number stays the same or decreases, depending on how similar subsequent items are.	`1` `2` `3` `4` `5`
4	**Emotion** *Definition: states elicited by obtaining rewards or avoiding punishments.* When we look at various stimuli around us, we evaluate and decode their value in terms of predicting what happens next. To the extent that the nature of the content we create is linked to receiving rewards or avoiding punishments, it can elicit an emotional reaction. When looking at a piece of content, ask: • "Is this getting me closer to receiving a reward or avoiding a punishment?" • "Is it neutral?" • "Is it getting me further away from a reward or toward a punishment?"	`1` `2` `3` `4` `5`

	Description	
5	**Facts** *Definition: truths known by actual experience or observation.* As you analyze your content, distinguish between what is abstract and opinion-based, such as "When one employee's morale goes down, everyone else in the office feels down"; and factual, such as, "30% of employees spend 2½ hours a day responding to e-mails." Assign a high score to content components that can be known by experience or observation.	1 2 3 4 5
6	**Familiarity** *Definition: knowledge or mastery of a subject.* We don't consciously think that certain things are familiar. We engage with them automatically and often tend to prefer them because they save cognitive energy. Familiarity may be brought to a conscious level when things deviate from what we're used to and we experience novelty. When analyzing a piece of content, ask, "Has my audience seen this before?" "Does it easily hook into something they already know?"	1 2 3 4 5
7	**Motivation** *Definition: the mental state we feel when we are willing to work to obtain a reward or avoid a punishment.* If we are hungry and see food, we are motivated to do the work to get it. If we are full, we are not willing to do much work to get food. Motivation is influenced by memory, and it contributes to memory: the more we remember, the more motivated we are to do (or not do) something; and the more we do something, the better we remember. Motivation is also driven by the amount of perceived effort, risk, time delay before obtaining rewards, and social impact if we act. When analyzing content, ask, "How motivated would an audience be to act on this content?" "Does it take a lot of effort to act on it?" "Will it be a long time before they see the rewards?" "Will they impress anyone if they act on this, or will anyone even notice?"	1 2 3 4 5

	Description	
8	**Novelty** *Definition: the quality of not being previously experienced or encountered.* We can also classify novelty in absolute versus relative terms: absolute novelty is something your audience has never experienced, whereas relative novelty provides familiar stimuli but in a *combination* they have not experienced before, like eating pickles dipped in peanut butter. When we encounter something new, we perform a quick memory search to map the experience against our existing memory inventory. When analyzing content, ask, "Have they seen this before?" "Have they seen this expressed in a different way?" "Have they seen it in the last few days, weeks, or months?"	1 2 3 4 5
9	**Quantity of information** *Definition: the amount of content we distribute to an audience at one time.* When we appeal to the senses and place things in context across a timeline, add facts and abstract ideas and meaning, and evoke emotion, we have the ability to create more memory traces. Short content does not always equal memorable content. But when presenters release too much content all at once, the result is that either viewers give up or they don't remember the specifics and just remember the gist. When you analyze content, ask, "Is this short enough so my listeners can stay focused but long enough so they can encode multiple memory traces that will help them remember later on?"	1 2 3 4 5
10	**Relevance** *Definition: importance of the matter at hand.* When the stimulus is considered relevant to obtaining rewards or avoiding punishments, it will receive preferential attention and stay active in memory until the goal is accomplished and the need dissipates. Analyzing your content, ask: "How important will this be to my audience at Point B, when they must remember and act on it?"	1 2 3 4 5

	Description	
11	**Repetition** *Definition: the occurrence of a stimulus multiple times.* Let's consider "multiple" a minimum of three, since MRI studies show that it takes the brain three impressions for something to be detected as repetitive and form a pattern. How many elements in your content repeat and how often? When scoring repetition, start with a 1 at the beginning of a set and inspect whether the score stays the same or increases based on how many items repeat within a certain segment (e.g., colors, layouts, words, images, etc.).	1 2 3 4 5
12	**Self-generated content** *Definition: implies interactive content that invites people to engage: answer a rhetorical question, complete an unfinished thought, or imagine a scenario.* When analyzing your content, ask, "Can my audience consume it passively, or does my audience have an opportunity to be involved in order to extract something meaningful from what I am sharing?" Asking questions or inviting the audience to imagine what you're proposing in abstract terms are great ways of turning passive into active communication.	1 2 3 4 5
13	**Sensory intensity** *Definition: the degree to which our senses are activated when we are exposed to a stimulus.* In business content, sensory intensity derives from visual and auditory information or from other senses that are triggered by provoking the imagination through words. When analyzing content, ask, "How many of my audience's senses am I activating?"	1 2 3 4 5

	Description					
14	Social aspects	1	2	3	4	5

14 Social aspects | 1 2 3 4 5

Definition: social advantages, such as power, prominence, and status that can be attained if your listeners remember and act on your content later.

Social expectations amplify motivations and drive action, which also have an impact on what we remember. Studies confirm that those who buy feature-rich smartphones, for instance, do so because they think others will believe they are technologically savvy and open to new experiences. When analyzing content, ask, "Will remembering and acting on this content bring my audience any social advantages?"

15 Surprise | 1 2 3 4 5

Definition: the result of encountering something suddenly or unexpectedly.

Expectations normally depend on cues that predict the occurrence of an event or on inferential processes that predict something will occur. We can also use the term "incongruity" to denote a stimulus that creates an expectation that is unfulfilled by other stimuli occurring at the same time.

This impacts memory because learning happens when we are surprised (we increase our biological fitness if we remember what to do next time to avoid surprises). In general, humans constantly want to revise their models or schemas to make more accurate predictions, which implies cognitive energy savings. Surprise leads to the improvement of predictions. When analyzing content, ask, "Will the audience expect something and receive something else?" (Example: "On this slide, I expected a giant graphic and instead see a small, tiny word." "Will they expect something formal and get something totally informal?" "Will they expect something static and suddenly something moves?")

Total

REFERENCES

Chapter 1: Memory Is a Means to an End

Einstein, G. O., & McDaniel, M. A. (1990). Normal aging and prospective memory. *Journal of Experimental Psychology: Learning, Memory, and Cognition, 16,* 717–726.

Graf, P., Uttl, B., & Dixon, R. (2002). Pro- and retrospective memory in adulthood. In P. Graf &N. Ohta (Eds.), *Lifespan Memory Development* (pp. 257–282). Cambridge, MA: MIT Press.

Heffernan, T. M., & Ling, J. (2001). The impact of Eysenck's extraversion-introversion personality dimension on prospective memory. *Scandinavian Journal of Psychology, 42,* 321–325.

Kliegel, M., MacKinlay, R., & Jäger, T. (2008). A life span approach to the development of complex prospective memory. In M. Kliegel, M. A. McDaniel, & G. O. Einstein (Eds.), *Prospective Memory: Cognitive, Neuroscience, Developmental, and Applied Perspectives.* London: Lawrence Erlbaum.

Neath, I., Brown, G. D. A., McCormack, T., Chater, N., & Freeman, R. (2006). Distinctiveness models of memory and absolute identification: Evidence for local, not global, effects. *Quarterly Journal of Experimental Psychology, 59*(1), 121–135.

Chapter 2: A Business Approach to Memory

Anderson, S. J., Yamagishi, N., & Karavia, V. (2002). Attentional processes link perception and action. *Proceedings of the Royal Society B: Biological Sciences, 269* (1497), 1225.

Breneiser, J. E. (2009). Implementation intentions and generative strategies in prospective memory retrieval. *North American Journal of Psychology, 11*(2), 401–418.

Bruine de Bruin, W., Parker, A. M., & Fischhoff, B. (2007). Individual differences in adult decision-making competence. *Journal of Personality and Social Psychology, 92*(5), 938–956.

Carr, V.A., Engel, S. A., & Knowlton, B. J. (2013). Top-down modulation of hippocampal encoding activity as measured by high-resolution functional MRI. *Neuropsychologia, 5,* 1829-1837.

Chasteen, A. L., Park, D. C., & Schwarz, N. (2001). Implementation intentions of prospective memory. *Psychological Science, 12*(6), 457-461.

Crovitz, H. F., & Daniel, W. F. (1984). Measurements of everyday memory: Toward the prevention of forgetting. *Bulletin of the Psychonomic Society, 22,* 413-414.

Ericson, K. M. M. (2011, February). Forgetting we forget: Overconfidence and memory. *Journal of the European Economic Association, 9*(1), 43-60.

Finucane, M. L., Mertz, C. K., Slovic, P., & Schmidt, E. S. (2005). Task complexity and older adults' decision-making competence. *Psychology and Aging, 20*(1), 71-84.

Holan, P. M., & Philips, N. (2004). Remembrance of things past? The dynamics of organizational forgetting. *Management Science, 50*(11), 1603-1613.

Jullisson, E. A., Karlsson, N., & Garling, T. (2005). Weighing the past and the future in decision making. *European Journal of Cognitive Psychology, 17*(4), 561-575.

Liu, L. L., & Park, D. C. (2004). Aging and medical adherence: The use of automatic processes to achieve effortful things. *Psychology and Aging, 19,* 318-325.

McDaniel, M. A., & Einstein, G. O. (1993). The importance of cue familiarity and cue distinctiveness in prospective memory. *Memory, 1,* 23-41.

McDaniel, M. A., & Einstein, G. O. (2000). Strategic and automatic processes in prospective memory retrieval: A multiprocess framework. *Applied Cognitive Psychology, 14,* 127-144.

McKelvie, S. J. (2000). Quantifying the availability heuristic with famous names. *North American Journal of Psychology, 2*(2), 347-357.

Meeks, J. T., & Marsh, R. L. (2010). Implementation intentions about nonfocal event-based prospective memory tasks. *Psychological Research, 74,* 82-89.

Orbell, S., Hodgkins, S., & Sheeran, P. (1997). Implementation intentions and the theory of planned behavior. *Personality and Social Psychology Bulletin, 23*(9), 953-962.

Percy, L., Rossiter, J. R., & Elliott, R. (2001). *Strategic Advertising Management.* Oxford: Oxford University Press.

Shah, A. K., & Oppenheimer, D. M. (2008).Heuristics made easy: An effort-reduction framework. *Psychological Bulletin, 134*(2), 207-222.

Sheeran, P., & Orbell, S. (1999). Implementation intentions and repeated behaviours: Enhancing the predictive validity of the theory of planned behaviour. *European Journal of Social Psychology, 29,* 349-369.

Terry, W. S. (1988). Everyday forgetting: Data from a diary study. *Psychological Reports, 62,* 299-303.

Wood, S. L. (2001). Remote purchase environments: The influence of return policy leniency on two-stage decision process. *Journal of Marketing Research, 38*(2), 157–169.

Chapter 3: Control What Your Audience Remembers

McKeown, G. (2009). *Essentialism.* New York: Crown Business.

Ochsner, K. N. (2000). Are affective events richly recalled or simply familiar? The experience and process of recognizing feelings past. *Journal of Experimental Psychology: General, 124,* 242–261.

Perneger, T. V., & Agoritsas, T. (2011). Doctors and patients' susceptibility to framing bias: A randomized trial. *Journal of General Internal Medicine.* Advance online publication.

Reyna, V. F. (2012). A new intuitionism: Meaning, memory, and development in fuzzy-trace theory. *Judgment and Decision Making, 7*(3), 332–359.

Sikström, S. (1999). Power function forgetting curves as an emergent property of biologically plausible neural network models. *International Journal of Psychology, Special Issue: Short-Term/Working Memory, 34*(5–6), 460–464.

Wixted, J. T. (2004). On common ground: Jost's (1897) law of forgetting and Ribot's (1881) law of retrograde amnesia. *Psychological Review, 111,* 864–879.

Chapter 4: Made You Look

Chun, M. M., & Johnson, M. K. (2011). Memory: Enduring traces of perceptual and reflective attention. *Neuron, 72,* 520–536.

Deco, G., & Rolls, E. T. (2005). Neurodynamics of biased competition and cooperation for attention: A model with spiking neurons. *Journal of Neurophysiology, 94,* 295–313.

Eger, E., Henson, R. N., Driver, J., & Dolan, R. J. (2004). BOLD repetition decreases in object-responsive ventral visual areas depend on spatial attention. *Journal of Neurophysiology, 92,* 1241–1247.

Han, S. H., & Kim, M. S. (2004). Visual search does not remain efficient when executive working memory is working. *Psychological Science, 15,* 623–628.

Killingsworth, M. A., & Gilbert, D. T. (2010). A wandering mind is an unhappy mind. *Science, 330,* 932.

Krauzlis, R. J., Bollimunta, A., Arcizet, F., & Wang, L. (2014). Attention as an effect not a cause. *Trends in Cognitive Sciences, 18* (9), 457–464.

Mason, M. F., Norton, M. I., Van Horn, J. D., Wegner, D. M., Grafton, S. T., & Macrae, C. N. (2007). Wandering minds: The default network and stimulus-independent thought. *Science, 315,* 393–395.

Posner, M. I., & Rothbart, M. K. (2007). Research on attention networks as a model for the integration of psychological science. *Annual Review of Psychology, 58*, 1–23.

Schloss, K. B., & McComb, M. (2013). Perceptual organization influences memory, search, and aesthetic judgment. *Journal of Vision, 13*(9), 805–818.

Strayer, D. L., Drews, F. A., & Johnston, W. A. (2003). Cellphone-induced failures of visual attention during simulated driving. *Journal of Experimental Psychology: Applied, 9*, 23–32.

Weissman, D. H., Roberts, K. C., Visscher, K. M., & Woldorff, M. G. (2006). The neural bases of momentary lapses in attention. *Natural Neuroscience, 9*, 971–978.

Chapter 5: The Paradox of Surprise

Aglioti, S. (2008). Action anticipation and motor resonance in elite basketball players. *Nature Neuroscience, 11*(9), 1109–1016.

Berridge, K. (2007). The debate over dopamine's role in reward: The case for incentive salience. *Psychopharmacology, 191*, 391–431.

Berridge, K., & Aldridge, J. W. (2008). Decision utility, the brain, and pursuit of hedonic goals. *Social Cognition, 26*(5), 621–646.

Berridge, K., Robinson, T., & Aldridge, J. W. (2009). Dissecting components of reward: Liking, wanting, and learning. *Current Opinion in Pharmacology, 9*(1), 65–73.

Bromberg-Martin, E., & Hikosaka, O. (2009). Midbrain dopamine neurons signal preference for advance information about upcoming rewards. *Neuron, 63*, 119–126.

Chennu, S., Noreika, V., Gueorguiev, D., Blenkmann, A., Kochen, S., Ibáñez, A., Owen, A. M., & Bekinschtein, T. A. (2013). Expectation and attention in hierarchical auditory prediction. *Journal of Neuroscience, 33*(27), 11194–11205.

Goldstein, R. (2008). Do more expensive wines taste better? Evidence from a large sample of U.S. blind tastings. *Journal of Wine Economics, 3*(1), 1–10.

Hermann, E. (2007). Humans have evolved specialized skills of social cognition: The cultural intelligence hypothesis. *Science, 317*, 1360–1366.

Hilke, P. (2008). Marketing actions can modulate neural representations of experienced pleasantness. *PNAS, 105*(3), 1050–1054.

Huron, D. (2008). *Sweet Anticipation: Music and the Psychology of Expectation.* New York: Bradford Books.

Kringelbach, M. L., & Berridge, K. (2009). Towards a functional neuroanatomy of pleasure and happiness. *Trends in Cognitive Sciences, 13*(11), 479–487.

Langer, E. (2007). Using mindfulness (mindfully) to improve visual acuity. *Psychological Science, 18*(2), 165–171.

Lee, L., Frederick, S., & Ariely, D. (2006) Try it, you'll like it: The influence of expectation, consumption, and revelation on preferences for beer. *Psychological Science, 17*(12), 1054–1058.

Lidstone, R., de la Fuente-Fernandez, R., & Stoessl, A. J. (2005). The placebo response as a reward mechanism. *Seminars in Pain Medicine, 3*, 37–42.

McKay, B., Lewthwaite, R., & Wulf, G. (2012). Enhanced expectancies improve performance under pressure. *Frontiers in Psychology, 3*, 8.

Morewedge, C., Eun-Huh, Y., & Vosgerau, J. (2010). Thought for food: Imagined consumption reduces actual consumption. *Science, 330*, 1530–1533.

Moseley, J. B. (2002). A controlled trial of arthroscopic surgery for osteoarthritis of the knee. *New England Journal of Medicine, 347*, 81–88.

Mueller, C., & Dweck, C. (1998). Praise for intelligence can undermine children's motivation and performance. *Journal of Personality and Social Psychology, 75*, 33–52.

Nelson, L., Meyvis, T., & Galak, J. (2009). Enhancing the television-viewing experience through commercial interruptions. *Journal of Consumer Research, 36*, 160–172.

Oettingen, G., & Mayer, D. (2002). The motivating function of thinking about the future: Expectations versus fantasies. *Journal of Personality and Social Psychology, 83*(5), 1198–1212.

Sharot, T. (2011). How unrealistic optimism is maintained in the face of reality. *Nature Neuroscience, 14*, 1475–1479.

Talbot, M. (2000). The placebo prescription. *New York Times Magazine, 9*.

Thompson, D., & Norton, M. The social utility of feature creep. *Journal of Market Research, 48*, 555–565.

Tinklepaugh, O. (1928). An experimental study of representative factors in monkeys. *Journal of Comparative Psychology, 8*(3), 197–236.

Weil, R. (2007). Debunking critics' wine words: Can amateurs distinguish the smell of asphalt from the taste of cherries? *Journal of Wine Economics, 2*, 136–144.

Wright, M. (2010). Functional MRI reveals expert-novice differences during sport-related anticipation. *NeuroReport, 21*, 94–98.

Zaki, J., Schirmer, J., & Mitchell, J. (2011). Social influence modulates the neural computation of value. *Psychological Science, 22*(7), 894–900.

Chapter 6: Sweet Anticipation

Adcock, R. A., Thangavel, A., Whitfield-Gabrieli, S., Knutson, B., & Gabrieli, J. D. (2006). Reward-motivated learning: Mesolimbic activation precedes memory formation. *Neuron, 50*, 507–517.

Baldwin, A., Kiviniemi, M. T., & Snyder, M. (2009). A subtle source of power: The effect of having an expectation on anticipated interpersonal power. *Journal of Social Psychology, 148*(2), 82–104.

Berridge, K. C. (2012). From prediction error to incentive salience: Mesolimbic computation of reward motivation. *European Journal of Neuroscience, 35*(7), 1124–1143.

Berridge, K. C., & Kringelbach, M. L. (2011). Building a neuroscience of pleasure and well-being: Theory, research and practice. *Psychology of Well-Being, 1*(3), 1–27.

Deci, E. L., & Ryan, R. M. (2000). The "what" and "why" of goal pursuits: Human needs and the self-determination of behavior. *Psychological Inquiry, 11*, 227–268.

Diener, E., Lucas, R. E., & Scollon, C. N. (2006). Beyond the hedonic treadmill—revising the adaptation theory of well-being. *American Psychologist, 61*, 305–314.

Galinsky, A. D., Gruenfeld, D. H., & Magee, J. C. (2003). From power to action. *Journal of Personality and Social Psychology, 85*, 453–466.

Huron, D. (2006). *Sweet Anticipation: Music and the Psychology of Expectation.* Cambridge, MA: MIT Press.

Jay, T. M. (2003). Dopamine: A potential substrate for synaptic plasticity and memory mechanisms. *Progress in Neurobiology, 69*, 375–390.

Kringelbach, M. L. (2010). The hedonic brain: A functional neuroanatomy of human pleasure. In Kringelbach & Berridge (Eds.), *Pleasures of the Brain* (pp. 202–221). Oxford: Oxford University Press.

Lemon, N., & Manahan-Vaughan, D. (2006). Dopamine D-1/D-5 receptors gate the acquisition of novel information through hippocampal long-term potentiation and long-term depression. *Journal of Neuroscience, 26*, 7723–7729.

Nadin, M. (2003). *Anticipation: The End Is Where We Start From.* Baden, Switzerland: L. Muller Verlag.

Redgrave, P., & Gurney, K. (2006). The short-latency dopamine signal: A role in discovering novel actions? *Nature Reviews Neuroscience, 7*, 967–975.

Salamone, J. D., & Correa, M. (2012). The mysterious motivational functions of mesolimbic dopamine. *Neuron, 76*, 470–485.

Salamone, J. D., Correa, M., Farrar, A., & Mingote, S. M. (2007). Effort-related functions of nucleus accumbens dopamine and associated forebrain circuits. *Psychopharmacology (Berl), 191*, 461–482.

Schevernels, H., Krebs, R. M., Santens, P., Woldorff, M. G., & Boehler, C. N. (2013). Task preparation processes related to reward prediction precede those related to task-difficulty expectation. *NeuroImage, 84*, 639–647.

Schott, B. H., Minuzzi, L., Krebs, R. M., Elmenhorst, D., Lang, M., Winz, O. H., Seidenbecher, C. I., Coenen, H. H., Heinze, H. J., Zilles, K., Düzel, E., & Bauer, A. (2008). Mesolimbic functional magnetic resonance imaging activations during reward anticipation correlate with reward-related ventral striatal dopamine release. *Journal of Neuroscience, 28*, 14311–14319.

Schott, B. H., Seidenbecher, C. I., Fenker, D. B., Lauer, C. J., Bunzeck, N., Bernstein, H. G., Tischmeyer, W., Gundelfinger, E. D., Heinze, H. J., & Duzel, E. (2006). The dopaminergic midbrain participates in human episodic memory formation: Evidence from genetic imaging. *Journal of Neuroscience, 26*, 1407–1417.

Shohamy, D., & Adcock, R. A. (2010). Dopamine and adaptive memory. *Trends in Cognitive Science, 14*(10), 464–472.

Sienkiewicz-Jarosz, H., Scinska, A., Kuran, W., Ryglewicz, D., Rogowski, A., Wrobel, E., Korkosz, A., Kukwa, A., Kostowski, W., & Bienkowski, P. (2005). Taste responses in patients with Parkinson's disease. *Journal of Neurology, Neurosurgery, & Psychiatry, 76*, 40–46.

Smith, K. S., Berridge, K. C., & Aldridge, J. W. (2011). Disentangling pleasure from incentive salience and learning signals in brain reward circuitry. *Proceedings of the National Academy of Sciences USA, 108*, E255–264.

Webber, E. U., Shafir, S., & Blais, A. R. (2004). Predicting risk-sensitivity in humans and lower animals: Risk as variance or coefficient of variance. *Psychology Review, 111*, 430–445.

Witmann, B. C., Bunseck, N., Dolan, R. J., & Duzel, E. (2007). Anticipation of novelty recruits reward system and hippocampus while promoting recollection. *NeuroImage, 38*, 194–202.

Zhang, J., Berridge, K. C., Tindell, A. J., Smith, K. S., & Aldridge, J. W. (2009). A neural computational model of incentive salience. *PLoS Computational Biology, 5*, e1000437.

Chapter 7: What Makes a Message Repeatable?

Alter, A. L. (2013). The benefits of cognitive disfluency. *Current Directions in Psychological Science, 22*(6), 437–442.

Alter, A. L., & Oppenheimer, D. M. (2006). Predicting short-term stock fluctuations by using processing fluency. *Proceedings of the National Academy of Sciences, USA, 103*, 9369–9372.

Alter, A. L., & Oppenheimer, D. M. (2008). Effects of fluency on psychological distance and mental construal (or why New York is a large city, but New York is a civilized jungle). *Psychological Science, 19*, 161–167.

Barsade, S. G. (2002). The ripple effect: Emotional contagion and its influence on group behavior. *Administrative Science Quarterly, 47*(4), 644–675.

Berger, J. (2011). Arousal increases social transmission of information. *Psychological Science, 22*, 7, 891–893.

Berger, J., & Milkman, K. (2012). What makes online content viral? *Journal of Marketing Research, 49*, 2, 192–205.

Bock, J. K., Dell, G. S., Chang, F., & Onishi, K. H. (2007). Structural persistence from language comprehension to language production. *Cognition, 104*, 437–458.

Bock, J. K., & Griffin, Z. M. (2000). The persistence of structural priming: Transient activation or implicit learning? *Journal of Experimental Psychology: General, 129*, 177–192.

Brunot, S., & Sanitioso, R. (2004). Motivational influence on the quality of memories: Recall of general autobiographical memories related to desired attributes. *European Journal of Social Psychology, 34*, 627–635.

Daniel-Niculescu-Mizil, C., Cheng, J., Kleinberg, J., & Lee, L. (2012). You had me at hello: How phrasing affects memorability. Retrieved January 19, 2015, from http://www.cs.cornell.edu/cristian/memorability.html.

Nagarajan, M., Purohit, H., & Sheth, A. (2010). A qualitative examination of topical tweet and retweet practices. In W. Cohen and S. Gosling (Eds.), *Proceedings of the Fourth International AAAI Conference on Weblogs and Social Media* (pp. 295–298). Palo Alto, CA: AAAI Press.

Pickering, M. J., & Garrod, S. (2004). Toward a mechanistic psychology of dialogue [Target article and commentaries]. *Behavioral and Brain Sciences, 27*, 169–226.

Reece, B. B., Vanden Bergh, B. G., & Li, H. (1994). What makes a slogan memorable and who remembers it. *Journal of Current Issues and Research in Advertising, 16*(2), 41–57.

Sanitioso, R. B., & Niedenthal, P.M. (2006). Motivated self-perception and perceived ease in recall of autobiographical memories. *Psychology Press, 5*, 73–84.

Schwartz, S. H., & Boehnke, K. (2004). Evaluating the structure of human values with confirmatory factor analysis. *Journal of Research in Personality, 38*, 230–255.

Simmons, J. P., & Nelson, L. D. (2006). Intuitive confidence: Choosing between intuitive and nonintuitive alternatives. *Journal of Experimental Psychology, 135*, 409–428.

Stieglitz, S., & Dang-Zuan, L. (2013). Emotions and information diffusion in social media—sentiment of microblogs and sharing behavior. *Journal of Management Information Systems, 29*(4), 217–247.

Sy, T., Côté, S., & Saavedra, R. (2005). The contagious leader: Impact of the leader's mood on group members, group affective tone, and group processes. *Journal of Applied Psychology, 90*, 2, 295–305.

Szmrecsanyi, B. (2005). Language users as creatures of habit: A corpus-based analysis of persistence in spoken English. *Corpus Linguistics and Linguistic Theory, 1*, 113–149.

Thomas, R. (2010, October). Hey, watch it! Have the movies run out of quotable lines? *Wisconsin State Journal*, 77Square, Pg.Web.

Verfaellie, M., Rajaram, S., Fossum, K., & Williams, L. (2008). Not all repetition is alike: Different benefits of repetition in amnesia and normal memory. *Journal of the International Neuropsychological Society 14*, 365–372.

von Helversen, B., Gendolla, G. H. E., Winkielman, P., & Schmidt, R. E. (2008). Exploring the hardship of ease: Subjective and objective effort in the ease-of-processing paradigm. *Motivation and Emotion, 32*, 1–10.

Chapter 8: Become Memorable with Distinction

Brown, G. D. A., & Neath, I. (2007). A temporal ratio model of memory. *Psychological Review, 114*(3), 539–576.

Bruce, D., & Gaines, M. T. (1976). Tests of an organizational hypothesis of isolation effects in free recall. *Journal of Verbal Learning and Verbal Behavior, 15*, 59–72.

Cimbalo, R. S., Nowak, B. I., & Stringfield, C. (1978). Isolation effect: Overall list facilitation and debilitation in short-term memory. *Journal of General Psychology, 99*, 251–256.

Conway, M. A. (2005). Memory and the self. *Journal of Memory and Language, 53*, 594–628.

Fabiani, M., & Donchin, E. (1995). Encoding processes and memory organization: A model of the von Restorff effect. *Journal of Experimental Psychology: Learning, Memory, and Cognition, 21*, 221–240.

Green, R. T. (1956). Surprise as a factor in the von Restorff effect. *Journal of Experimental Psychology, 52*, 340–344.

Gumenik, W. E., & Levitt, J. (1968). The von Restorff effect as a function of difference of the isolated item. *American Journal of Psychology, 81*, 247–252.

Hunt, R. R. (1995). The subtlety of distinctiveness: What von Restorff really did. *Psychonomic Bulletin & Review, 2*, 105–112.

Hunt, R. R., & Lamb, C. A. (2001). What causes the isolation effect? *Journal of Experimental Psychology: Learning, Memory, and Cognition, 27*, 1359–1366.

Hunt, R. R., & Seta, C. E. (1984). Category size effects in recall: The roles of relational and individual item information. *Journal of Experimental Psychology: Learning, Memory, and Cognition, 10*, 454–464.

Hunt, R. R., & Worthen, J. B. (2006). *Distinctiveness and Memory*. New York: Oxford University Press.

Jenkins, W. O., & Postman, L. (1948). Isolation and the spread of effect in serial learning. *American Journal of Psychology, 61*, 214–221.

Jones, F. N., & Jones, M. H. (1942). Vividness as a factor in learning lists of nonsense syllables. *American Journal of Psychology, 55*, 96–101.

Kothurkar, V. K. (1956). Learning and retention of an isolated number on the background of meaningful material. *Indian Journal of Psychology, 31*, 59–62.

Kramer, T. H., Buckhout, P. F., Widman, E., & Tusche, B. (1991). Effects of stress on recall. *Applied Cognitive Psychology, 5*, 483–488.

McCaul, K. D., & Maki, R. H. (1984). Self- reference versus desirability ratings and memory for traits. *Journal of Personality and Social Psychology, 4*(5), 953–955.

Pillsbury, W. B., & Raush, H. L. (1943). An extension of the Kohler-Restorff inhibition phenomenon. *American Journal of Psychology, 56*, 293–298.

Rosen, H., Richardson, D. H., & Saltz, E. (1962). Supplementary report: Meaningfulness as a differentiation variable in the von Restorff effect. *Journal of Experimental Psychology, 64*, 327–328.

Smith, M. H., & Stearns, E. G. (1949). The influence of isolation on the learning of surrounding materials. *American Journal of Psychology, 62*, 369–381.

Chapter 9: "I Write This Sitting in the Kitchen Sink"

Anderson, A. K., & Phelps, E. A. (2001). Lesions of the human amygdala impair enhanced perception of emotionally salient events. *Nature, 411*, 305–309.

Andersson, L. M. (1996). Employee cynicism: An examination using a contract violation framework. *Human Relations, 69*(11), 1395–1419.

Ashby, F. G., Isen, A. M., & Turken, A. U. (1999). A neuropsychological theory of positive affect and its influence on cognition. *Psychological Review, 106*, 529–550.

Bacon-Macé, N., Kirchner, H., Fabre-Thorpe, M., & Thorpe, S. J. (2007). Effects of task requirements on rapid natural scene processing: From common sensory encoding to distinct decisional mechanisms. *Journal of Experimental Psychology: Human Perception and Performance, 33*, 1013–1026.

Bower, G. H., Black, J. B., & Turner, T. J. (1979). Scripts in memory for text. *Cognitive Psychology, 11*, 177–220.

Bower, G. H., & Clark, M. C. (1969). Narrative stories as mediators for serial learning. *Psychonomic Science, 14*, 181–182.

Brewer, W. F., & Lichtenstein, E. H. (1982). Stories are to entertain: A structural-affect theory of stories. *Journal of Pragmatics, 6*, 473–186.

DiCarlo, J. J., Zoccolan, D., & Rust, N. C. (2012). How does the brain solve visual object recognition? *Neuron, 73*, 415–434.

Fabre-Thorpe, M. (2011). The characteristics and limits of rapid visual categorization. *Frontiers in Psychology, 2*, 243.

Hunt, R. R., & Smith, R. E. (1996). Accessing the particular from the general: The power of distinctiveness in the context of organization. *Memory & Cognition, 24*, 217–225.

Lipman, D. (1995). *The Storytelling Coach*. Atlanta: August House.

McGaugh, J. L. (2000). Memory—a century of consolidation. *Science, 287*, 248–251.

Ostir, G. V., Markides, K. S., Black, S. A., & Goodwin, J. S. (2000). Emotional well-being predicts subsequent functional independence and survival. *Journal of the American Geriatrics Society, 48*, 473–478.

Potter, M. C., Hagmann, C. E., & McCourt, E. S. (2014). Detecting meaning in RSVP at 13 ms per picture. *Attention, Perception, & Psychophysics, 76*(2), 270–279.

Salovey, P., Rothman, A. J., Detweiler, J. B., & Steward, W. T. (2000). Emotional states and physical health. *American Psychologist, 55*, 110–121.

Schank, R. C. (1986). *Explanation Patterns: Understanding Mechanically and Creatively*. Hillsdale, NJ: Lawrence Erlbaum Associates.

Schank, R. C., & Abelson, R. P. (1977). *Scripts, Plans, Goats, and Understanding*. Hillsdale, NJ: Lawrence Erlbaum Associates.

Simmons, A. *Whoever Tells the Best Story Wins: How to Use Your Own Stories to Communicate with Power and Impact* (Kindle Location 454). Kindle Edition.

Srull, T. K. (1981). Person memory: Some tests of associative storage and retrieval models. *Journal of Experimental Psychology: Hitman Learning and Memory, 7*, 440–462.

Todd, R. M., Ehlers, R. M., Mueller, D. J., Robertson, A., Freeman, N., Palombo, D. J., Levine, B., & Anderson, A. K. (2015). Neurogenetic variations in norepinephrine availability enhance perceptual vividness. *Journal of Neuroscience, 35*(16), 6506–6516.

Vuilleeumier, P., Richardson, M. P., Armony, J. L., Driver, J., & Dolan, R. J. (2004). Distant influences of amygdala lesion on visual cortical activation during emotional face processing. *Nature Neuroscience, 7*, 1271–1278.

West, R., Herndon, R. W., & Ross-Munroe, K. (2001). Event-related neural activity associated with prospective remembering. *Applied Cognitive Psychology, 14*, 115–126.

Zirkle, G.A. (1946). Success and failure in serial learning: Isolation and the Thorndike effect. *Journal of Experimental Psychology, 36*, 302–315.

Chapter 10: How Much Content Is Too Much?

Cary, M., & Reder, L. M. (2003). A dual-process account of the list length and strength-based mirror effects in recognition. *Journal of Memory and Language, 49*, 231–248.

Cowan, N., Donnell, K., & Saults, J. S. (2013). A list-length constraint on incidental item-to-item associations. *Psychonomic Bulletin and Review, 20*, 1253–1258.

Criss, A. H., & Shiffrin, R. M. (2004). Context noise and item noise jointly determine recognition memory: A comment on Dennis and Humphreys (2001). *Psychological Review, 111*, 800–807.

Dilip, S., & Zhao, M. (2011). The fewer the better: Number of goals and savings behavior. *Journal of Marketing Research, 48*(6), 944–957.

Gilchrist, A. L., & Cowan, N. (2011). Can the focus of attention accommodate multiple separate items? *Journal of Experimental Psychology: Learning, Memory, and Cognition, 37*, 1484–1502.

Howard, M. W., Jing, B., Rao, V., Provyn, J., & Datey, A. (2009). Bridging the gap: Transitive associations between items presented in similar temporal contexts. *Journal of Experimental Psychology: Learning, Memory, and Cognition, 35*, 391–407.

Oberauer, K., & Hein, L. (2012). Attention to information in working memory. *Current Directions in Psychological Science, 21*, 164–169.

Sederberg, P. B., Gershman, S. J., Polyn, S. M., & Norman, K. A. (2011). Human memory reconsolidation can be explained using the temporal context model. *Psychonomic Bulletin and Review, 18*, 455–468.

Thomas, E. A. C., & Weaver, W. B. (1975). Cognitive processing and time perception. *Perception and Psychophysics, 17*, 363–367.

Underwood, B. J. (1978). Recognition memory as a function of length of study list. *Bulletin of the Psychonomic Society, 12*, 89–91.

Wang, S. H., & Morris, R. G. M. (2010). Hippocampal-neocortical interactions in memory formation, consolidation, and reconsolidation. *Annual Review of Psychology, 61*, 49–79.

Wertheimer, M. (1938). Gestalt theory. In W. D. Ellis (Ed.), *A Source Book of Gestalt Psychology* (pp. 1–11). London: Kegan Paul, Trench, Trubner & Company.

Zakay, D., & Block, R. A. (1997). Temporal cognition. *Current Directions in Psychological Science, 6*, 12–16.

Chapter 11: How Does the Brain Decide?

Bannerman, R. L., Milders, M., de Gelder, B., & Sahraie, A. (2009). Orienting to threat: Faster localization of fearful facial expressions and body postures revealed by saccadic eye movements. *Proceedings of the Royal Society B, 276* (1662), 1635–1641.

Bargh, J. A. (1994). The four horsemen of automaticity: Awareness, intention, efficiency, and control in social cognition. In R. Wyer & T. Srull (Eds.), *Handbook of Social Cognition* (pp. 1–40). Hillsdale, NJ: Lawrence Erlbaum Associates.

Beisswanger, A. H., Stone, E. R., Hupp, J. M., & Allgaier, L. (2003). Risk taking in relationships: Differences in deciding for oneself versus for a friend. *Basic and Applied Social Psychology, 25*, 121–135.

Benoit, R. G., Gilbert, S. J., & Burgess, P. W. (2011). A neural mechanism mediating the impact of episodic prospection on farsighted decisions. *Journal of Neuroscience, 31*, 6771–6779.

Bradley, R., & Drechsler, M. (2013). Types of uncertainty. *Erkenntnis*, online, 1–29. ISSN 0165-0106.

Broemer, P. (2002). Relative effectiveness of differently framed health messages: The influence of ambivalence. *European Journal of Social Psychology, 32*, 685–703.

Buytendijk, F. A. (2010). *Dealing with Dilemmas.* New York: Wiley.

Cialdini, R. *Influence: The Psychology of Persuasion.* New York: Harper Business Review.

Cooper, N., Kable, J. W., Kyu, B. K., & Zauberman, G. (2013). Brain activity in valuation regions while thinking about the future predicts individual discount rates. *Journal of Neuroscience, 33*(32), 13150–13156.

Dalal, R. S., & Bonaccio, S. (2010). What types of advice do decision-makers prefer? *Organizational Behavior and Human Decision Processes, 112*, 11–23.

Förster, J., Friedman, R. S., & Liberman, N. (2004). Temporal construal effects on abstract and concrete thinking: Consequences for insight and creative cognition. *Journal of Personality and Social Psychology, 87*, 177–189.

French, R. M. (2003). Catastrophic forgetting in connectionist networks. In L. Nadel (Ed.), *Encyclopedia of Cognitive Science*. London: MacMillan.

Gallagher, K. M., Updegraff, J. A., Rothman, A. J., & Sims, L. (2011). Perceived susceptibility to breast cancer moderates the effect of gain- and loss-framed messages on use of screening mammography. *Health Psychology, 30*, 145–152.

Grant, A. M. (2008). Does intrinsic motivation fuel the prosocial fire? Motivational synergy in predicting persistence, performance, and productivity. *Journal of Applied Psychology, 93*, 48–58.

Graybiel, A. (2008). Habits, rituals, and the evaluative brain. *Annual Review of Neuroscience, 31*, 359–387.

Harbaugh, W. T., Mayr, U., & Burghart, D. R. (2007). Neural responses to taxation and voluntary giving reveal motives for charitable donations. *Science, 316*, 1622–1625.

Izuma, K., Saito, D. N., & Sadato, N. (2008). Processing of social and monetary rewards in the human striatum. *Neuron, 58*, 284–294.

Kable, J. W., & Glimcher, P. W. (2007). The neural correlates of subjective value during intertemporal choice. *Natural Neuroscience, 10*, 1625–1633.

Kirchner, H., & Thorpe, S. J. (2006). Ultra-rapid object detection with saccadic eye movements: Visual processing speed revisited. *Vision Research, 46*, 1762–1776.

Kray, L. (2000). Contingent weighting in self-other decision-making. *Organizational Behavior and Human Decision Processes, 83*, 82–106.

Lebreton, M., Jorge, S., Michael, V., Thirion, B., & Pessiglione, M. (2009). An automatic valuation system in the human brain: Evidence from functional neuroimaging. *Neuron, 64*, 431–439.

McGaugh, J. L. (2000). Memory: A century of consolidation. *Science, 14*, 248–251.

Milosavljevic, M., Koch, C., & Rangel, A. (2011). Consumers can make decisions in as little as a third of a second. *Judgment and Decision-Making, 6*(6), 520–530.

Mori, S., & Shimada, T. (2013). Expert anticipation from deceptive action. *Attention, Perception, & Psychophysics, 75*, 751–770.

O'Doherty, J. P., Hampton, A., & Kim, H. (2007). Model-based fMRI and its application to reward learning and decision making. *Annals of the New York Academy of Sciences, 1104*, 35–53.

Parsons, S. (2001). *Qualitative Methods for Reasoning Under Uncertainty*. Cambridge, MA: MIT Press.

Plassmann, H., O'Doherty, J., Shiv, B., & Rangel, A. (2008). Marketing actions can modulate neural representations of experienced pleasantness. *Proceedings of the National Academy of Sciences USA, 105*, 1050–1054.

Pronin, E., Olivola, C. Y., & Kennedy, K. A. (2008). Doing unto future selves as you would do unto others: Psychological distance and decision making. *Personality and Social Psychology Bulletin, 34*, 224–236.

Savage, L. J. (1954). *The Foundations of Statistics.* New York: Wiley.

Spreng, R. N., & Grady, C. L. (2009). Patterns of brain activity supporting autobiographical memory, prospection, and theory of mind, and their relationship to the default mode network. *Journal of Cognitive Neuroscience, 22*(6), 1112–1123.

Tricomi, E., Balleine, B. & O'Doherty, J. (2009). A specific role for posterior dorsolateral striatum in human habit learning. *European Journal of Neuroscience,* 29, 2225–2232.

Trope, Y., & Liberman, N. (2010). Construal-level theory of psychological distance. *Psychological Review, 117,* 440–463.

Tusche, A., Bode, S., & Haynes, J. D. (2010). Neural responses to unattended products predict later consumer choices. *Journal of Neuroscience, 30,* 8024–8031.

Villas-Boas, S. B., & Villas-Boas, J. M. (2008). Learning, forgetting, and sales. *Management Science, 54* (11), 1951–1960.

Weaver, W. (1964). *Alice in Many Tongues: The Translations of Alice in Wonderland.* Madison: University of Wisconsin Press.

Weber, J. A. (1997). Certainty and uncertainty in decision making: A conceptualization. In R. T. Goembiewski & J. Rabin (Eds.), *Public Budgeting and Finance* (4th ed., pp. 449–473). New York: Marcel Dekker.

Wilson, T. D., & Gilbert, D. T. (2005). Affective forecasting: Knowing what to want. *Current Directions in Psychological Science, 14,* 131–134.

Yaniv, I., & Kleinberger, E. (2000). Advice taking in decision making: Egocentric discounting and reputation formation. *Organizational Behavior and Human Decision Processes, 83,* 260–281.

Yin, H.H., Knowlton, B.J. & Balleine, B.W. (2004). Lesions of dorsolateral striatum preserve outcome expectancy but disrupt habit formation in instrumental learning. *European Journal of Neuroscience,* 19, 181–189.

INDEX

ABOUT THE AUTHOR

Carmen Simon, PhD, is a recognized cognitive scientist who specializes in neuroscience research and takes a daring approach to persuasion by placing memory at the heart of all decision-making. She advocates that people make decisions in our favor based on what they remember, not on what they forget. Carmen suggests that if we want to persuade others, it is not practical to simply help them remember the past. It is more profitable to know how to influence what they will remember in the future, where decisions happen.

Carmen is the cofounder of Rexi Media, a presentation design and training firm that uses brain science to help business professionals stay on their audiences' minds long enough to make a difference.

For more information, visit http://www.reximedia.com/.